Building a Home Within

Building a Home Within

Meeting the Emotional Needs
of Children and Youth in Foster Care

edited by

Toni Vaughn Heineman, D.M.H.

and

Diane Ehrensaft, Ph.D.

A Home Within
San Francisco

·P·A·U·L·H·
BROOKES
PUBLISHING CO®

Baltimore • London • Sydney

Paul H. Brookes Publishing Co.
Post Office Box 10624
Baltimore, Maryland 21285-0624

www.brookespublishing.com

"Paul H. Brookes Publishing Co." is a registered trademark
of Paul H. Brookes Publishing Co., Inc.

Typeset by Integrated Publishing Solutions, Grand Rapids, Michigan.
Manufactured in the United States of America by
Versa Press, Inc., East Peoria, Illinois.

Cover photograph used courtesy of Tamisha Carlson and Ghita Riane.

The stories in this book are based on the authors' experiences. Some
of the cases represent actual people and circumstances. Individuals'
names and identifying details have been changed to protect their
identities. Other vignettes are composite accounts that do not
represent the lives or experiences of specific individuals, and
no implications should be inferred.

Library of Congress Cataloging-in-Publication Data

Building a home within : meeting the emotional needs of children
and youth in foster care / edited by Toni Vaughn Heineman and
Diane Ehrensaft.
    p.   cm.
   Includes bibliographical references and index.
   ISBN 1-55766-839-6 (pbk.)
   1. Foster children—Psychology.   2. Foster children—Mental health.
3. Child psychotherapy.   4. Adolescent psychotherapy.   5. Children's
Psychotherapy Project (San Francisco, Calif.)   I. Heineman, Toni
Vaughn.   II. Ehrensaft, Diane.
HV873.B87 2006
362.73'3—dc22   2005019175

British Library Cataloguing in Publication data are available
from the British Library.

To our best teachers—
the children and youth in the
Children's Psychotherapy Project

Contents

About the Editors

Toni Vaughn Heineman, D.M.H., is the founder of the Children's Psychotherapy Project (CPP) and Executive Director of A Home Within, the national nonprofit organization that houses the 12 chapters of CPP across the United States. She received her master's degree in social work from the University of California, Berkeley, and her doctoral degree in mental health from the University of California, San Francisco. Dr. Heineman has taught for the Psychoanalytic Institute of Northern California, the San Francisco Psychoanalytic Institute, and many local and national training programs. She is the author of numerous articles and presentations about clinical work with foster children and of *The Abused Child: Psychodynamic Understanding and Treatment* (The Guilford Press, 1998). Dr. Heineman has been in private practice in San Francisco since the late 1970s and is Associate Clinical Professor of Pediatrics and Psychiatry at the University of California, San Francisco.

Diane Ehrensaft, Ph.D., is a senior clinician and founding member of the Children's Psychotherapy Project and Vice President of the board of directors of A Home Within. A developmental and clinical psychologist, she received her doctoral degree from the University of Michigan. She has lectured and published nationally and internationally on the subject of parenting and child development. Dr. Ehrensaft has served on the faculty of The Wright Institute in Berkeley, the Psychoanalytic Institute of Northern California, and the University of California, Berkeley, and has been in private clinical practice in the San Francisco Bay Area since the late 1970s. She is the author of *Mommies, Daddies, Donors, Surrogates: Answering Tough Questions and Building Strong Families* (The Guilford Press, 2005); *Spoiling Childhood: How Well-Meaning Parents Are Giving Children Too Much but Not What They Need* (The Guilford Press, 1997); and *Parenting Together: Men and Women Sharing the Care of Their Children* (The Free Press, 1987).

Contributors

Susan R. Bernstein, M.S.
Marriage and Family Therapist
Children's Psychotherapy Project
San Francisco, California

Christopher Bonovitz, Psy.D.
Clinical Psychologist
Psychoanalyst
William Alanson White
  Institute
New York, New York

Peter G.M. Carnochan, Ph.D.
Instructor and Graduate of the
  Psychoanalytic Institute of
  Northern California
San Francisco, California

**Thetis Rachel Cromie,
  D.Mn., Ph.D.**
Psychotherapist
Private Practice
South Holland, Illinois

Martha P. Harris, Ph.D.
Developmental and Clinical
  Psychologist
Private Practice
Lafayette, California

Michael LoGuidice, L.C.S.W.
Psychotherapist
New York, New York

Barbara Reed McCarroll, Ph.D.
Consulting Psychologist
Therapeutic/research child care
  center
Northern California
Clinical Psychologist
Kentfield, California
Clinical Director
Children's Psychotherapy Project
Marin County, California

Isabelle Reiniger, L.C.S.W.
Psychotherapist
New York, New York

Richard Ruth, Ph.D.
Psychologist/Psychoanalyst
Private Practice
Wheaton, Maryland
Steering Committee, Faculty, and
  Supervisor
Child and Adolescent
  Psychotherapy Program
Washington School of Psychiatry
Washington, D.C.

**Julie Stone, B.A., B.M.,
  FRANZCP**
Infant, Child, and Family
  Psychiatrist
Consultant to Child Protective
  Services and Health Department
Western Australia

Barbara Waterman, Ph.D.
Clinical Psychologist
Ann Martin Children's Center
Oakland, California

Rebecca B. Weston, J.D.,
L.C.S.W.
Clinical Director
Children's Psychotherapy
    Project–Brooklyn
New York, New York

Norman Zukowsky, Ph.D.
Clinical Psychologist
Private Practice
Children's Psychotherapy Project
San Francisco, California

Foreword

Building a Home Within: Meeting the Emotional Needs of Children and Youth in Foster Care is a pioneering book, and the editors' and contributors' vision, determination, charity, and courage are extraordinary. It offers real hope both to those at the bottom of society and to those professionals who despair of ever getting to grips with effecting real change at the grimmest of levels. The children described in this book have suffered multiple bereavements and traumas, some unfortunately and unknowingly inflicted by the care system itself. They usually have great difficulty in trusting in the reliability and decency of adults, so they may also have great difficulty in respecting adult helpers or in finding them interesting. In the worst cases, the damage is not only emotional: The children's early lives have been so chaotic that their mental and cognitive abilities, their capacity to think and learn, have been damaged, too. If such children are to have sufficient peace and pleasure in their lives to develop the capacity to think, they need some degree of consistency in the world and in their emotional lives. The therapists who contributed to this book do not claim to erase old traumas or to prevent new injuries to the children in their care, but they can and do build emotional and cognitive buffers against what further blows may come. The children begin to build—to varying degrees—better internal representations of what other human beings are like and can offer. Many of the children described in *Building a Home Within* learned to overcome despair instead of freezing up against it.

I am writing this in England, where the profession of Child and Adolescent Psychotherapist is a specialized profession recognized in its own right within the National Health Service, and there are now hundreds of therapists working in Child and Family Mental Health Clinics in England. In England there is some acknowledgment that there are no quick fixes for children who have been damaged by trauma; indeed, work with foster and adopted children, as well as their families and their social workers, is becoming something of a subspeciality within the wider profession. It is shocking to think how few such resources there are for U.S. children who have undergone deprivation or other disturbing circumstances. The therapists in the Children's Psychotherapy Project (CPP) are making a bold step forward in helping these children overcome adversity.

The generosity of the therapists in CPP concerns not only their time and labor—for which they have decided to receive no pay—but also the degree of distress, desperation, and sometimes horror they have to experience, tolerate, and yet somehow use and transform. They are honest about their passionate rescue fantasies and the ways in which their own attachment to their clients—which is often stronger than to well-parented children—can lead to dangerous denials in themselves and also in other workers. The awareness of a difficult child's terrible history and relentless deprivation and abuse can often soften our hearts so much that we fail to see exactly how demanding and manipulative the child may be and the ways in which his or her identifications with troubled parents may have shaped his or her character. As the authors note, we need both the insights of attachment theory and the psychoanalytic understanding of the darker side of human nature if we are to treat such children.

The authors also examine the frequent desire to blame people or systems for the unacceptable and destructive realities to which their child and adolescent clients are continually exposed. They know, however, that the small comfort of self-righteous blame can lead to the dead end of sullen resignation. They have learned to work hard with each other in their consultation groups to process these feelings, hang in there, and find new energy to go on—not only to give "one child one therapist for as long as it takes," but also to support or collaborate with the myriad other people concerned with the children in the network for as long as that takes. They understand the enormous psychic toll that the cruelty and indifference of societal deprivation exacts on foster care agency workers as they try to respond to the needs of individual children experiencing never-ending abuse and neglect.

Because of the great distortion or delay in these children's development, the therapists have been challenged to rethink issues of psychoanalytic technique: They have learned to go more slowly and not to try to dismantle a child's protective defenses too rapidly. They have found that playing together and thinking about the play can often foster a carefully calibrated development in reflective capacities, whereas in many cases a more direct interpretive approach to the child's past or current crises can serve to traumatize a child all over again.

The therapists have also been forced to rethink a second question of method. In more traditional therapies, a client's treatment is usually protected from a therapist's interventions into the child's outside life; in these more desperate circumstances, the therapists have found it at times necessary to act and to let the child know they have acted to protect him or her in some way. In general, they have had to be involved in far more collaboration, cooperation, and discussion with the whole network of other professionals, parents, and foster parents than is usually the case. CPP's clients seem to have survived all of this very well! My view is that with children who are deprived of ordinary parenting, outside contacts of this kind tend not to be experienced as disloyalty on the part of their therapists. On the contrary, many children who have never had the experience of two parents working together to think about them and to parent them experience it not as a betrayal but as something more like a protective arch over them. I have also seen many cases in which overwhelmed parents or foster parents have been helped by support from the therapist, and this in turn has helped to protect a child's therapy. In other cases, it has sometimes been a relief to a burdened child who knows all too well that his or her parent's need is as great as his or her own.

Building a Home Within shows that in the first 10 years of CPP, therapists have already developed enormous expertise in understanding the complexity of the children's struggles to find an identity and a sense of belonging to an internal family. The therapists who contributed to this book have much to say about a multitude of issues, including, for example, the timing and nature of reunifications with biological parents. This is a wise and compelling book, and we can all learn from it.

Anne Alvarez, Ph.D., MACP
Consultant Child and Adolescent Psychotherapist
Tavistock Clinic
London

Acknowledgments

How does one build a home within? How does one make a safe place inside oneself—a place that holds the important people, values, ideas, and feelings from childhood and adolescence? How does one use that internal place as a base that provides comfort and stability for moving away and returning home?

It takes a long time to build a home. Building a home that lives inside oneself takes much longer than building a house to live in. Building any house or home that is both sturdy and customized to the needs of the inhabitants takes the foresight, skills, and dedication of many people. We are fortunate to have many people to thank for their contribution to the building of A Home Within and to the creation of this book.

Fittingly, this book takes its name from the nonprofit organization that sustains the work of the Children's Psychotherapy Project (CPP). We have been able to build A Home Within as an organization only because of the confidence of the families and individuals in the social service agencies who understood, shared, and trusted our mission of bringing lasting relationships to children and youth in foster care. In particular, we owe a debt of gratitude to the Department of Human Services and Community Mental Health in San Francisco for joining with us in our fledgling efforts to develop CPP and assisting us in laying the foundation for the 10 years of work that we chronicle in this book.

This book could never have happened without the contributions of all of the clinicians in CPP. The therapists who work with individual children, the clinicians who provide ongoing consultation, and the clinical directors who guide the work of each chapter of CPP each volunteer time to help children and youth in foster care build an internal home that protects and nurtures them.

Our founding members, whose important work is described in Chapter 1, were instrumental in developing the underpinnings of A Home Within and served as an informal board. A decade later, we have a legally recognized organization with an active and energetic board of directors who offer a wide range of skills and perspectives on foster care. Without their individual and collective support, this book would not have been possible. We take this opportunity to thank Linda Fitzpatrick, Leeann Borton Harvey, William Luby, Cheryl Polk, Pat Reynolds-Harris, Ellen Salwen, Diana Sanders, and Kira Steifman.

We also extend our special appreciation to Brian Dunn, one of our first board members. Brian offered us consistent and steady leadership and connected us with Paul H. Brookes Publishing Co. At Brookes Publishing, we found enthusiastic backing for our ideas. Our editor, Jessica Allan, understood our vision and brought our far-ranging proposal into focus. Her assistant, Sarah Shepke, steadily guided us through the process of turning an idea into a book, and Nicole Schmidl's careful and attentive copyediting made all of us better writers. Our gratitude goes to all of them for their patience and dedication to this undertaking.

Of course, this book would not exist without the inspired and insightful writing of the clinicians who share their work here. Through the time, effort, and thoughtfulness they have devoted to presenting their clinical work, these authors have given voice to all CPP clinicians and the work that goes on each week in the therapy sessions and consultation groups of CPP.

Although the therapists volunteer their time, they could not do the work of CPP without an administrative infrastructure to maintain direct services. We have benefited greatly from the generous financial assistance and guidance of the foundations who embraced our ideas and had faith in our ability to carry out our mission. We thank the Andrus Family Fund, the Bella Vista Foundation, the Brotman Foundation, the California Endowment, the California Wellness Foundation, the David L. Klein Foundation, the Eva Leah Gunther Foundation, the FAR Fund, the McKesson Foundation, the Morris Stulsaft Foundation, the Potrero Nuevo Fund, the Pottruck Family Foundation, the Richard and Rhoda Goldman Fund, the San Francisco Foundation, the Stuart Foundation, the Trio Foundation, the Walter and Elise Haas Fund, the Y & H Soda Foundation, and the Zellerbach Family Foundation.

We could not have built A Home Within without the help and direction of many professionals who offered their pro bono services in the process of creating a home for our volunteer clinicians. We are particularly indebted to the many attorneys at Morrison & Foerster, LLP, for their advice and ongoing legal services. We continue to enjoy and benefit from the talented designers at Cahan & Associates, who created the logo (see p. xxi) that has opened so many hearts and doors for us.

We are also indebted to the corporations, family funds, and hundreds of individuals in the communities we serve. Their emotional and financial support has given us the confidence to hold to our commitment to bringing lasting relationships to all children and youth in foster care. We thank each and every benefactor for the words of encouragement and the donations that enable our work.

Finally, our deepest appreciation goes to our program administrator, Veronica Pontes. Her unflinching attention to detail, persistent good humor, and consistent and sensitive care sustain our day-to-day work. Above all, her passionate understanding and unwavering commitment to our vision is a model for all of us involved in A Home Within.

More About A Home Within

A Home Within is a nonprofit organization dedicated to helping current and former foster children and youth build healthy and lasting relationships.

For more information, contact us at

2481 Clay Street
San Francisco, California 94115
415-474-6365

Or visit our web site: http://www.ahomewithin.org

Building a Home Within

Introduction

The Children's Psychotherapy Project (CPP) started as an idea for a very simple means of bringing lasting, high-quality mental health services to children and youth in foster care. Good ideas are not hard to come by; good programs are more difficult to start and maintain.

This section describes the forces that gave rise to the initial idea for CPP. It chronicles the life of the program from its inception in San Francisco in 1993 to its current incarnation as a national program with clinicians in large and small communities coming together in local chapters of CPP. Each local chapter draws on the unique resources of the clinicians in the community to meet the particular needs of the foster children and families in that community. The chapters cannot and should not be identical. However, each is recognizably part of a larger group and, as such, has an impact beyond the local community.

The importance of the words that pass between any individual CPP therapist and child is magnified when clinicians come together to join their voices in a unified message about the importance of stable, lasting, therapeutic relationships for children and youth in foster care. As CPP grows in numbers across the country, the strength and reach of its message grows. In this section, we illustrate the ways that the whole of CPP is truly greater than the sum of its parts.

CHAPTER I

The Children's Psychotherapy Project

One Child. One Therapist. For as Long as it Takes.

Toni Vaughn Heineman

Like most grassroots organizations, the Children's Psychotherapy Project (CPP) grew out of frustration with the status quo and a belief that, with luck and pluck and ingenuity, a few people might be able to make a significant difference. In the years since a group of clinicians in the San Francisco Bay Area first took up this challenge, we have enjoyed much good luck, have had our resolve tested many times over in expected and unexpected ways, and have discovered seemingly boundless sources of creativity among the clinicians who have joined CPP and the foster children and youth they serve.[1]

A confluence of factors sparked my initial thinking about the need for alternatives for mental health services for children in the foster care system. None of the events were unusual at the time nor, unfortunately, are they now. Had they not occurred so closely together, I might have dismissed each of them individually. People working in and around the foster care system can easily become numb to the consistent and pervasive mistreatment of children and come to accept the small and large transgressions as business as usual. It is often so painful to recognize the intentional and unintentional hurts that are inflicted on these young people that we learn to look away and to assume that it cannot be different. However, despite the concerted attention and devotion of literally thousands of individuals and

---

[1]As interest in replicating CPP in other communities grew, we needed the more formal structure of a nonprofit organization. We built A Home Within to house the growing chapters of CPP. I write this introductory chapter as a therapist and consultant in the San Francisco chapter of CPP and as the Executive Director of A Home Within.

organizations, the system that serves foster children and families did not and does not function well. At times, children suffer greater harm in the system designed to protect them than they suffered while with their abusive or neglectful families. Sometimes it becomes impossible to look away.

The events that led me to gather a group of highly respected clinicians to talk about how to help address the unmet psychotherapeutic needs of foster children and families occurred within a few weeks of each other in the spring of 1993. At that time I was supervising a psychology intern in a very well-regarded clinic. The time for the intern to move on to a new training site was fast approaching, and we talked extensively about how difficult her leaving would be for the little boy she had seen during the training year. He was a foster child who had seen several therapists over the years he had been in treatment at the clinic. Although they all had reportedly been attentive and devoted to helping him, he had become increasingly unresponsive during his tenure at the clinic, content to play board games with little apparent interest in talking about the events in his present or past life or his feelings about his internal or external worlds. With the agreement of the trainee, I called the director of training at the clinic with the strong recommendation that this child be assigned to a member of the staff, explaining that the changes in therapists so completely replicated the changes he had endured coming into and staying in foster care that he was closing off, rather than opening up, to relationships. In response, I received a stern lecture about the importance of trainees learning to work with transfers and terminations. Of more importance, the director carefully explained to me that the repeated, but planned, separations from therapists afforded the foster child opportunities to master the unexpected and traumatic losses of parents and foster parents. Unfortunately, this stance often remains relatively unchanged, despite the overwhelming clinical experience and research that demonstrates the importance of lasting relationships for the healthy development of trust, emotional stability, cognitive gains, and social competence. Indeed, one does not have to look hard to find programs that are built on the premise that long-term relationships— whether with foster parents, social workers, or therapists—merely create an unhealthy dependency and must not be encouraged.

During this same period, I was asked to complete a bonding study involving an 18-month-old girl, Susan, and her mother, Martha. Like her mother, Susan had spent most of her life in foster care. The social worker felt that Martha would never be able to assume full parenting responsibilities and that her parental rights should be terminated so that the child could be placed for adoption while still young. These may be among the most difficult evaluations facing clinicians—assessing whether a parent, usually the mother, is capable, even minimally, of providing safe and basic care for her child or whether it is in the child's best interests to be adopted by a family that can presumably provide loving and lasting care. These cases are particularly tragic when the parent herself is a product of the foster care system. When a young girl who has grown up in a series of foster placements (whether family or group homes) and has had no stable, loving relationship herself bears a child, she usually will not know how to provide for the child whom she may have knowingly or unknowingly borne in an attempt to fill the aching need for a special human relationship. When the system is compelled to remove the child from parental care in such instances, it is as if the mother were being punished for the system's failure to have provided adequate care during her childhood and adolescence. Little during the course of the evaluation gave me hope that this young mother could develop the empathy or skills necessary for even minimally adequate parenting. However, it seemed to me that she was entitled to at least one more chance and that the possibility of sustaining the mother–daughter ties should not be so easily foreclosed. When I made referrals for psychotherapy that would focus on the infant–parent relationship and individual therapy for the mother, I could not help wondering whether Martha might have had a happier outcome if she had had a long and lasting relationship with a therapist throughout her childhood and adolescence. Certainly psychotherapy cannot avert every misfortune, but it might have mitigated an apparently inevitable and tragic separation for this mother and child.

At about the same time, I completed a psychological evaluation of Billy, a young boy in foster care. I had recommended to the social worker that Billy be referred to a therapist who could provide long-term treatment. To help the social worker follow through on this recommendation, I called the group of therapists to which I usually referred. They either had no time available or were working with as many foster children as they believed they could manage. The same was true of those on the list of potential therapists that I had compiled from the recommendations made by the initial group of therapists. In the course of trying to find a therapist for this little boy, I repeatedly heard a profound sense of discouragement and anger. These people felt deeply committed to making long-term treatment available to every child or adult, regardless of the individual's ability to pay. They all relied on a sliding fee scale to make space available in their practices for people from diverse economic backgrounds, including students and young adults with entry-level incomes, parents working at low-wage jobs, and foster children and families whose fees were set by county guidelines. They felt overwhelmed and undervalued in their relationships with the foster care system—the fees were often less than half of what they regularly charged, and they could not bill for missed sessions, phone calls, or meetings on behalf of the child. They struggled with seemingly endless paperwork and late payments, and they felt lost in a system of unreturned phone calls, misplaced forms, and lack of information about the children they were supposed to be helping. They also expressed frustration at having no one to blame—no one to whom they could look to fix the problems. The social workers, foster parents, and attorneys involved with their young clients often shared this frustration and discouragement. Impotent rage seemed to have melted into a pervasive and hopeless gloom.

As noted previously, none of these situations is unusual—individually or in combination, they arise hundreds of times each week in foster care communities across the United States. That none of them results from malice or intentional harm merely adds to the pathos. The interns in the clinic all meant well and did what they could to help the children assigned to them. Unfortunately, in the process of justifying the education and training of interns as a top priority, the service system often creates a theory of psychotherapy that actually creates the psychological mistreatment of foster children. When a director's main task is preserving and protecting the training program, the needs of one individual child must be balanced against the needs of the trainee group. Allocating precious staff time to direct service leaves less time available for teaching and supervision. This is an uncomfortable but not unusual or psychologically dangerous situation—individuals, families, and organizations struggle with competing demands on limited finances, time, and emotional resources all of the time.

What *is* dangerous in such situations is the self-deception that is passed along explicitly to trainees as best practice and implicitly to children, who are told that enduring multiple new losses will help them master previous losses. Anticipating, planning for, and talking about the feelings and implications of losing a therapist may provide an opportunity to revisit earlier unexpected and traumatic losses; however, this does not create a good opportunity but merely offers the chance of being less bad. The unfortunate truth is that life in foster care is fraught with losses; we need not generate more. Rather, children need to be provided stable, lasting relationships that will help them confront and absorb the feelings engendered by losing important people. A series of short-lived relationships merely underscores what foster children learn too early and too well: "Don't count on others. They don't stick around."

Such situations demand something that is so elusive in the foster care system: a simple, straightforward statement of the truth that trainees and clients may have competing needs. On the one hand, trainees draw on a range of experiences in a variety of settings in order to appreciate the scope of emotional problems that they will most likely encounter as therapists. This usually means that they need to move around—either within a hospital setting or among community agencies. On the other hand, foster children need to hold still. They need a secure base and a solid relationship that promotes the capacity for reflection—for thoughtful attention to feelings and the meaning of actions, both their own and those of people around them. In short, foster children need a lasting relationship with a therapist in order to develop the trust necessary for lasting relationships with friends, teachers, foster parents, and partners.

The truth is sometimes painful. For example, it is extremely painful to tell small children that their parents cannot care for them and that they will have to live—for a short or long time—with people they may not know. It is also painful to tell these children that the system cannot care for them in the way that they would like or that might be best for them—that personal or professional needs take priority over the children's needs for a lasting relationship. This does not mean that trainees and therapists should be encouraged to make undue sacrifices for their clients who are foster children or to become embroiled in enactments of unconscious rescue fantasies. It simply means that all involved in providing therapy must hold the truth about the therapeutic relationship's rich possibilities and limits.

Part of therapy's work is helping children and adolescents recognize and manage the competing needs and desires inherent in any relationship. For children whose primary relationships have been abusive or neglectful, it is tempting to assume for and with them that any better relationship is worth cultivating or preserving—that something beats nothing, that a little bit of a good relationship is better than no good relationship. In addition, although we might prefer to work from the theory that every cloud has a silver lining, sometimes enduring the downpour is not worth the tiny ray of sunshine that comes before the next storm. Foster children learn early that it is easier to stay in out of the rain; they avoid relationships out of the knowledge and fear that the relationships will not last. When foster children repeatedly lose therapists, they understandably become as wary of therapists and what we have to offer as they do of the help and support offered by the social workers, foster parents, attorneys, and myriad other people who populate the system that runs their lives.

At any given time in the United States, there are approximately 500,000 young people in foster care. They are right to be wary of the system. Although it certainly helps some, and perhaps even saves their lives, it fails to give others the basic emotional, social, or educational foundation necessary for adulthood, let alone for parenting or for finding fulfilling work and relationships. Fifty percent of the approximately 20,000 teenagers who age out of the foster care system each year have not graduated from high school. The consistent finding that fully one third of young people leaving foster care will work below grade level, be incarcerated, be unemployed, and/or be homeless (EMT Group, n.d.) supports the anecdotal evidence that foster care does not offer the support or skills necessary for building a successful, fulfilling adult life.

Martha's case can be counted among the failures of the foster care system. She was shuttled through foster homes and group homes throughout her childhood and adolescence. Certainly these changes, along with a significant learning disability, contributed to her academic failures, including the failure to graduate from high school. Beginning in early adolescence, Martha had a succession of "boyfriends"—men usually closer to her father's age than hers. At age 18, she gave birth to Susan, who was removed from her care when she wandered away from her mother during an outing to a neighborhood park and was molested before being taken into protective custody by the police. The social worker described Martha as consistently angry, belligerent, and unresponsive to Susan, who reportedly cried during all of their visits. The social worker also expressed concern about Susan's somewhat delayed development and bland affect. The social worker was confused and angered by Martha's failure to ask for help or to make use of reunification services. Martha's version of events was somewhat different.

She had little to say about the circumstances that resulted in Susan's being in foster care but was extremely angry that she had not been notified in a timely manner that Susan had been removed from her first foster home because of a suspicious bruise. During the initial sessions with me, Martha did not play with Susan unless encouraged to do so; she did not seem to know what to do. However, Martha came to the final evaluation session with Susan's favorite fruit and a delightful, age-appropriate toy. When Susan was not brought to one of our scheduled evaluation sessions because of a mix-up in the driver's schedule, Martha's rage effectively masked her enormous disappointment and sadness. In this context, she talked about the many losses she had suffered in foster care. She particularly suffered from the death of her first foster mother and the loss of contact with the girls with whom she had lived in a group home. She left foster care with no meaningful relationships.

It was hardly surprising that Martha did not turn to the system for advice, support, or help in having Susan returned to her care. Martha's consistent refusal to talk with the social worker about how she had failed to supervise Susan provides a glimpse into the complexities of relationships within the foster care system. The social worker believed that Martha's failure to assume responsibility for her actions was a sign of poor judgment and an indication that Martha did not recognize her shortcomings as a parent. She reasoned that Martha would not be able to accept help until she could admit that she needed it. Her argument was logical, and she was understandably concerned about Martha's future ability to protect Susan if she could not consider what had gone wrong in the past. However, that position failed to take into account Martha's suspicion of a system that had neglected her needs and seemed to punish rather than help her when she made mistakes. From Martha's perspective, admitting that she did not know much about children or how to be a good parent virtually guaranteed that Susan would never be returned to her. Largely because I was an outside evaluator, Martha was able, even if only fleetingly, to give me a glimpse into her worries about being able to care for Susan and to consider a referral for help. Fortunately, Martha and Susan had access to a program where they could receive the intensive psychotherapy and sensitive support that their relationship so desperately needed.

The picture for Billy, whom I mentioned previously, was not so bright. I cast a wide net in trying to find a good therapist for him. Clinicians who have the skills, experience, and sensitivity to the particular needs of foster children and are willing to accept the severely reduced fees offered for their treatment constitute a relatively small pool. They are easily overwhelmed by requests for their services.

The absence of a consistent, loving caregiver creates multiple deficiencies in a child's life, some more obvious than others. We readily think of the enormity of the emotional loss for the child. Those working with foster children—social workers, teachers, doctors, coaches, and therapists—quickly confront the impact of the loss of the organizational function of parenting. Parents hold extraordinary amounts of interrelated information for and about their children—they know not only the important events in a child's life but also the social and emotional context in which these occurred. They know not just the names but also the personalities of the important people in a child's life. For example, with one simple question to a parent, a therapist may learn that the birth of a sibling occurred at about the same time as a grandparent's move to a neighboring community during a particularly difficult school year, which was marked by the loss of the child's best friend and a series of minor respiratory illnesses. This kind of information about the life of a child in foster care, if available at all, might require numerous phone calls to several different people, each of whom has a small bit of information and none of whom knows the whole story. Ferreting out the important information about a foster child's life can be a daunting and time-consuming task.

Not merely the child's history is difficult to discover; routine events in the foster child's life can be equally hard to grasp. For example, a child might fail to appear for a therapy session because the social worker, unaware of the child's regular weekly routine, scheduled an educational evaluation at the same time. In the flurry of arranging multiple appointments for multiple children, social workers and foster parents often forget or do not have the time to change or rearrange schedules or call to cancel standing appointments. Although making a few extra phone calls is time-consuming and can be annoying, the greater toll comes from not even knowing whom to call or discovering that there is no one to call. The demoralization arising from this kind of confusion and lack of cohesion takes a toll on therapists and leads many either to limit the number of foster children they see or to simply give up and leave the world of foster care to others.

GOALS OF THE CHILDREN'S PSYCHOTHERAPY PROJECT

These are the experiences that gave rise to CPP. They, and the stories in the chapters that follow, do not all end happily. In many cases, we only know the very beginnings of the stories. Yet, one thing is clear from our work and from countless reports, interviews, and studies: *The single most important factor in the lives of children and youth in foster care is a stable and lasting relationship with a caring adult.*

CPP represents one means of meeting this crucial need. It is based on a very simple premise, namely that children and adolescents in foster care should have the opportunity to work with a therapist until the therapy draws to its natural conclusion. That is, they should have the same opportunities as children whose parents can afford treatment. In general, an adult or a child embarks on a course of psychotherapy with a clinician in private practice with the understanding that the process of psychotherapy has a beginning, a middle, and an ending. Client and therapist expect, whether explicitly or implicitly, that they will work together until the process comes to a natural conclusion. Simply put, when clients find sufficient relief from the suffering that propelled them to seek treatment, therapy typically draws to a close, with both parties participating in the decision and the process of bringing closure. Of course, not all therapy continues to its natural conclusion; external events may necessitate a premature ending, or the emotional distress that often accompanies psychic change may bring therapy to an abrupt halt. However, the possibility of an open-ended relationship—one that might continue as long as it is needed—offers young people time to develop trust and a sense of safety in the therapeutic relationship. Foster children and teens who have repeatedly been hurt and disappointed by those who are supposed to care for them, do not trust easily. They test the stability of the therapeutic relationship over and over again. This process takes time.

The simple formula of "One Child. One Therapist. For as Long as it Takes." attempts to capture the profound and complex compact that emerges between a therapist and a client who begin working together with the expectation that they will be able to finish what they start, even when they do not know how long the process will take or where it will lead them. For

client and therapist alike, open-ended therapy differs from therapy that begins with a predetermined, externally imposed ending. For example, if an
adolescent starts therapy knowing that she is leaving for college at the end
of the summer, or a young adult contacts a therapist with an understanding
that his insurance company only allows for 10 sessions, or an intern explains
that she will only be at a training site for 6 months, or an adolescent in
foster care knows that funding for his therapy will end when he turns 18,
both parties in the therapeutic process are aware of the time limits on the
relationship. Of course, this does not mean that one or both may forget
about this externally imposed limitation as they become involved in the
work and the relationship. Just as the anticipation of the parting can intensify a summer romance, a time limit can also bring an enhanced and
useful intensity to the therapeutic relationship. However, foster children
and youth typically need less, rather than more, intensity in their lives; they
often lack a time and place for quiet reflection in the context of a non-
judgmental relationship.

When embarking on a therapeutic journey, neither therapist nor
client knows for certain what psychological terrain they will traverse together. Certainly, the client's history—which for foster children and youth
often includes a combination of multiple losses, neglect, abuse, poverty,
and instability—will offer some clues about what lies ahead. However, despite the commonalities that bring children to foster care and the recurrent
themes in the lives of foster children and adolescents, each has traveled a
unique path to the therapist's office and the beginning of the therapeutic
journey. When someone enters therapy with a history of chronic and traumatic life events, the therapist reasonably expects that the journey will not
be an easy one—perhaps interesting and full of unexpected discoveries, but
not easy. For these reasons, not surprisingly, clients often feel tempted to
leave therapy. Sometimes they announce clearly and directly that the work
is just too hard or the feelings are just too frightening. Other times, their
wish to avoid the painful scenery on the psychic journey is less conscious
and less direct—transportation becomes too difficult, after-school activities interfere, or therapy is written off as being boring. In these instances,
the therapist, who may share the client's trepidation, may be inclined to
collude with the wish to avoid knowing and experiencing the painful emotional realities. The therapist may agree that the client is too fragile or not
ready to examine the events in her past and the way that they influence her

present unhappiness. In other cases, the therapist may also become overwhelmed by the difficulties of finding reliable transportation or establishing a schedule that can accommodate both therapy and after-school activities or may succumb to a mutually dissatisfying boredom that eventually results in a quiet, gradual ending of the relationship.

Therapists attempting to work with foster children and adolescents often find that these young clients somehow fall between the cracks. The transportation fails so often that the therapist believes that she cannot reasonably keep open an hour that is not being used and, consequently, for which she cannot charge. The accumulated attempts of therapist, social worker, and foster parents to speak by phone often create such a burden that one of the parties stops returning calls and the therapy drifts off with no formal ending.

We were acutely aware of these as examples of the complicated dynamics facing therapists and families in foster care when we[2] first gathered to discuss the best way to address the needs of the foster care community. We were also acutely aware of the limitations of our resources; we numbered 14 people working in private practice and community agencies. Our professional lives were filled by a variety of activities—teaching, supervision, consultation, psychotherapy, psychoanalysis, administrative duties, writing, and presenting at local and national meetings. We were also deeply committed to our own children and families and to maintaining a balance between our personal and professional lives. In short, as individuals and as a group, we had limited time and energy to devote to increasing the availability of long-term psychotherapy to children in the foster care system. We were also acutely aware that the clinics that typically served the foster care community were closing or reducing services at an alarming rate. This meant not only fewer services for children and families but also fewer training opportunities for psychiatrists, social workers, psychologists, and marriage and family therapists. When training institutions reduce or eliminate their programs, the faculty, staff, and former trainees also lose their professional home. This can be a particularly devastating loss for young clinicians, who need a base from which to venture into the larger professional community. At all developmental milestones—from toddlers who use

---

[2]The initial working group included Joe Afterman, Marian Birch, Carolyn Block, Victor Bonfilio, David Donner, Diane Ehrensaft, Graeme Hanson, Barbara Kalmanson, Alicia Lieberman, Velora Lilly, Jeree Pawl, Judy Pekarsky, Steve Seligman, and me.

their parent as a home base to explore the world, to college- or work-bound young adults who leave home with the expectation of returning for special meals and family gatherings, to the new parents who return to their child-hood homes to gather advice and artifacts from their own childhoods—people like returning to the familiar in order to gather their resources be-fore moving into unfamiliar territory.

In our initial conversations, we were keenly aware of the disparity be-tween the resources 14 people could offer and the enormous need facing San Francisco's foster care system. Simultaneously, we were developing a better understanding of the desire of young therapists to join a community of like-minded peers and mentors as they moved into the world of private practice. In response, and with the certain knowledge that therapeutic work with foster children and youth often presents overwhelmingly daunt-ing challenges, we arrived at a model designed to maximize the resources of the therapeutic community. We elected to draw on the experience of senior clinicians within our group by establishing them as consultants who would each offer a weekly pro bono consultation group for a small group of CPP therapists. With the groups in place, we would invite other clini-cians to join our fledgling project as therapists, each of whom would be asked to take one foster child or adolescent into weekly psychotherapy and provide treatment, without charge, until the therapy drew to a natural close. We believed that this model made the best use of the range and va-riety of skills and experiences in our small community. At the time, we felt certain that the consultation groups would form a core element of the proj-ect—without them, we would simply be offering a referral service to clini-cians in private practice with openings for foster children.

We also wanted to address a persistent complaint of therapists work-ing with foster children and families: too much paperwork for too little pay. When we organized the first chapter of CPP, payments were frequently delayed and statements often had to be submitted many times. This be-came particularly annoying and demoralizing when therapists had devoted many hours making phone calls to social workers, foster parents, attorneys, or teachers. Agencies that serve numbers of foster children and families often receive a flat fee for treating foster children; in these instances, trainees and/or staff members may be able to include the necessary collat-eral work as part of their routine activities. However, at that time, thera-pists in private practice could charge only for face-to-face contact, not for the work to support the treatment and certainly not for the hours that the child simply failed to appear even without prior notice. A therapist who already feels underpaid and undervalued will likely feel uncomfortable about continuing to keep an appointment time available that could be filled with a paying client.

The initial group at CPP elected to address this problem by establishing a community of clinicians who would work on a volunteer basis. We took this approach for a number of reasons, including the reality that no one in the group wanted to take on the task of fundraising! Working without pay also meant eliminating the monthly headache of billing. Paradoxically, it also underscored the value of the work; people feel very differently about making a choice to donate their time than about spending it in underpaid work. In addition, we envisioned establishing a level playing field for the clinicians in CPP, in contrast to the very wide differential in fees paid according to degree and specialty, which can result in three therapists who are seeing three siblings being paid at three wildly different rates.

Then, too, we wanted to minimize the chances of children's having to stop therapy for administrative rather than clinical reasons. The administrative interruptions often resulted from the financial constraints that local, state, and federal agencies imposed on the foster care agency and passed along to therapist and child. If the therapist received no income from the process, then the therapy would not depend on the stability or variability of income streams.

Over several months of meetings, we created the previously described model designed to incorporate the variety of needs and resources we had identified. We envisioned a structure that took maximum advantage of the considerable expertise presented by the group of psychodynamic clinicians, provided a home base for younger therapists, placed minimal time demands on any one person, and created a network of skilled and experienced clinicians committed to providing long-term treatment to foster children and families. Above all, we wanted to keep it simple. No one had the time to create or manage a complicated organization.

The model we created in 1993 has served us well for more than 10 years. We ask therapists who volunteer to offer weekly psychotherapy sessions with one child or adolescent until the therapy draws to a natural, clinically indicated termination. We recognized at the outset that the quality of work expected of the therapists would demand ongoing education and support, which we offer through the consultation groups. Some of these consultation groups have remained relatively stable since the inception of the project. Others have varied more—for example, when therapists' working hours change, when a therapist takes maternity leave and another takes her place in the group, or when a therapist wants the opportunity to work with a different consultant. Therapists are not assigned to consultation groups; they select a group that meets their scheduling and clinical needs.

This model creates a place and space for therapists to reflect on and talk about their clinical work with children and families in the foster care system. This model provides a particularly important counterpoint to the frequent demand from and within the foster care system to act and react. It is a system fueled by and infused with action. It puts enormous pressure on those in and around the system to act and to act quickly, often before they have time to consider the meaning of action or response. For example, missed sessions are ubiquitous and problematic parts of therapy with foster children that often result in the premature ending of the therapeutic relationship. However, in the CPP consultation groups we have the time and space to consider the meaning of the child's absence from therapy with the same care that we consider the meaning of what happens when the child or adolescent is present. Since the beginning of CPP, we have undoubtedly devoted hundreds of hours to missed sessions. The time includes the hours that therapists spend waiting for children and adolescents who do not show up or come at the tail end of the session, along with the time spent in the consultation groups discussing the meaning of the missed sessions and trying to understand how best to respond, because every missed session has a particular story and a unique meaning. We know that children who have repeatedly been let down by people who are supposed to care for them will inevitably do unto others what has been done to them and leave adults waiting and wondering when they will appear.

Of course, young children are not responsible for getting themselves to therapy or any other appointments. However, the foster parents who care for them may also consciously or unconsciously demonstrate that they, too, feel abandoned and mistreated by forgetting appointments or failing to call to cancel. As surrogate parents in a system with too few human and financial resources, they often feel that the system does not make good on its promise for help and support, which seems to offer implicit permission for them to treat others in like fashion. Sometimes negotiating these complex dynamics leaves the child, the foster parents, and the therapist in very uncomfortable positions—all waiting for and feeling let down by the others when therapy sessions do not occur.

Adolescents or young adults may also repeatedly question the therapist's availability through actions rather than words. For example, Marvella, a young woman who had grown up in foster care, called CPP wanting to begin therapy as soon as possible because of pervasive and chronic depression. She called numerous times in subsequent days, with an increasing sense of urgency. However, when a therapist called to set up an appointment, Marvella did not return the call for several days. When she did call back, she explained that her schedule was very full for the next few weeks. Marvella missed the first session, explaining that she had forgotten about a previously scheduled appointment. Again Marvella and the therapist scheduled a time to meet. Marvella called 10 minutes before the appointment to ask how to get to the office from her home about 40 minutes away by bus. After a brief conversation, the therapist and Marvella elected to reschedule the appointment rather than meet for the first time in a shortened session.

When Marvella did arrive, about 20 minutes late for the rescheduled session, she barely paused for breath in her urgency to describe the anxiety that made her seek therapy. She explained that she could not figure out how to make friends or avoid relationships that were not good for her, unaware that she had begun to tell the therapist her story in actions before putting it into words.

The therapist took Marvella's story back to the consultation group, four people who had never met her and did not know her name but were beginning to care about her and wonder how her story would unfold. Marvella and her therapist had entered into a community ready to support them on the therapeutic journey that had taken several turns before they had even met.

A community of concerned people who keep the foster child, teen, or young adult in mind is one of the crucial gifts that CPP offers clinicians and the individuals they serve. Even if the concerned community sits quietly in the background, the way in which the therapeutic couple is upheld and supported is transmitted to the child through the therapist's words and actions. In addition to offering a place to share concerns and problems, CPP offers a place to share successes, something missing when parents are not available for a collaborative relationship with a child's therapist. When the therapist who had worked with a young girl through the trials, tribulations, and triumphs of high school brought news of the girl's acceptance to the college of her choice, a collective cheer rose up from the consultation group. Other than the girl and her therapist, those in the group comprised the only people who really understood the incredible work and sense of partnership that went into this important developmental milestone. It was incredibly valuable to the therapist to be able to share this moment with people who knew the history of the accomplishment. Often, a therapist knows more of a child's history than any other adult. Like parents who want to reminisce with friends and relatives as their children move through life, therapists—whose work would otherwise be very isolated and isolating—appreciate a community of people who know the small and large pieces of a therapeutic relationship's history.

LOOKING AHEAD

We started CPP in 1993 with feelings of excitement, adventure, purpose, trepidation, and disbelief. More than 10 years later, as I write about our work and the lessons we have learned, I hold the same feelings. In that time, 250 clinicians have been involved with CPP, touching the lives of more than 200 children in 12 communities. We have been cited as a Promising Practice by the Administration for Children and Families of the U.S. Department of Health and Human Services (2004). As we continue to talk and write about our work, clinicians from communities across the country contact us for more information. Clearly, we are not alone in our recognition of the limitations of the current means of matching experienced therapists with an interest in long-term therapy with foster children and youth who truly need a lasting relationship. We and those who come to us for advice and consultation know that we can and must do better.

In many ways, the founders of CPP saw a simple problem—foster children did not have access to long-term psychotherapy—which we planned to address with a simple solution—matching therapists willing to offer pro bono psychotherapy with children who needed it. Viewed through one lens, this *is* a simple problem with a simple solution. The public funds available to meet the mental health needs of these children and adolescents are insufficient. Often the available money is stretched by offering every child a little bit or by allocating the most money to those in greatest need. Surely, compelling arguments can and have been made for these approaches to the distribution of scarce resources. However, others have argued and continue to argue with equal conviction that anything short of political action addressing the allocation of federal, state, and local revenues is wasted effort that tacitly supports a fundamentally unfair system.

Certainly, we have always sensed the complex historical, social, economic, and political realities that shaped the problems facing foster children and those responsible for their care. As a group, members of CPP had and continue to have connections to clinics, training institutions, and public agencies that are charged with meeting the mental health needs of underserved children and families. We recognize both the importance and limitations of individual psychotherapy. From the time when we began the creation of this book, we have learned more than we ever could have imagined when we started. CPP chapters have sprung up in small and large communities across the United States.

Of course, we cannot know what lessons the next 10 years will offer. As I write this, unprecedented deficits threaten to inflict further funding cuts on the already tenuous foster care system. Children will have fewer supportive services. Adolescents will be moved out of the foster care system earlier and with fewer services to help them make a successful transition to independent living. Young parents who grew up in foster care will find fewer preventive mental health programs to help them raise emotionally and physically healthy children.

We offer the material in this book as a way of sharing our appreciation for the unique needs of children and youth in foster care and our deepening conviction that offering them a lasting therapeutic relationship is one very important key to breaking the intergenerational cycle of trauma in the foster care system. We hope that the ideas, techniques, and stories in the following chapters will help sustain therapists who work in isolation or without the support of a community of like-minded peers and mentors. We know that the journeys that bring foster children and youth to all of our consulting rooms are fraught with many dangers. We also know that they need a steady, guiding presence on their journey out of the foster care system into a healthy adulthood that promotes self-confidence, encourages the capac-

ity to care for self and others, and allows for the pleasures of both independence and interdependence. We invite you to explore some of the journeys
CPP therapists and clients have shared.

REFERENCES

Administration for Children and Families, U.S. Department of Health and Human
     Services. (2004). Meeting the mental health needs of foster children: The Children's
     Psychotherapy Project. *Children's Bureau Express, 5*(1). Retrieved April 5, 2005,
     from http://cbexpress.acf.hhs.gov/articles.cfm?issue_id=2004-02&article_id=772
EMT Group for the California Department of Alcohol and Drug Programs. (n.d.).
     Life after foster care: Foster youth mentorship training for program managers. Folsom,
     CA: Author.

Holding the Child, Knowing the System

Theories for Bridging Internal and External Worlds

Most children grow up in a family system—a system composed of interdependent relationships that, for better or worse, create a context of meaning and connections to the immediate and larger community. From a very young age, children know who is in their family and who is not, regardless of how that family is defined. For example, in a family where cousins are called and treated as siblings, children know who is a brother or sister and who is a cousin. Similarly, in families defined both by friendship and legal agreements, children know the difference between those they call Aunt or Uncle or Granny or Grandfather as a sign of honor and those to whom they are bound by biology or the courts.

Some children grow up in the foster care system—a system of fragmented relationships that often fails to create a context of meaning and connections to the immediate and larger communities. It is sometimes very hard for young foster children to know who is in their family and who is not. The children's biological parents may not know their foster parents, and the tenth foster parents may not know the first or second or third foster parents. If a social worker leaves the system or is transferred, then only the case record holds the history that the social worker had kept in his or her mind. When foster children move to a new community, they usually make the move by themselves, without parents or siblings or extended family to help them maintain internal and external connections to the community left behind.

This section explores the theories that guide our understanding of the inner world of children who grow up in the foster care system—the ways that they are like and different from children who grow up in a family system. It also focuses a theoretical lens on the foster care system as a system with a mandate to provide care in the face of impossible and contradictory tasks. Looking through that lens will provide the vision for understanding the day-to-day clinical work of Children's Psychotherapy Project (CPP) clinicians.

CHAPTER 2

Walking Through Walls

The Mind of a Foster Child

Peter G.M. Carnochan

It is not easy being a foster child. Something has gone wrong with the birth family's ability to sustain the child within the family. Perhaps this is because of a death, but more commonly the breakdown involves forms of neglect or abuse. For these children there was a beginning, but it went wrong. The difficulties continue: Although the loss of the birth family is in the past, the tragedy is not yet resolved. Foster children have lost one family and have yet to find another where the terms are guaranteed. To be a foster child means to be taken in, but not fully claimed. The *foster* part of the term, a word that in ordinary usage denotes care, points to the tentative status of the child. In a foster home, the child does not have ownership rights, cannot rely on the bonds of love and law to ensure the constancy of the attachment. At any moment, placement in the foster home can be suspended, and the child can find him- or herself bounced to a shelter or a new home.

A foster child lives in the midst of constant transition, like a business traveler on the road. The question the traveler has to ask at each new hotel, or each new foster home, is "Will this stay merit unpacking my suitcase?" For the business traveler this is a question about shirts and socks, but for the foster child at issue are rumpled items of love, pain, and memory. Before this luggage can be unpacked, the child must wait to see whether the stay in the foster home will be more than a brief visit. The question is "Will this become a home, a place where new attachments can be permitted to form?" Before we can help foster children, children who have suffered loss and are living in a state of transition, we must first try to imagine what it is like to be in their shoes. It is only from this vantage that we can offer help that navigates the narrow gap between sentimentality and resignation.

Foster children live in a suspended state. Maybe they will be returned to the family of origin after a reconciliation process, maybe they will move on to an adoptive family, but neither of these outcomes can be taken for granted. This sense of not fully being home, of not belonging, lends a stigma to foster children. Given our own insecurities, we tend to want what is wanted. If a line forms, we imagine that what is being waited for must be really good. Yet, if something has been discarded, we regard it with suspicion, wondering about its flaws. Foster children suffer not only from their initial loss but also from the ongoing uncertainty and doubt that accompanies the status of being discarded.

In trying to imagine the interior experience of being a foster child, we need to penetrate this stigma in a way that neither sentimentalizes nor demonizes. This chapter seeks to illuminate the mind of the foster child. To do this, the chapter discusses psychoanalytic perspectives on how children develop the capacity to think about emotional experience. It touches briefly on Klein's work on object relations and on Bion's theory of thinking and containment. In addition, the chapter presents case material from four children in the foster care system to illustrate the double challenge that they face: Their past is hard to think about, but their present, dominated by uncertainty, does not provide a stable foundation for thinking.

PROBLEMS IN THE BIRTH FAMILY

To thrive, babies need good parents. As Winnicott (1965) made clear, we cannot even conceive of the child apart from the parent. This need goes beyond what is required for survival. Food and protection are not enough. In addition to the provision of basic needs, babies need to be held within a relationship that helps them develop the capacity to modulate feeling and to think about experience. It is through the attachment to caregivers that children develop the affective–relational skills that make effective living possible. When children suffer from abuse and neglect, they must bear a double hardship. Violence and deprivation are hard for anyone. They tend to overwhelm one's capacity to make sense of the world and leave residue in memory that act like the aftershocks from a violent earthquake. Yet, when these events happen to infants and young children, the difficulty is more fundamental. The traumatic events are also a failure in provision. An infant, rather than being received with the care and understanding that support the development of the mind, receives abuse. A child, because of this fundamental failure in developmental provision, is left unequipped to work through the difficult events of his or her life.

Psychologists have made a sustained effort to study how the infant–parent relationship supports development. The results of this work have provided multiple lenses for understanding the interactive processes that shape an infant's maturation. Attachment theory, Piagetian theories of skill development, infant observation, and models of affect regulation, among many others, point to the critical role that early experience plays in supporting the child's emotional and cognitive development. Gaining an understanding of these theories is an important part of understanding foster children. Clearly, trying to provide a map to all of this material is beyond the scope of this chapter; instead, it offers something more modest: a brief account of mental and emotional development from the world of contemporary psychoanalysis.

Although psychoanalysis began with Freud, it has been extended and reshaped in the years after his death by an international community of analysts. A key part of this reshaping has been trying to understand how the mind develops during the first years of a child's life. During the years surrounding World War II, Klein (1992) recognized that for children, play is a means for communicating and making sense of their emotional world. As Klein developed the practice of child therapy, she saw how the world of monsters, witches, and superheroes—that is, the characters of play—are representations that have their origin in the immature mind of the infant. She recognized that infants organize their first perceptions around the poles of the positive and negative emotions. Rather than seeing his or her mother as sometimes comforting and sometimes frustrating, an infant instead builds up representations of two separate mothers: the good mother who offers unlimited help and the bad mother who withholds help and subjects the child to torments from the body (i.e., the infant does not experience hunger and discomfort as internal states). In this black-and-white world of understanding, the infant feels free to direct his rage at the bad mother, seeking to annihilate her in fantasy as a strategy for regaining his contact with the good mother. It is only as the infant matures and the mother is able to withstand these sometimes violent demands that the infant comes to understand that the two mothers in his mind are in fact one.

This realization is not easy for the child; it brings on feelings of guilt and dread over the moments of attack. It also awakens feelings of concern and a wish to make reparation. For foster children who have endured neglect and abuse, this process of integration is more difficult. Abusive and neglectful parents *are* a study in extremes. At times they really are almost witchlike in their cruelty. The split between the good and the bad representation, then, is reinforced by reality. This makes the step toward integration more complicated. The children can oscillate between feeling tremendously persecuted by the harsh parent and tremendously worried that they were in some way responsible for creating this harshness through their own infantile aggression. The confusion between self and other, about the lines of responsibility, can be extreme.

Klein's portrait of the infant looked at the earliest relationship between infant and parent. Yet, her account begins with the baby already being able to think about self and other, about good and bad experience. The question of how thinking itself emerges, however, required an answer. This is the project that Bion (1962) took on in his work on the development of the mind through the process of containment. Bion saw that experience is unthinkable for the baby outside the matrix of the mother's understanding and concern. When the new baby experiences a discomfort or a bodily need, it comes on with an intensity that is amplified by the baby's inability to comprehend its meaning. The somatic experience of need is felt as a distress that does not yet have a significance or purpose; it can be felt like an attack on the mind. The painful quality of the need, rather than being represented in the mind—for example, a thought such as "I'm hungry"—is translated into somatic expression, an urgent cry, and is projected outward. When things go well, the mother is ready to receive this projected state of need within her own mind. Through a process of reverie[1] and concern, she recognizes the baby's need, and through the act of a tender feeding, she returns the projected distress, now satisfied as an experience of knowable hunger. The feeding infant can think, "Oh yes, that's hunger, the need for milk." Bion calls this process *containment*. The mother takes in the baby's raw sensory experience, digests it, and returns to the infant in modified form that is

---

[1]For Bion, reverie is a form of affective–intuitive understanding. It allows the parent, through a daydream-like empathetic extension, to know something of the baby's state of mind.

suitable for thinking. It is through repeated moments of this kind of projection, containment, and provision that infants develop an increased capacity to think about experience. Slowly, infants become able to tolerate moments of frustration without having tantrums; they begin to think about what is being felt, what is missing but needed. In moments of suffering, infants can come to believe in the presence of a concerned adult who wants to help them make sense of their experience.

For foster children, containment can be in short supply. Many times, the level of chaos in their birth families disrupts parents' capacity to offer containment. Parents who are struggling with poverty and abuse can feel so desperate in their own states of need that it is virtually impossible for them to have the composure to contain their children's needs. For some of these parents, the insistent cry of a newborn can be felt as a grating, greedy demand rather than a vulnerable state of dependency. In other cases, the family struggles with chemical dependency. The parents, trying to turn down the volume of their own suffering, become lost in the excitement or somnolescence of the altered state. In these cases, an infant's projected distress fails to get through. The cry becomes lost in a fog, and no clear meaning is returned to the infant. Now the infant's experience, which has been projected into the parent, is not contained, is not received within a field of reverie. The overstressed parents experience the infant's need as an unimportant distraction, as an attack, as an impossibly greedy demand, and this is the meaning that is returned to the infant. The infant, then, comes to know him- or herself not through the mediation of the parents' love, but through the filter of the parents' stress, apathy, or even hatred. It is a knowing that is permeated with aggression and misunderstanding, in which the boundary between self and other is hugely confused and the capacity to believe in the value of understanding is undeveloped.

Foster children experience a double deficit in the realm of containment. Not only do they suffer from inadequate containment in their earliest relationships but they also must endure the rupture of their family and contend with the porous world of the foster care system. The loss of a family, even one permeated with violence, is a profound insult. For the children who face this kind of loss, it comes as a shocking blow, something that precipitates great fear and pain but that can barely be known as an experience. It is an emotional experience that overwhelms the capacity to think.

These children are left to try to manage such experiences while they are placed in an unfamiliar family with little reason to expect that their confusion and suffering will be contained and made manageable.

LIVING IN TRANSITION

Foster families are needed when birth families break down. Perhaps drug abuse undermines the capacity to parent; perhaps there are other difficulties that lead to neglect and abuse. These kind of events make children suffer and demand their rescue. Yet, it is an odd thing to be rescued from your home. From the families' point of view and for the children, the question is whether the removal is best understood as a rescue or a kidnapping. Even in the most problematic families, there are moments of care. The fact that the child, although maybe battered, is still alive attests to that. The child has counted on her birth parents, and this leads to some form of attachment. To disrupt this bond, even if it is a matter of life and death, is inevitably traumatic. The child somehow knows that her parents conceived her and that she emerged from the mother's body, creating an unseverable link to her biological parents. The foster child, then, cannot help but feel ambivalence about her lost birth parents. Their failures in care lead to anger and hurt, but the attachment leads to feelings of loss and longing. Perhaps the child knows something of the parents' suffering and is left wishing she could have restored them through her love.

In an ideal system, children who need to be removed from their family of origin would be placed in a home they could count on. When the foster family is dependable, there is a better chance that children will be able to accept that the removal from their families involved elements of rescue. Although many good families take on the responsibility for providing foster care, the foster care system as a whole often fails to provide this kind of constancy. It is not unusual for children to go through a string of foster placements. They are moved from family to family until their sense of location becomes blurred.

James's Story

James was a 5-year-old boy who had already lived in 10 foster placements by the time I met him at a therapeutic nursery school. It was a few weeks after he had been removed from his last foster home. That family had taken him in with the plan of adopting him, but within 2 days, the foster parents called James's case worker to say that the family would not keep him; his behavior was too much to handle. When James was removed from this home, social services had to scramble to find a new placement, and he ended up missing school for a week until the school administration was able to track him down and work out transportation for him. He was now living in a new home. The report suggested that his new foster parent was very capable and that she might take steps to adopt him. Yet, it was still far too early to know anything with confidence about the final reliability of his new placement.

When James returned to school, he was uncontrollable. He had constant tantrums, throwing toys and hitting teachers. To keep the classroom safe, the teachers had to restrain him several times a day. Moving is hard enough on adults, but for a boy like James, the disruptions were more than he could bear. What was he meant to do with the feelings that roared through him? He felt both enraged at the school for losing him and desperately in need of the comfort and containment that comes with being held. In the face of things that are too horrible to bear, one's mind and body says, "This is too much; I'm leaving." It is like closing one's eyes and screaming, refusing to see and hear, during a scary movie. When we are faced with trauma and events of horror that we do not have the resources to halt, the attempt to defend against the moment moves from the external world to the internal. We work to keep the onslaught from becoming a perceptual event. Although we cannot prevent the assault to our body or to the conditions of our living, it is possible to close the doors to the mind. I believe that the loss of yet another family threw James into a state of trauma. This trauma had force both because of uncertainty and fear about the new placement and because the disruption reawakened the loss of his first family.

On the day I met James, he was in another restraint. A teacher had him in the corner and he was not talking. His eyes were closed and he was alternating between crying and yelling. In his tantrum, he blocked out what was happening around him, but the tantrum also served to drown out the thoughts and feelings that threatened him from within his own mind. I tried to talk to him, but he was not able to say much. From one point of view, this was quite reasonable behavior. Why should he expect that talking would help him feel any better? He had little experience with the value

of words. Even worse, talking about his situation brings the pain of his experience back to his mind. Why would he want that? Pain is the very thing
he sought to escape. Maybe I could have said to him, "I think your screams
are telling us that none of this should have happened and are a way of making it stop happening inside. You need the grown-ups to know this and to
do something about how awful it feels." However, rather than talk, James
took from his pocket a quarter that his new foster mother had given him;
he held it tight. A lot of things had been taken from James, but he was not
going to let us take this coin from him. The worth of a quarter is indis-
putable and portable. He stuck it in his mouth as though it were a sweet, as
though he was a baby who still wanted to know the world through his
tongue. Then he took it out of his mouth and began to grind it against the
wall with its rough edge. The grinding reminded me of a prisoner who
etches his initials into the cell wall: a kind of proof that he had been there.
Foster children run the risk of being forgotten, and to be forgotten is to
become insubstantial. This move from regressive sucking to aggressive cutting shows how feelings of rage and need can become intertwined for children who have to endure repeated dislocation.

I talked with James about his quarter, and finally he calmed down
enough to return to his class. It was circle time, and the children were singing
with their teacher. James was still upset, and rather than joining in with the
singing, he kept sliding off his chair and using his quarter to carve on the
walls. It was as though James lived in a world of ice surfaces where he just
kept slipping away. For the rest of circle time, I had to take him by the arm
and hold him in place. In this constant slipping, I think James was showing
a wish to slip away from his current reality as well as a wish to be held. Escape or containment: It was a real dilemma for him.

After circle time, it was snack time, and James settled down. Maybe
talking to him about his losses and how he wanted to hold onto the quarter had helped calm him some. He ate a bunch of sandwiches, cleaned up
his plate, put away his name card, and worked at the puzzle table while
waiting for his turn to go outside. I talked with him as he worked on a
puzzle. He was good at it—could see how it went together. I was surprised
at his puzzle-building skill; it suggested that somewhere he had gotten help
with learning how to think. Then he wanted to show me his Buzz Light-
year wristbands. They were bright green, with decals picturing various knobs
and controls. When another boy asked him what they did, James said,

"They don't do anything; they're just pretend." The other child, though, could see that pretend or not, the wristbands were cool. So James and the other boy each put on a wristband. The other boy opened up the plastic flap and pushed the imaginary buttons while making zapping noises to show that he made a power ray shoot out, laying waste to all enemies. Yet, James took a different route. When he fired his wristband, he made a vibrating noise and announced that he was coated with ice. He said, "I'm frozen; your rays just bounce off me." For a foster child who has suffered so many losses, so many aborted attachments, what would be adequate protection? For James, the danger was not so much that something was going to be done to him by an attacker, who could be fended off, killed by a ray of fire. Instead, the danger was that something would be lost, and the damage was to himself, to his heart. Yet, such damage could only be done if he was foolish enough to let someone matter to him. By freezing himself, James kept his loving under control and avoided the constant threat of loss.

When we come across a boy coated in ice, it is natural to think that what is needed is to bring forward some warmth. Yet, if we understand that this is a self-freezing boy, we have to be more cautious. To melt away the encasing ice would be to leave him exposed to further injury. Perhaps James could be composed enough to solve a complicated puzzle because he knows how to freeze himself. Instead of cajoling such a child prematurely into the warmth of another attachment, we should pay close attention to the creativity of the icing mechanism. Perhaps we might say, "Wow, what a great idea using ice to protect you. If something came through and bruised you, you'd already have on an ice pack." Rather than trying to disable such protective mechanisms, it is better to help these children find the capacity to use them selectively, to turn the jets on and off, to vary the depth of the freeze. This would be the game that, with time, I would want to play with James. I would then ask him, "When you're frozen like that how do you move? Ice is so stiff. Do you get cold? How do you stay warm under all that ice?" When you let the ice melt, what happens to the water that runs off?" In playing like this, my goal would not be to turn off the protective mechanism but to help him gain more subtle, volitional control over the self-icing process.

After working on the puzzle, it was time to go outside. James and his friend began playing a game about monsters and superheroes. He wanted me to be a monster, to give chase. In the middle of the yard, there was a play structure with a rope ladder that formed a square column. Each wooden rung was approximately 18 inches long; together, they formed a series of ascending bars. In the middle of the monster chase game, James stopped running, crawled inside the rope ladder column, and announced that he was inside my trap. Immediately my imagination was captured by this moment in the play. What is it like for a foster child to be brought into a new family, a new school, a new therapy? In some ways, it would be good if I had a nice trap for this boy, one with bars that could keep him in for a change. A place like that might be strong enough to restrain his aggression and fear and act as a container of sorts. Yet, if you are playing a game about traps, it is clear that the goal is to get out, to master the art of escape. It would be a mistake to assume that this foster child's only fear when placed in a new home is that he will be set loose too soon. Perhaps, at least initially, the fear is more of being held forever by strangers. The child might reasonably think, "Who are these people? Why are they choosing me when I didn't get a voice in choosing them?" Therefore, it is not surprising that some foster children act in ways to escape the trap of the foster home. By trying to break free (as James symbolically indicated by cutting the wall with his quarter), these children put their fear into action and investigate the quality of the new home's physical and emotional walls.

As the monster chase game continued, James told me that he could walk through walls; my trap could not hold him. To be that diaphanous is quite a superpower, although a bit tragic. Where does a foster child—a boy without the solidity of home, just the presence of houses and caregivers—get an identity that feels solid? When a child moves through so many placements so quickly, it is natural to feel somewhat ghost like. His tangibility involves more than a physical body; it emerges from the constancy of relationships, from having his past remembered by someone who loves him. To know that he is wanted is a way that his presence is made more real.

In trying to help children who are in the middle of transition and uncertainty, there can be a temptation to extend concern about the trauma that has been endured. For children who are in the midst of ongoing upheaval, however, this attempt to offer understanding can be felt as more of a threat that an offer of help. The child has all that he or she can handle in trying to manage the anxiety that comes with being moved from placement to placement; the invitation to reflect on devastating memories is merely a further demand and burden. It would be like an accountant offering tax advice in the middle of the earthquake: "Thanks, but now is not the time." For foster children, though, the problem with trying to offer understanding can go further. Many of these children have suffered from profound deficits in containment. They may be more accustomed to misunderstanding than to understanding. The attempt to name what has occurred can be perceived not as help, but as taunting and insulting. For instance, several weeks after I met James, I returned to his school. While we were outside, James revived the monster chase game. He pretended that he had snuck into my house and was eating my food. We were having fun. I said to him that I know he has been moved to a new home and that maybe he is trying to understand what will be offered to him there. He said, with some irritation, "I know that." I had hoped my comments would be perceived as a form of understanding and a way to clarify his anxiety, but James apparently heard my comments as a potential belittlement. It was as though I had said to him, "I know you better than you do; you don't even know what has happened to you." One of the first tasks in working with children who have suffered from abuse and neglect is to try to establish the possibility and value of understanding. This work may have to start with more ordinary concerns before the most painful events of the child's life can be approached.

SETTLING INTO A NEW HOME

Although disruption and transition mark the first part of the foster care experience, many of these children are eventually placed in a more stable situation. Sometimes, this is a long-term foster placement; other times, a family shows an interest in adoption. The child is finally invited to unpack his or her bags and to begin thinking in terms of home. In more romantic notions of adoption, the temptation is to think of this provision as the happy conclusion, as the moment of rescue that will mend past hurts. This fantasy, often held by politicians and adoptive parents, is that love and affection will overcome all. However, in my experience working with adoptive and long-term foster placements, the reality is more complicated and uneven. For children who have endured abuse and neglect, love is a potentially dangerous emotion. They have known love before and come away bruised. The process of settling into a new home takes time, and there are many difficulties that must be negotiated with care and awareness before the goodness of the new home can become clear.

Foster care and adoption are a bit like an arranged marriage. The state locates a family for a child and makes the placement. However, from the child's point of view, this is not a union based on love—the child has not been involved in the choosing. The child is told, "Here is your new family," and must try to make sense of what this situation will mean. Foster children have had experiences with family—often frightening ones. This is the template that they bring to bear as they settle into the new home. In the first months of a new placement, there can be a tendency for a foster child to swing between extremes. At one moment, the child may be all smiles and appreciation. In the next moment, this can dissolve into loud outbursts and uncontrolled behavior. Maybe the foster child offers hugs and his or her most engaging behavior to the new parents. In part, this is an expression of genuine gratitude. After a history of neglect and abuse, to be treated with warmth and predictable care is a great relief. Yet, this initial wave of loving behavior can also be an expression of fear. If the child holds the conviction that families are unpredictable and dangerous, it is good strategy to placate the disposition toward cruelty. These first versions of loving must be accepted by the foster family, but gobbling them up too eagerly can subtly confirm the foster child's anxious convictions about the terms of attachment.

In new placements, the moments of feeling positive and calm tend to be punctuated by frequent outbreaks of more disturbing feelings. When foster children become anxious or frustrated, they can fall into tantrums and defiance. At these moments, words lose their ability to reassure. Battles for control often ensue, and overwhelming fears frequently emerge. Control battles can be pronounced, and there are frequent fears. Children can be beset by nightmares and other troubling fantasies. One foster child, David, refused to brush his teeth for months after moving to his new home. At night he would dream of vampires with bloody teeth. For this boy, his own oral needs had become fused with a great deal of biting aggression, and having to brush his teeth remained a tangible reminder of these anxieties. When a child has lived in the midst of sustained unpredictability, it takes a long time to accept that the stability of the new home can be trusted. Predictability lurks as a new form of unpredictability, possibly a trick of apparent consistency.

For children who have lived with neglect, it is odd to finally be with adults who are prepared to help. After enduring such deprivation, foster children can be unsure of what constitutes help. Bion suggested that when there is a failure of containment, the hope for understanding and emotional provision can be diverted into a more empty wish for material provision. The child may turn away from relationships and express need in battles over sweets or toys. These tokens of provision cannot really address the child's needs, but this is not an easy thing to understand. Another boy showed this confusion about provision in a remarkable way during a therapy session. My therapy playroom contains a set of toys that are available to and shared by all of the children in my practice. All of the children have their own boxes, too, where they can keep things that they make. Matt came to realize that the ball of string I kept with the art supplies was part of the common property of my playroom but that if he cut off a length of string, it became his, something that he could place in his box. In one session, he slowly, mischievously, began to cut up the string. As he gauged my reaction to his avarice, he cut the whole ball of string into a set of 12-inch lengths. Although we might say that this act of cutting up the string was a way of expressing how many times the continuity of his home life had been cut into pieces, at that moment I would argue it was a way of trying to get something through a kind of theft. At the end of the session, he had a box full of string scraps, useless but abundant. The cutting up of the string was a kind of experiment for Matt as he tried to see what I would offer him, how I would react to his need and greed. It was several months before he was able to return to his box of string. With a kind of tentative wonder, he asked me to help him tie the bits of string together. His unspoken question seemed to be, "Would you actually help me with this project; would you feel misused?" When we got it all tied together, Matt had a large ball of string, and he began to play with it as a lasso, as an escape ladder, and as a way of barring the door to keep out intruders. Through this sequence, which reportedly was repeated many times at his new home, Matt began to understand how grown-ups can be of help beyond simply offering material goods.

When foster children come to live with a family, they often lie or steal. This can be a difficult behavior for the new family to confront. It creates uncertainty and suspicion. Family members may worry about this being a sign of sociopathy, of delinquent behavior, and about how this child will turn out. David, the boy who dreamt of vampires, went through a phase where he frequently lied and stole candy from convenience stores. When confronted by his foster parents, he would insist that he was telling the truth and that someone had given him the candy. When he came to my office, he would often run into the room and sit in my chair. In a way, he was stealing my seat. In trying to make sense of this behavior, which can be so disturbing to parents, it is important to see beyond the delinquent act. Rather than saying, "You don't care about the rules; you're being dishonest"—comments that point to aggression and deficits in superego functioning—it is both more accurate and helpful to point to the wish that is embedded in these moments of transgression. When David ran into my office and stole my chair, I tried to say to him, "You find it hard to believe that I will make sure that there is a good chair for both of us." When foster children lie or steal, they express a wish about how they think the world should have been. We might say to a child who steals, "I think you're showing me that there was a time when there wasn't enough. Back then, things should have just been given to you. Babies aren't meant to have to think about what things cost, about buying them from a store." Pointing to the implicit sense of justice in the antisocial act offers a truer understanding of the child and begins to build the possibility of a conscience based on care rather than fear.

It is hard to build a life when one's infancy has gone poorly. Experiences during this time are foundational and shape how children view themselves and the world. A bad beginning can make it hard for the child to tolerate the infantile parts of the self. This hatred of vulnerability shows up in play. Foster children often become aggressive toward a doll, saying things such as "Eehw, a baby, gross," before throwing it down and maybe giving it a kick. This hatred of the baby shows a rejection of their own experience of dependency. When foster children find a new family that offers stability, there is a chance to rework these experiences and, at least in play, to have a kind of second infancy. Some foster and adoptive families give these children permission to play at regressing to earlier relationships of dependency. As David began to settle into his new family and the worst of his fear receded, he began to play with his foster mother that he was a baby. He would pretend to cry or to soil himself, and his foster mother would offer cooing sounds and wrap him in a blanket. In this game, David began to consolidate a sense of trust and reclaim his need for a sane relationship of dependency.

FACING THE PAST, RECOVERING THE MIND

The previous section touched on how foster children can engage in behavior that attempts to ameliorate conditions from their infancy. Nonetheless, many foster children have good reasons to want to leave the past behind. It can be a mistake to prematurely pursue the memories and feelings connected with their troubled beginnings. Before the past can be faced in therapy, safety and provision must be secured. However, stabilization of the good is not enough. For foster children, remembering the past is a painful and frightening experience. To survive, these children had to learn how to shut out those thoughts; they had to learn some form of self-icing. Before they can make any sense of the suspension of these self-protective mechanisms, they must first have experience with the value of understanding. It can take a long time for these children, who have little experience with containment, to believe that adults can take in their emotional experience, think about it, and return it in a form made more bearable by being contained in words.

The pain of memory can be so great that we may reasonably ask whether reflection on the past is a process that actually holds value. Maybe the child, having found a new family, should be allowed the freedom to forget. Charles, a former foster child who was later adopted, made this claim. One day he brought a decommissioned cellular phone to his therapy session. It was a cool gadget, and he was clearly captured by the technological thrill. By pushing the buttons he could make it go through its custom rings. Again and again he made the phone ring out "Take Me Out to the Ball Game." It was an irritating sound, all tinny and hollow. It struck me that the grating ring was like an intruding thought that would not leave him alone. I told him, "I think you are showing me what it's like to think about your birth mom. The thoughts just keep bugging you, but when you try to answer them, no one is there." Immediately Charles told me I had it completely wrong: "I don't have any memories of my birth mother," he said; "I erased them." In making this claim he was equating his mind with a computer. By pretending he was a computer or some other object from technology, Charles could maintain a fantasy that he could be upgraded and perfected. These machines can be reprogrammed; they do not have the disadvantage of having to manage painful feelings. However, unlike computers, human minds, do not readily delete files. Despite assertions to the contrary, thoughts that are unwanted cannot be discarded. If we refuse to think them, they must be dealt with through other modes of displacement or suppression. I am going to talk about two ways that foster children can attempt to keep troubling thoughts and feelings out of mind: runaway fantasy and constricting repetition.

Fantasy

In some cases, a child can feel that reality has been his enemy. Now, like the queen in *Alice's Adventures in Wonderland*, the child passes sentence on the real and proclaims "off with its head." When a troubling feeling and memory threaten to intrude on the child's sense of security, he or she retreats into the imaginary and uses fantasy to invalidate and displace the encroaching perceptions. This is what Charles did when he tried to neutralize my interpretation by imagining himself to be a computer boy. When things felt painful or humiliating, rather than trying to find a way of managing these feelings, Charles claimed that he was the boss of reality. His birth mother was a drug addict who exposed him to significant chaos during his first 4 years. She could be quite cruel, and there were times when the only refuge Charles could find was in the detached recesses of his own mind. This use of fantasy can lead to quite vivid forms of play, but because it inverts the hierarchy of the real and the imaginary, it leads to confusion. The refusal to face what *is* can prevent the child from learning modes of coping that function in the ordinary world.

One day Charles told me that he was not real. This was a kind of play, but there was little playfulness in the interaction. He insisted that he was a hologram and showed me how his image was projected up from the soles of his shoes. In a way, the insistence was part of the game, and part of the fun was trying to make me believe that something crazy was actually a fact. I am sure that he often had that experience when he was living with his birth mother. Crazy acts of mothering were treated as though they made good sense, as though they were a natural corollary of who Charles was.

Yet, the insistence also pointed to a way that Charles began to cut his contact with reality. He deliberately punctured the boundary between the real and the pretend. I tried to see if he could accept some understanding between us about his immersion in the game. I whispered an aside to find a few seconds outside of the pretend world, but he told me, "You're so stupid. I am a hologram; I'm not kidding." I said, "I think what you're trying to tell me is that it has been very stupid of me to mistake this image of you for real." He replied that the real Charles was back in the town where he lived with his birth mother. In a way, he was telling me something true. To survive what he went through with his mother, he had to substitute a false self for his actual self. Charles told me that when things touched him, they wiped some of the color away. Perhaps this was a way of saying that when he came into contact with a present that felt solid, it wiped away some of the bright affect of his psychotic reality. It left him grayer, more within the depressed world of mourning. For Charles, the question had to be, "Why would I want to trade the vibrancy of my omnipotent fantasy for the pain of depression?" It is hard to believe that moving through mourning, accepting the pain of the past and the vulnerability of new attachments could lead to something good.

The problem with this mode of defense goes beyond the loss of contact with what is real. The use of fantasy to negate painful memory is not easily kept in control. Like Mickey Mouse in *The Sorcerer's Apprentice*, the imaginary creatures brought into being can spin out of the child's control. For instance, when Charles returned for his next therapy session, he was quite scared. He worried that I had not signed a confidentiality form and that he would be humiliated and exposed because I posted his secrets on his school's web page. Because of his habit of asserting the reality of the imagined, it was hard for Charles to keep in mind that this concept was a worry—a scary imagining—rather than a fact. For Charles, it was a frightening thing for him to begin to acknowledge that there was a real boy who lived through what he did back in the town where he lived with his mother. At present, as he begins to tolerate this truth, his adoptive parents report that he is making friends at school and doing better academically. Part of the payoff that comes from relinquishing omnipotent fantasy is a better ability to make sense of and negotiate the ordinary world.

Repetition

For other children, the problem of memory is handled in less vivid ways. Rather than relying on an insistent assertion of fantasy, they dampen their imagination. They know that to let the mind roam is to risk encountering painful images from the past. These children protect themselves by staying with familiar forms of play, even if the familiar becomes mundane. David, after I worked with him for many years, came to a point in his therapy where his play became quite repetitive. Session after session, he was content to make the same paper airplanes or play out the same race between toy cars. These activities had once been fresh, but eventually their capacity to generate meaning and possibility had expired. I knew I was bored by this play, and I believed that David, too, was bored by his play but had not yet realized this. The soothing relief of the predictable was welcome to David because it kept painful memory and fantasy at bay, even if it left the present monotonous. The problem with this way of managing trauma is that it involves a truncation of mind. It cuts the child off from important internal resources that are the source of creativity and liveliness.

After many months of this repetitive play, I began to talk to David about the problem of boredom. During one session, David again tried to have us play a game in which our two cars would race. Although David was always pleased when I introduced new twists to the game, he had not yet allowed himself to imagine new possibilities in the narrative. Racing, winning, losing—that seemed enough to him. On this day, I told David that I would not play the racing game. Instead, I wanted to tell the story of his play. Immediately David protested; he told me I had to play. He shoved a car toward me. This was my character, he insisted. I said no and instead I got my harmonica and started to play a quiet soundtrack. David could not decide whether to laugh or get angry. He told me if I did not stop playing, he would throw my harmonica case into the garbage. Now I started to sing my interpretations: "David's really mad; when I don't play, he feels like I've thrown him away." He laughed but got increasingly angry, pretending to throw the case into the trash. In this act of pretend, he showed how, over the long course of the therapy, he had established a realm of imaginary and playful aggression. Yet, because it was pretend rather than actual, the play could continue. Finally, I said that he worried that I cared more about the harmonica than about him, but that I did care about him and that was why I wanted to hear the story. When I said this, David immediately said, "Well, if you care about me, then I'll kill myself." I think the first logic of this statement was that he would find some leverage with me by depriving me of the thing I cared about. Never mind if the thing I cared about was him; it had to go to get revenge. David began to play out a suicide of stabbing himself in the heart with a pen. It was simultaneously disturbing, beautiful, and funny. We were on to something with bigger meaning, and I said, "Now you're telling me a story. I think this is what you feel when I don't play with you. It brings you back to a very painful feeling when you weren't sure what you could do to make people take care of you." This mock suicide began to express something about how David must have felt while with his birth mother. Despite her difficulties, she had clearly loved him. What was David to do in the face of her failures? Should he attack her? Should he attack himself? Maybe if he stabbed himself in the heart, the pain of loving might stop. In a way, David had killed parts of his own imagination. The problem with trying to refuse memory is that the mind does not operate in such focused ways. Although the pain of the past may be avoided, it is a relief that does damage to the wider realm of imagination. The mind becomes muted and gray. Part of what we must try to show children in such situations is that facing the moments where the heart was pierced offers the promise of recovering the vividness of feelings and the possibility of new ways of playing.

CONCLUSION

Children who have suffered neglect, abuse, and dislocation have a difficult time thinking about their experiences. They need extended help before they can work through the painful experiences of their past and find the capacity to trust again. The difficulty in thinking, though, is not limited to foster children. Those of us living in the United States often fail to extend our thought to the reality of these children's suffering and need. Services for foster children are underfunded, and social workers are asked to carry such heavy caseloads that there is little time to think carefully about the needs of each child. As a result, it is the exception rather than the rule for foster children to receive the consistent treatment that they need if they are to recover from their early deprivations and trauma. It is a puzzling thing that this wealthy country seems unable to make a commitment to tending to all of its children. Perhaps it is uncomfortable to open our minds and fully imagine what it is like to be a foster child. My hope is that this book will serve as an invitation to our collective imagination. Foster children deserve to be thought about.

When foster children find a stable and caring long-term placement, there is a chance for recovery. I have worked with children who have shown the courage to trust again, to believe that something good can happen in loving relationships. These are children who have reclaimed their capacity to think and have faced the pain of thinking through their past. When these two things happen, the result can be quite amazing. Because of what they have endured, these children can show a remarkable sensitivity to other children. I feel richer because of my contact with these children, and a wise country would recognize that extending compassion to foster children would be an investment well repaid.

REFERENCE

Bion, W.R. (1962). *Learning from experience.* London: Karnac Books.

Klein, M. (1992). *Love, guilt and reparation and other works (1921–1945).* London: Karnac Books.

Winnicott, D.W. (1965). *The maturational processes and the facilitating environment.* New York: International Universities Press.

CHAPTER 3

In Search of the Fuzzy Green Pillow

Fragmented Selves, Fragmented Institutions

Rebecca B. Weston

An enduring problem that psychotherapists face in working with foster children is that we are deeply affected by—but usually unable to think fully about—the larger institutional and socioeconomic conditions in which we work and in which our clients live. Either we are already working in beleaguered mental health agencies that have precious few resources to allocate to thinking or we are private practitioners, often tossed about by the foster care agency. Depending on where we work[1], we bump up against the broader world differently. On the one hand, we get overwhelmed by the need to act because of an always-urgent, never-ending waiting list. On the other hand, we are uncertain how to handle new case management demands that come with the foster care territory. Either way, it is hard to actually find space to understand the complex ways in which broader socioeconomic conditions influence not only clients but also social workers and ourselves.

This chapter attempts to make that space. Taking the life and a year of therapy of one foster child, Roberta ("Bobbie"), as a point of departure, this chapter addresses fragmentation—the myriad ways in which the internal and external worlds of foster children are split and fractured. It explores how maternal loss (and abuse) and, more broadly, societal scarcity may ultimately lead foster children into a material and psychological world that is

---

[1]In his book, *The Analyst in the Inner City: Race, Class, and Culture Through a Psychoanalytic Lens*, Altman (1995) took on these questions more broadly—addressing the theoretical and clinical aspects of psychoanalytic work with clients who lived in poverty, lived in urban settings, and were non-Caucasian. Altman's analysis of the split between public and private mental health systems is relevant to my work with Roberta (discussed later in the chapter); however, spatial constraints are such that the chapter will not focus on these broader issues.

incoherent—riddled with half-truths and twisted distortions. Consequently, too often foster children have little choice but to navigate an external world that is by turns overcompensating and neglectful. Only rarely are they able to do so with an integrated, stable, and good-enough internal world.

This chapter explores fragmentation as it was manifested at three different levels: in Roberta's internal world, in the foster care system as a whole, and finally, in my own work with Roberta. The chapter concludes by emphasizing the need for space to think, to integrate, and to become whole.

ROBERTA'S STORY

Roberta, a young Latina, was 13½ years old when her social worker referred her for therapy. Roberta's involvement with the system began at birth when a paramedic found her on the floor of an apartment. Later, doctors determined that she was addicted to cocaine. Roberta was immediately removed from her biological mother, placed in a hospital detoxification unit, and transferred to an emergency foster home. Her first few years were precarious—her birth weight was low, and she required tube-based feeding for at least a year.

"Too much" for her foster parents, Roberta was adopted at 2½ years old by Mr. and Mrs. Harrison, who had already raised five children. Mrs. Harrison explained that despite their ages and the fact that Mr. Harrison was in ill health, they adopted Roberta because they were also raising their 12-year-old grandson, Christian, who reportedly wanted a sibling.

Upon arriving at the Harrison's, Roberta had verbal and specific gross motor delays. Because she also had behavioral difficulties, Roberta's child care program provided special education and individual therapy.

When Roberta was 5 or 6 years old, she engaged in sexually provocative behavior at school (usually involving underwear or comments about her vagina). When her school reported these incidents to child protective services (CPS), Roberta disclosed that Christian—then 14 or 15 years old—had repeatedly "tried to sex her." Although Roberta's story remained consistent when she talked to nurses trained to interview sex abuse victims, her account was convoluted in subsequent interviews by the police, CPS, and

Mrs. Harrison. The record corroborates Roberta's contemporaneous allegation that her adoptive mother did not believe her and that she and Christian were beaten after her disclosure.

After the disclosure, Roberta became more sexually provocative, impulsive, and distracted. Mrs. Harrison beat Roberta in response. After finding scars all over Roberta's body, her teachers filed a second report. CPS dropped the case, stating that Roberta "embellished" and "was a handful." Although both Mrs. Harrison and Christian confirmed her physical abuse, most services provided to Roberta addressed her attention-deficit/hyperactivity disorder (ADHD) diagnosis (she was prescribed methylphenidate) or specific learning disabilities rather than her experience of fragmented and abusive caregiving.

Mrs. Harrison and Roberta did take part in family therapy. During my treatment with Roberta, her adoptive mother permitted me to speak with their family therapist. From this therapist, I learned the extent to which Roberta had been abused: She stated that Mrs. Harrison's discipline *improved* because she had succeeded in confining her abuse to just making threats—including, for example, a threat to throw Roberta out the window.

When Roberta was 8 years old, the foster care agency permitted another infant, Ruby, to be fostered and subsequently adopted by the Harrisons. Ignoring their advanced age and disregarding all signs that their parenting was deeply problematic, it is plausible that both the Harrisons and the foster care agency needed to repair broken "romance fantasies." They needed to believe that the Harrisons could once again be perfect parents to an untainted new baby (Heineman, 1999).

In collateral discussions with me, Mrs. Harrison said that Roberta's "mental problems"—habitual lying, nervousness, and impulsivity—began when she was 9 years old. Mrs. Harrison remembered frequent and volatile battles with Roberta over strict rules regarding curfews and going outside without supervision. Two significant events occurred that same year: Roberta began menstruating and Mrs. Harrison told her that she was adopted—something Mrs. Harrison had denied previously when asked by Roberta.

At the request of both Mrs. Harrison and Roberta's school, Roberta underwent both neuropsychological and psychoeducational testing over the next couple of years. The results of these tests were inconclusive: One examiner found specific learning disabilities, whereas another did not. However, both examiners noted that Roberta experienced cognitive and emotional difficulties. Thus, it was found that Roberta had trouble organizing her social perceptions, that she often reacted impulsively, and that she could not sustain reflection. In addition, the examiners noted that she drew a picture of herself behind barriers, was underconfident, was wary of human closeness, and was "psychologically inaccessible." One examiner noted that Roberta often set up competitive and envious triangular relationships with two other girls. Neither examiner speculated about the cause of Roberta's symptoms, and she was prescribed imipramine and continued individual therapy with her then-current therapist.

Roberta's life deteriorated in the following years. She stopped taking methylphenidate, discontinued all therapy, and failed seventh grade due to poor attendance and oppositional and occasionally dangerous behavior. At least two reports were made alleging physical abuse, although the foster care agency accepted Mrs. Harrison's claim that Roberta was beaten because of her "mental problems."

When Roberta was 13, things at home reached a breaking point. After rifling through papers on Mrs. Harrison's desk, Roberta discovered that her biological mother was addicted to crack and that she herself had been exposed to cocaine in utero. In addition, two more reports were filed; one against Roberta for physically abusing Ruby and her young cousin and another against Mrs. Harrison for abusing Roberta. Mrs. Harrison complained that she could not control Roberta and that Roberta punched walls, refused to attend school and was threatening. In the same year, according to credible disclosures Ruby made while I was working with Roberta, Roberta asked Ruby to perform oral sex.

After Roberta snuck a boy into the house and had sex with him in the room she shared with Ruby, Mrs. Harrison gave up: She asked the foster care agency to take Roberta to a homeless shelter for youth and to terminate her parental rights. Reports indicate that Roberta was utterly distraught, unable to believe that her adoptive mother did not want her back.

Two months after she was abandoned and placed in a foster home, I began seeing Roberta for weekly psychotherapy, which lasted until she was placed in a residential program approximately 1 year later. Throughout our work together, the agency had no long-term plan for Roberta. However, without informing Roberta, both her social worker and her adoptive mother told me that she would not return home.

Within a short period of time, Roberta went through three foster and/or group home placements, living for less time in each successive placement. Academically, Roberta did relatively well in nonpublic schools. Yet, in each placement, Roberta lived under constant threat of removal due to argumentative, ring-leader behavior—including behavior designed to sexually humiliate other foster or group home residents.

In her first foster home, where she lived for 8 months, Roberta lacked sufficient supervision and structure. She frequently left school to return to her adoptive mother's house and to her home neighborhood. During these visits, her adoptive mother gave mixed messages about returning home. After one such visit on her fourteenth birthday, Roberta was removed because she fought with another foster child living in the home.

Because no homes were available locally, Roberta's second placement was in another county. After 4 months, she was removed for disrespecting her foster mother, violating house rules, and generating competitive and humiliating conflict among the other foster children living in the same home.

Roberta lived for 2 months at her third placement—a notoriously unstructured group home. While there, Roberta once again humiliated another resident, was arrested for stealing, and was taken to juvenile hall for assaulting another female resident.

Roberta was transferred to a higher-level residential group home, whose rules forbade outside therapists. Roberta and I terminated our work together over the course of several sessions. Later, Roberta's social worker told me that after 11 months, Roberta fought with another resident and was transferred to the most restrictive level of care available.

ROBERTA'S FRAGMENTED SENSE OF SELF

Much can be said about the seemingly endless traumas, relational ruptures, and failures of parenting that had taken place in Roberta's young life. This chapter focuses on the process by which Roberta psychically survived these traumas—however unconsciously and painfully—through splitting her sense of self. Roberta was neurologically fragile at birth, and it is likely that she lacked consistent, good-enough care in the early years of her life. Without such care, Roberta had few internal resources with which to resist pressure to blame herself or deny the traumatic impact of the physical and sexual abuse that she later experienced. Unable to integrate these traumas into her sense of self, their impact resurfaced and exploded during puberty—precisely when she learned of her adoption.

Confronted with the developmental demands of adolescence—a time in which children are expected to separate from their families, integrate their increasingly complex inner world, and relate more maturely to the demands of living—Roberta coped first with the news of her adoption and then her subsequent abandonment by hardening a split within her sense of self. By the time I met Roberta, she had two relatively separate states of mind. On the one hand, there was the conscious persona of Bobbie, who had banished most feelings of shame, vulnerability, and loneliness. By far the more visible self, Bobbie was masculine, grandiose, charismatic, and powerful. Bobbie claimed that she did not care what anybody said, that she did not need anyone, and that she smiled "'cause I'm Bobbie." Bobbie protected and bullied, drew a crowd, humiliated, and showed beneficence. On the other hand, at an unconscious and rarely accessible level, Roberta was convinced that at her core, she was vulnerable and bad. From this perspective, Roberta risked further sexual abuse, yearned for parental structure and nurturance, wanted forgiveness, cared about her talents, and longed to be a baby with a new beginning.

As a consequence of her internally split and fragile world, Roberta was only partially able to utilize positive relationships. Although she felt deeply deprived of, craved, and expressed her right to such relationships, she could not sustain them. Arriving too little and too late to be integrated, relationships that offered positive regard and intimacy terrified Roberta. Often, she sabotaged, devalued, or utterly rejected what appeared to be a good thing.

Lack of Containment:
Cocaine Exposure, Tube Feeding, and Attachment

To understand the impact of Roberta's fragile infancy on her psychological development, one must have a balanced perspective regarding the impact of Roberta's in utero cocaine exposure. This is particularly important because Mrs. Harrison, the foster care agency, and ultimately Roberta herself found some degree of psychological comfort and moral exculpation by explaining Roberta's problems through the reductive and unifying clarity of organic neurological damage.

Research indicates that cocaine exposure affects an infant's ability to think flexibly, react in a purposeful manner to stimuli, modulate arousal levels, and regulate attention (Bennett, Bendarsky, & Lewis, 2002; Black, Schuler, & Nair, 1993; Lester et al., 2002). However, studies also indicate that such effects are transient. Although effects may later appear at school age, when the child faces greater cognitive and regulatory demands (Lester et al., 2002), most researchers agree that a child's current environmental factors—especially maternal depression, hostile maternal discipline, and access to support services—are of far more consequence to the child's behavioral, emotional, and cognitive development (Bendarsky, Gambini, Lastella, Bennett, & Lewis, 2003; Bennett et al., 2002; Black et al., 1993; Frank, Augustyn, Knight, Pell, & Zuckerman, 2001; Frank et al., 2002; Lester et al., 2002; Messinger et al., 2004).

That said, it is likely that the subtle and complex neurological damage that Roberta sustained through in utero cocaine exposure—and that was possibly identified in her neuropsychological evaluations—made her all the more vulnerable to the trauma of inadequate early parenting or stressful environmental conditions. Indeed, Roberta's fragile neurological system probably made it harder for her first foster parents to develop predictable, soothing patterns of care that could facilitate positive attachment (Heineman, 1998). The stress on this parent–infant relationship was certainly compounded by the fact that Roberta had to be tube fed for the first full year of her life. Roberta was probably given food before she experienced herself to be hungry and was probably satiated without having to initiate elemental forms of relating to a maternal presence. Deprived of the active physical and relational aspects of feeding meant that Roberta also lacked what Dowling described as "an important stimulus and organizing force for a variety of [sensory-motoric] developmental accomplishments" (1977, p. 251). Perhaps more important, her history suggests that she was deprived of the relational experience of communicating a primary bodily need that was then met empathically and consistently by a benign, responsive mother—an experience that is central in infants' developing capacity to both relate to people outside of themselves and to notice and feel safe in their own inner world (Winnicott, 1965a, 1965b).

As is so often the case for foster children, little specific information was available about Roberta's first foster family. Given that people need to have coherent narratives of their own history in order to make meaning of both their own behavior and feelings and those of others, this gap in Roberta's history constituted its own harm (Fonagy, 2001; Hickman, 2004). Court records indicated that her first foster parents were overwhelmed by Roberta's needs. Because the family chose not to provide Roberta with a long-term relationship, it is likely that their attachment was not particularly positive or secure. Notwithstanding their limited ability to care for Roberta, it is nevertheless true that when she lost her first foster family, she lost the only caregivers she had known. It is probable that Roberta's post-adoption behavioral difficulties at child care were at least partially related to her insecure and then ruptured attachment with her foster parents.

In conversations with me, Mrs. Harrison stated that Roberta did not miss her first foster family, which speaks more to Mrs. Harrison's inability to imagine the needs, thoughts, and feelings of a young adopted child than to Roberta's grief and confusion. Indeed, Roberta told me an anecdote that conveyed the emotional tone of her relationship with her adoptive mother. After being abandoned at the homeless shelter, Roberta learned that an elderly family friend had died. Roberta became afraid that her adoptive mother would die. Looking for empathy and reassurance, Roberta told Mrs. Harrison, who simply stated, "You'd get over it." Both because she had a loss outside of conscious memory and because no one helped her explore feelings of abandonment, Roberta had to find her own answers. The circumstances of Roberta's life left her vulnerable to negative fantasies that she was simply not good enough for people to keep (Kleinerman, 2004).

Each of Roberta's early childhood traumas compounded the effects of the other—the result being that Roberta was unable to regulate her emotions or her impulses (Schore, 2003) and lacked the vital mirroring and containing experience that she needed in order take within herself a stable, nurturing, and protective maternal presence (Kenrick, 2000, 2004; Winnicott, 1965a). Lacking such an attachment, Roberta also lacked the psychological sense of safety and security that she needed to develop an awareness of, a sense of trust in, and a capacity to reflect on her own inner world and the inner world of others (Fonagy, 2001). That is, she was unable to "acquire a space within [her]self for thinking thoughts" (Kenrick, 2000, p. 395). As a result, Roberta's internal world was lonely, anxious, and hostile.

The Bad Child: Coping with Sexual and Physical Abuse

Conveying the emotional landscape in homes where sexual abuse occurs without empathic or substantial intervention by caregivers, Hunter wrote that it is a "world where [a child] cannot trust, where weakness is exploited, where dependence is betrayed" (2001, p. 89). At age 5 or 6, Roberta was beaten by her adoptive mother for telling her experience of sexual abuse. One can hardly imagine an experience for Roberta that would have been more destructive, lonely, or psychically terrifying. In that single act, Roberta learned that she was not worthy of protection, that her experience did not matter, and that truth was too dangerous to speak.

Roberta had no place to turn, no one to help make sense of her experience of sexual abuse or the subsequent beating. To explain and cope with such horror, Roberta was forced to patch together her own set of explanations and psychological defenses. Already primed to fear maternal loss, Roberta had to choose between preserving her own sense of internal coherence and preserving both the actual presence and internal image of the only mother she had (Heineman, 1998). As her individual therapist suggested at the time, Roberta was terrified that the foster care agency would remove her from the Harrison's home. As a result, Roberta recanted, shifted, and disassembled a story that had previously made sense. Yet, because she lacked an internal source of comfort and integrity, Roberta needed to do far more than "un-tell" or "not tell" in order to cope with her unbearable psychological dilemma. Roberta herself had to stop knowing and experiencing the trauma in her own terms. She had to distort her own reality.

Terrified to direct blame, rage, and aggression toward her mother, Roberta repressed full awareness of her horrific situation and psychically adapted to her mother's explanation of events. Roberta turned her feelings inward, blaming herself (Hunter, 2001)—something she had learned to do from early childhood. That she was later diagnosed with ADHD and other organic, neurological deficits only made it easier for both Roberta and her mother to deny the power of relational trauma and to concretize the problems into Roberta's body.

In our sessions, Roberta found a way to tell me about her self-blame. Though she only tentatively and briefly emerged behind a wall of nonstop boy talk to reflect upon her life with the Harrisons, scattered comments enabled me to catch a glimpse of the "bad" Roberta—the one who kept blame away from her mother by turning it onto herself. For example, Roberta identified herself as "greedy" for wanting money and food; she called herself "bad" as if it were a matter of common sense, an unsentimental statement of fact. She remembered that her mother canceled her ninth birthday party because, in Roberta's words, "I was bad; I must have been bad, because my mother wouldn't do that, but I don't remember what I did." Once, while fantasizing about marrying her boyfriend, Roberta literally adopted her mother's perspective on children. When I asked if Roberta wanted children, she said, "No way. Labor would be difficult and it wouldn't be worth it to have kids disrespect you and disappoint you."

Poignantly, Roberta came to believe not only that her essence was bad, but also that she was bad luck, that her badness magically caused bad things to happen. After she moved out of the county, Roberta achieved an intimacy on the phone with me that she was unable to achieve in person. In so doing, Roberta revealed how she desperately explained the chaos of her world; she said, "Bad things happen on [this street] because of me. My foster mother lost her job because I came to live with her."

As she blamed herself, Roberta absolved her mother. In interviews following an abuse report that was filed when Roberta was 11, Roberta blamed herself for moving out of the way of her mother's belt and, thus, getting hit in the face. She said, "I don't want my Mom to get in trouble; she got in trouble when I was in fourth grade." After being abandoned at the homeless shelter, Roberta denied that she had been physically abused and asked, "You trying to get my mother into trouble?" Unable to bear the terrible reality of her own literal and psychological abandonment, Roberta believed, implausibly, that she could not return home because her mother was too busy.

Adoption, Adolescence, Abandonment, and Identification with Power

Given their occurrence within the same approximate time frame, it is impossible to fully determine the complicated ways in which learning about her adoption and subsequently being abandoned diminished Roberta's already compromised ability to negotiate the developmental tasks of adolescence. However, Roberta solidified her identification with badness and engaged in escalating antisocial behavior as she externalized newly reopened feelings of abandonment, betrayal, shame, and vulnerability. As she did so, Roberta consciously blurred her own gender identity. Calling herself Bobbie, she hardened her identification with masculine power—with those who can abuse and humiliate and also protect and command a space.

Crack Baby

Not having learned of her adoption until such a late age, Roberta had no frame of reference with which to incorporate the information. "She's a liar," Roberta said, furious that her mother had lied when Roberta previously asked about being adopted. This was the only criticism of her mother that Roberta allowed herself. Lying, in fact, was central to Roberta's acting out, just as it was a theme in our first several sessions: Roberta both hoped and feared that I could differentiate her truths from her lies.

Finding out during early adolescence—precisely when children crave real information about their origins (Levy-Warren, 1996)—Roberta must have felt as though she were falling into a black hole, as though she were endlessly dropping (Winnicott, 1996). Indeed, she might have wondered— if her parents were not her parents, then who was she? No longer trusting the shifting sands of her adoptive home, Roberta was desperate for more information about her biological mother—searching for a stable story, a place to belong (Winnicott, 1996). It is therefore not surprising that Roberta discovered that her biological mother was a crack addict by rifling through papers on Mrs. Harrison's desk. She called herself a "crack baby." It was awful for Roberta to learn this history. Seeing herself as a monster, Roberta expressed hatred toward her biological mother for "turning her [Roberta] into this." At the same time, Roberta's sense of relief was palpable. Identifying with her biological mother, Roberta's story about her badness made sense. "Crack baby" was a psychological home, a connection to a reality she knew to be true. Indeed, in one session, Roberta proudly wrote what she regarded as her "real name"—the name that was given by her biological mother and that Roberta usually disavowed. As Winnicott wrote, for an adopted adolescent, "Almost [any information] is of value if it is factual. . . . [T]he need is so urgent that even unpleasant facts can be a relief. The trouble is *mystery*" (1996, pp. 141–142).

Trauma and Gender Identity

As Roberta entered adolescence—a time when children try to forge their own gender and sexual identity (Levy-Warren, 1996)—old feelings of dirtiness, badness, vulnerability, shame, and sexual confusion resurfaced and intensified (Anastasopoulos, 1997; Campbell, 1994). Despite her conscious attempts to deny the traumatic impact of her sexual abuse, its enduring resonance was evidenced in the several occasions that Bobbie brought up the incident with me—both directly and in a veiled way. Yet, for Bobbie, naming the abuse was not the same as integrating it.

Instead, in various ways, Bobbie attempted to externalize and push away these deeply painful feelings by identifying with those who had masculine sexual power. Purging these feelings and projecting her fear onto others, Bobbie bullied and assaulted other young women (Hunter, 2001). Thus, when Bobbie was 13, she asked her 5 or 6-year-old adopted sister, Ruby, to perform cunnilingus—a horrific repetition of her own abuse by Christian. Just as she had been in early childhood, Roberta was preoccupied with underwear, with the vagina hidden underneath, and with things "soiled" by the female body. On at least two occasions, Roberta stole the dirty underwear of other foster girls and put it on public display. As Campbell wrote, victims of sexual abuse may protect the self by splitting off self-disgust and "projecting that disgust onto the organs exposed by the abuse. Furthermore, the abused child may project [his or her] . . . self-disgust via an abusive act onto another's body which is treated with contempt. In this way, the abused child becomes the abuser" (1994, p. 316).

Yet, Bobbie's identification with masculine sexual power did not only appear through abusive behavior. Paradoxically, she also repressed feelings of sexual vulnerability by asserting a kind of omnipotent "badness." Bobbie called herself "the pimp." When I asked her about this nickname, Bobbie expressed thinly veiled hostility toward boys, coyly stating that she was "reversing it on the guys." Manically defending herself against feelings of loss, Bobbie regaled me with stories of relationships with boys and of her own sexual victimization (Horne, 2001). As she rebuffed my attempts to show protective concern, I held her fear and helplessness. After telling me about a particularly violent sexual experience with four boys (I wondered, *Was that experience real? A lie?*), Bobbie referred to her experience with Christian and explained that she "liked it like that; that [she] was brought up that way." When I asked how she would handle the violent experience, Bobbie gave a cavalier shrug and said, "I dust my problems off."

Finally, Bobbie's identification with male power also expressed her healthy yearning for safety and a position to occupy. Equating vulnerability and loss with femininity, Bobbie consciously rejected those aspects of herself. In an unusually open session with me, Bobbie said that when she was younger, she thought she was a boy and that she sometimes wished that she were because girls are "too messy." When I asked her what she meant by *messy*, she stated that she meant that girls are "backstabbers." She did not seem conscious of the more bodily connection: that girls make "messes" in their underwear. Bobbie went on to say, "[Boys] don't back stab and don't get hurt. They're more powerful."

In the face of extreme adolescent pressure to act her gender (Levy-Warren, 1996), Bobbie was admirably courageous in fronting a masculine self in her efforts to withstand the terror of foster care and stake turf in the dog-eat-dog atmosphere of group homes. For example, Bobbie told me that she initiated friendships with other foster girls by offering to "cover their back." One teenage girl even called Bobbie "brother" after receiving Bobbie's protection. When I reminded her of our discussion about wanting to be a boy, Bobbie explained that because she was a tomboy, she did not mind the nickname.

Impotent Rage

In discussing how adolescents accomplish a sense of "autonomous selfhood," the central developmental task of adolescence, Levy-Warren (1996) emphasized that in order to successfully separate and individuate from their families, early adolescents need to periodically return to their maternal secure base. Yet, that assertion begs a fundamental question: If the maternal home base is gone, how is a teenager able to launch a coherent self? For Bobbie, the painfully short answer is that she could not. Already lacking the capacity for internal reflection, her adoptive mother's abandonment was catastrophic. Abandoned when she was desperately trying to establish a sense of self—when she most needed secure footing—Bobbie's sense of inner badness, her "crack'ed-ness," solidified. Lacking information about her first foster family and knowing only that her biological mother was addicted to crack, Bobbie defended herself by triumphantly and omnipotently renouncing all dependency (Hunter, 2001). Proud of her ability to "run fast," Bobbie proclaimed to me that she did not need help and did not care what others thought of her.

Bobbie was stuck, unable to separate but desperately needing to act. Already more action prone as an adolescent than she was as a younger child (Fingert-Chusad, 1990), Bobbie could not launch a more mature sense of self without a parental base. At some level, the healthier part of Roberta knew what she needed. To my consistent surprise, Roberta repeatedly expressed enthusiasm—however muted—for structure and supervision. For example, at the beginning of our work together, Roberta was willing to consider a structured classroom because, in her words, she "didn't want to get into it with people" and "wanted to ask more questions." When she took part in a demanding, highly structured music and drama program, she was well liked by her teachers and flourished; she loved the disciplined practice and she wanted to fit in with others.

Bobbie's grandiose defense made it impossible for her to consciously ask for help, even as she expressed worry that she would "wind up in juvenile hall." So she raged out of control—stealing, lying, running into the street, and fighting. Illustrating Winnicott's (1992) point that antisocial behavior is an expression of hope, a way of making a righteous demand on the environment, Roberta found her way toward structure: first at a group home, then at juvenile hall, and, finally, in a secured residential treatment program. Raging, bad, and abusive, Bobbie gathered around herself a pseudo-parental boundary.

The Fuzzy Green Pillow

In our work together, I almost always saw Bobbie, Roberta's masculine, grandiose persona. Hiding behind constant talk about boys, this young girl rarely gave voice to her more feminine self—the self that was vulnerable, despairing, and wishing to be a baby so that she could experience maternal care. Most of the time, this version of Roberta needed to be approached indirectly and from a distance. Thus, our most intimate conversations took place over the phone. Buffered by the miles between us, Roberta found it safer to express vulnerability. In such discussions, for example, Roberta was able to say that she feared rejection by an arts program and feared returning from the other county.

Similarly, Roberta found it nearly impossible to verbalize sadness, pain, or a positive yearning for connection and nurturance. Although Roberta used several different modes of mediating her longing for intimacy (including silent, collaborative picture drawing), one mode in particular stands out: the fuzzy green pillow. I had spontaneously offered the pillow during one session when she was sick. In that first session with the pillow, Roberta lay down and played with toys—a regression and use of symbolic play that she had never allowed previously. In the following session, Roberta asked to use the pillow and repeated her play. From then on, the pillow became a regular feature of our work. Somehow, my offering the pillow reached Roberta's unconscious, desperate need for direct maternal tenderness (Lanyado, 2001). Roberta witnessed my carrying the pillow to the treatment room for each session, regardless of where we met. In this way, she could see that the pillow uniquely belonged to our shared space and it became a source of reassuring continuity in the face of chaos.

Over the course of our work, Roberta's use of the pillow changed. In retrospect, it is clear that in this pillow, Roberta found a symbolic maternal lap that was consistently available for regression, for comfort, for a place to continue feeling, for idle banter, for a secure base, and—finally, painfully—for rejection. In the beginning, it provided an essential sense of security that she needed to suspend her usual, very concrete thinking. After long gaps in our work due to transportation difficulties or placement changes, the pillow eased her transition back into the therapeutic space. For instance, after Roberta had moved to her first residential placement, I brought the pillow to our first termination session. Conveying her extreme ambivalence about and fear of relating, Roberta initially made a gesture to hold the pillow but then withdrew. At other times, the pillow provided Roberta a refuge from her own constant chatter—a space to be quiet and, maybe, a space to feel. Still again, Roberta occasionally spent a few minutes on the pillow before she took a chair and began to talk, thereby using the pillow as a secure base from which to initiate interaction. However, most poignant was the way in which Roberta used the pillow to express her deep longing to start over, to be a baby once again. After being removed from the out-of-county foster home and before she entered the group home, Roberta sank into the pillow, turned her back toward me, and fell asleep, sucking her thumb. Sleeping in the small room, sucking her thumb, wearing her always-new and never-comfortably-worn-in clothes (with their tags still on)[2], Roberta communicated the depth of her vulnerable despair in a way that no words ever could. (Roberta later found another way to communicate her desire to be a baby. For Halloween that year, she dressed as a baby and said to me over the phone: "Wanna hear me? Goo goo ga ga . . . Wahhhhh.")

That Roberta showed me her vulnerable self was extraordinary, but should not be overstated. Except when transportation was provided, Roberta skipped nearly every other session—unable to tolerate the feelings of dependency and deprivation that the sessions stirred up (Kenrick, 2000). For every session in which Roberta used the pillow, there were several more in which she reminded me that she had more important things to do, rolled her eyes in exaggerated boredom, voiced resentment that we met weekly, or communicated her annoyance by saying, "What's the point of therapy anyway?"

As Kenrick wrote, "Just at the moment when hopes begin to rise, or at times when people begin to feel really contained and understood . . . , they seem almost compulsively to destroy what they have" (2000, p. 401). As Roberta destroyed our relationship during our terminating sessions, I felt the burning edge of humiliation, the shame and rage that she felt at wanting to be loved. Because Roberta's residential program did not permit us to continue working together and did not provide her with transportation to my office for our final sessions, I drove to the program to conduct our termination sessions there. During these sessions, Roberta also began seeing the program's in-house therapist.

In our first of six scheduled termination sessions, it seemed possible that Roberta could tentatively grieve the loss of our relationship, as she complained to me that her new therapist "didn't have a green pillow." However, as the weeks went by, Roberta could not endure the ambiguity or the suspense inherent in the situation. Unable to experience termina-

---

[2] While children living in secure environments often get pleasure out of wearing new clothes and showing off designer tags, this experience is radically different for foster children. Often, foster children are deprived of the chance to get comfortable, to assume that things will stay the same, day to day. If they are able to accumulate "stuff" that takes on personal significance, foster children are often unable to keep track of their belongings when they move to a new home. When foster parents actually spend their state-allotted "clothing allowance" on clothing, foster children must not only replace the old with the new, but also navigate frequently changing house rules regarding acceptable clothing. Robbed of the security of "lived-in familiarity," foster children are unable to derive real pleasure from new clothes. Just as relationships become fungible and unpredictable, new clothes come to represent the always changing, never certain nature of their environments.

tion as a way of internalizing the comfort of the green pillow, the six ending sessions felt like a ticking time bomb. As if she were anticipating the dreaded 7-day notice that foster children are given before being removed from a placement, Roberta was waiting to be dropped. In our second termination session, Bobbie disdainfully pushed away the green pillow, as if to say that she needed neither the pillow nor me. Before the third termination session, she refused to come to our assigned room; the program staff coaxed her into showing up. "Why are you here?" she asked when she saw me, "Don't you know that I died?" In the therapy room, Bobbie refused to talk and asked if she had to be there. At the precipice of another involuntary rupture, Bobbie cut her losses. Psychic survival required that she "dust herself off" and turn to face the always new staff and foster care siblings. Proactively, Bobbie took charge and killed our connection. In so doing, a part of her—that part that remained open to a genuine and specific relationship—did in fact die.

Our fourth session ultimately proved to be our last. With bone-chilling hostility, Bobbie very publicly and loudly rejected me. Screaming and laughing as she taunted me down the hallway, Bobbie surrounded herself with friends as she leveled accusations that cast me as a scorned lover: "Why can't you let go?", "Why are you stalking me?", and "Can't you accept that I have a new therapist now?" Whether it was out of a masochistic need to endure the session, to maintain a coherent sense of my therapeutic self, or to somehow remain present for Roberta, I stayed in the therapy room for the full hour. As I struggled to understand and respond to Roberta's conscious and unconscious communications, I felt deeply humiliated, confused, ashamed, and filled with self-doubt (Anastasopoulos, 1997). I wondered, *Had I been stalking her? Was I wrong to insist on a termination period? Was it me who couldn't say good-bye?*

Although I came to care a great deal about Roberta and was invested in continuing our work, I do not believe it "was me." It was not that I clung helplessly to a one-sided relationship. For Roberta, losing our relationship opened raw wounds of maternal abandonment. Through my countertransference, I understood what it felt like to be her, to feel horrific shame and despair, and to be "dropped." It felt like dying. Seeing herself as a wretched, disgusting, sexualized, and clinging girl, Roberta projected those feelings onto me—and attacked with a vengeance the vulnerable part of herself.

SYSTEMIC FRAGMENTATION

The dreadful and basic unfairness of the current socioeconomic and political world pervades and circumscribes our work with foster children. Although the United States is the richest country in the world, social workers
and therapists working with foster children constantly hit the brick wall of
artificial scarcity: not enough to go around. There is not enough for basic
human care—for well-paying jobs, addiction recovery programs, sustained
mental health services, affordable child care, enriching educational programs, or supported housing. As will be discussed later, therapists working
with profoundly traumatized children react with an array of fantasies and
defenses; the same is true for CPS social workers. Indeed, the larger context
of enormous societal deprivation exacts a powerful psychic toll un social
workers as they try to respond effectively to the wrenching and seemingly
never-ending reality of child abuse and neglect.

Anxiety and the Role of a Child
Protective Services Social Worker

Like the nurses studied by Menzies Lyth, foster care social workers must
"contend with very strong and mixed feelings [. . .]: pity, compassion and
love; guilt and anxiety; hatred and resentment of the . . . [clients] who
arouse these strong feelings; envy of the care given to the patient" (1988,
p. 46). Moreover, for many families, social workers embody the intolerable
inequities of the entire socioeconomic system. Consequently, even as they
must manage their own strong and conflicted feelings, social workers must
negotiate the actual and projected anxiety, rage, despair, and fear of the
numerous children, parents, and foster parents for whom they are responsible. As if that were not enough, social workers are expected to coordinate
care plans involving children, parents, foster parents, schools, courts, and
any other professionals involved in caring for the child—all of whom may
have differing or even conflicting agendas. Ultimately, as Waddell wrote,
"the problem of the social work profession is a structural one: in attempting to meet the needs of the individual client with inadequate resources
[. . .] when underlying causes cannot be addressed—the social worker" un-
wittingly takes up tasks that more properly belong to the state (1985, p. 5).

Absent broad societal restructuring, social workers have no choice but to defend themselves against the anxiety and feelings of inadequacy aroused by their work. To some extent, the defenses activated are unique to each social worker. However, some generalizations can be made about the various ways in which social workers keep overwhelming feelings at bay—and often it is precisely those commonalties that define the emotional tone, culture, and responsiveness of the larger foster care system. In my work with Roberta, social workers relied on at least three different strategies to defend themselves against the unbearable sadness that Roberta's life evoked in them: First, through neglectful identification with Roberta's adoptive mother; second, through an abject refusal to identify with or see Roberta's need for relational continuity; and, third, through grandiose expectations of finding "the perfect placement."

Identification with Adoptive and Foster Parents

Given the shortage of adoptive and foster parents available to take care of children once they are brought into the system, there is a propensity for social workers to prioritize and identify with the perspective of adoptive and foster parents. Facing overwhelming numbers of children needing homes and finite placements, social workers are under enormous pressure to satisfy the psychic or material demands of these substitute parents—even when those demands are inappropriate for the child (Emanuel, 2002). On a daily basis, it is very difficult for social workers to remain conscious of such a potentially explosive conflict of interest and they must find a way to reconcile the contradiction. At a critical juncture in Roberta's life, one social worker coped with this psychic dilemma by identifying with the adoptive parent—a response that had dire consequences.

When reading Roberta's file, I was stunned to observe how the workers in the social service system minimized or even denied the abuse that Roberta endured in the Harrison home. At the crucial point in which Roberta disclosed sexual abuse, they seemed unable to accept the reality of what had happened—precisely the defense utilized by Mrs. Harrison when Roberta spoke to her. Issuing a mild cautionary to Mrs. Harrison about beating Roberta, nothing in the record explained why more protective action was not taken. Without knowing more about the people involved at the time, I could only assume that in order to maintain the stability of Roberta's placement, it may have seemed as if there were no choice but to look help-lessly the other way. Illustrating the way in which workers' defenses be-come systemic, the fact of Roberta's sexual abuse simply dropped out of the agency record. Over time, with new reports and additional workers, refer-ences to her sexual abuse completely disappeared. Because they did not know about the original sexual abuse report, it is not surprising that subsequent workers solidified their identification with Mrs. Harrison and accepted her perspective that Roberta was "a handful," had "mental problems," and "embellished." Just as Mrs. Harrison could not imagine the point of view of her child, the foster care agency allowed Roberta's truth to disappear. The system was literally in denial.

Devaluing Relational Continuity

In an effort to protect front line staff, such as social workers and nurses, from overwhelming anxiety, institutions both deliberately and inadver-tently foster a culture of detachment. Although it seems counterintuitive from the perspective of the child, the foster care system often builds in discontinuity, rather than continuity, of care. It tends to keep children moving and social workers rotating. For example, a different social worker may be assigned as the child reaches different stages within the system. If a child's home is under investigation, he or she is assigned one worker; if the child is removed from the home, he or she receives a new worker; when he or she is adjudicated to be a dependant of the court, another worker takes over. In such cases, no single social worker works with a child con-tinuously throughout his or her involvement with the system.

Anxiously guarding against "overinvolvement," this defense creates an-other contradiction. Ostensibly, the purpose of the foster care system is to ensure that children are provided with appropriate, nurturing care. Although detached discontinuity reduces one source of anxiety for the social worker, it gives rise to another. Not only does detachment and discontinuity re-produce the endless fragmentation that has taken place in the lives of chil-dren who are brought into the system (Rustin, 2001), but it also eliminates the opportunity for sustained, meaningful, and potentially transformative contact with the children and, thus, deprives social workers of the chance to feel truly significant.

Therefore, when an outsider demands continuity, the system often responds defensively. In a system that actively undermines their own continuous relationships with the children, many social workers simultaneously devalue the importance of continuity for the foster children and denigrate other service providers for being too involved. Continuity was essential for Roberta (and is for all children). As patchy as our relationship was, it allowed Roberta to experience one person who stood for connection rather than rupture, who stood for hope rather than despair, who stood for consistency rather than chaos, and who stood for reflection rather than action (Hunter, 2001).

The residential program and the CPS team assigned to handle Roberta's case each gave to the other the power to determine whether I would continue working with Roberta. With no one officially in charge, the foster care culture prevailed. The residential program remained adamantly opposed to my continued involvement. The social workers did not think it was worth pursuing because relationships are interchangeable and Roberta's entire residential program was a therapeutic environment. To the extent that the social workers were trained to be detached, to repress their own needs for ongoing, meaningful relationships with their clients, it was extremely difficult for them to promote my demand for continuity. If they had done so, it is likely that they would have aroused their own needs for meaningful engagement (Emanuel, 2002), which would then leave them vulnerable to internal and external accusations of overinvolvement.

Maintaining personal and institutional equilibrium, CPS workers gradually assigned less importance to my relationship with Roberta, suggested that I was too demanding, deferred to the residential program, and eventually dropped me. In his article about systemic deprivation, Sutton wrote, "Within the overall organization, the professionals working with the children and representing the children may become unconsciously viewed as being the children by other members of that organization" (1991, p. 74). Within CPS, it seemed that I was increasingly identified with Roberta and was unconsciously viewed as an enraged child begging to be noticed. In so doing, CPS not only seemed to be mirroring Roberta's own defense against loss (framing the problem as one in which I, the therapist, could not say good-bye) but also seemed to be reinforcing her experience that relationships do not matter and cannot last.

Grandiosity: Setting Up for Failure

Although the system discourages social workers from identifying with or becoming attached to the children with whom they work, such detachment ultimately runs counter to the reasons that most people become social workers in the first place. Sometimes, in order to preserve their own sense of values and conviction, social workers break through the barrier of detachment and go to the other extreme. Thus, in their work with a particular child, social workers may shift from detachment to overcompensation. Suspending their own anxiety about scarce and often-inadequate resources, they fantasize that finally *they* have found the perfect placement.

Partially rooted in unconscious longings for the pre-Oedipal romantic family, in which both the child and the parents are in complete harmony, such grandiose fantasies are based on false but deeply held beliefs that such placements exist (Heineman, 1999). Such "breakthrough" moments are often motivated by social workers' unconscious need to both preserve their faith in the curative powers of the family and to maintain a coherent sense of themselves in the face of overwhelming scarcity and need (Zagier-Roberts, 1994). Afraid to jeopardize the perfect placement, social workers may deliberately or unconsciously omit facts about foster children's behavior (fragmenting their histories once again) or overlook occasionally obvious but usually subtle inadequacies in the placement. When such placements fail, social workers feel surprised and resentful, wondering, "How could they do this to me, to the placement I found?" (Mawson, 1994).

This too happened in Roberta's life. Because her previous social worker resigned just before Roberta was removed from her first foster home, Roberta was assigned to a coordinated team of social workers. At this time, there were no local foster homes available for Roberta. Consequently, she had to be placed in another county. When I learned about a prospective home, it seemed almost too good to be true—the foster parent had a fabulous track record, kept children until they left the system, and was not easily daunted. As various workers spoke about this home, the team deepened its conviction that it was "perfect for Roberta." Although I had qualms about moving Roberta so far away because it meant that she had to endure a radical change in her surroundings and substantial distance from both her adoptive home and me, I had no alternatives to suggest.

Within a few weeks of the move, Roberta was already on a 7-day notice; her new foster mother could not tolerate that she lied, stirred up the other children in the home, and failed to follow ordinary household rules about cleanliness without argument. No parent likes to put up with such behavior; however, the foster parent's vehemence and surprise regarding Roberta's conduct was stunning, making me wonder whether she had previously worked with teenagers, particularly foster children. For a few weeks, CPS and I worked with Roberta and the foster parent to maintain the placement. However, the foster parent gave up and demanded Roberta's immediate departure.

I have no way of knowing what had been communicated to the foster mother about Roberta, but it seems unlikely that she was fully aware of Roberta's behavior. Had she known how difficult Roberta could be, it is doubtful that this foster parent would have accepted Roberta for placement in her home. In retrospect, it is not surprising that Roberta was removed. Nevertheless, after Roberta lost that placement, the entire social work team seemed to substantially distance itself from Roberta. The team was generally more resigned, more deferential to authority, and less passionate about Roberta's case. Although no one voiced hurt or deflated feelings, Roberta was subsequently assigned an intern while team members focused on other, perhaps more gratifying children. Daunted by the inadequate resources available for Roberta, perhaps the CPS workers defended against feelings of hopelessness and disconnection by idealizing the second foster home and its potential impact on Roberta. When Roberta's placement failed, the team appeared to feel injured—perhaps even punished for caring too much—and retreated into the cold comfort of detachment. Things that burn twice as brightly last half has long.

Crashing against their own diminished expectations about what they can accomplish and faced with chronic lack and overwhelming need, social workers in the system have a limited number of coping strategies. Unfortunately, these strategies often undermine the workers' original aspirations and provide only short-term relief as they replicate and reproduce the ruptured, fragmented inner and outer lives of foster children.

THERAPEUTIC FRAGMENTATION

Challenged by Roberta's intrapsychic deprivation and fragmentation on the one hand and by systemic deprivation and fragmentation on the other, it is not surprising that I gradually developed an internal split parallel to the one manifested by Roberta and the system. I frequently moved between two poles—namely, grandiosity and self-deprecating devaluation—struggling to know what was good enough and what was possible. At times, my internal self-image was of a righteous maternal angel—alone in the shattered ruins of Roberta's life, within the alienated foster care system, trying to save Roberta. At other times, I felt myself to be a naïve, needy child—inadequate, ashamed to care, and deserving of scorn by both Roberta and the foster care system.

Grandiose Rescue Fantasy

Even before meeting Roberta, my first reaction to learning why she was in foster care was stunned horror. I thought, *Her adopted mother abandoned her? Does she know what damage that will cause?* Having only limited information about Roberta or her family, I already cast Roberta as a young victim.

In subsequent weeks, I met with Mrs. Harrison, who told me nothing about Roberta's history of abuse and explained her daughter's behavior in terms of neurological damage. Mrs. Harrison framed her own decision to abandon Roberta as one that Roberta made by her own behavior. She stated, "Bobbie left. She knew she was working her way out of the house." I also met with Roberta's first post-abandonment foster mother, whose vague and somewhat scattered, flighty manner accounted for the fact that she often had no idea where Roberta was during the day. Unable to gain more information from Roberta's social worker, who knew little about her case and was about to leave the job, I ploughed through Roberta's voluminous record. As I pieced together a narrative of Roberta's life—the tube feeding, the buried sexual abuse, the physical abuse—I found myself thinking, *She was just a tiny baby. . . . She was beaten after she told her mother. . . . Why didn't anyone do anything? . . . Can ADHD explain everything?*

As I read the record, met with Roberta's caregivers, and implored the foster care agency supervisor to assign Roberta's case to an individual social worker rather than to a leaderless team, grandiose rescue fantasies came easily. Like most fantasies, these had some basis in reality—no one had made Roberta a priority, and she desperately needed help. She was falling through the cracks. Yet, also like most fantasies, mine impaired my vision of psychological complexity.

What did that mean for my work with Roberta? First and foremost, it made it difficult for me to see—much less contain and reflect on—Roberta's aggression, rage, and sexually perverse behavior. Because it fit well into my fantasy, I oriented toward the vulnerable Roberta—the part of her that was hidden and split off. I even resisted calling her Bobbie. Of course, I did know and talk about the grandiose, abusive, and rage-filled aspects of Roberta's personality. I knew that she landed in juvenile hall for assaulting another girl; I knew that she stole dirty underwear. I even knew that she had sexually abused her adoptive sister. Despite my knowledge of and theories about this behavior, it is obvious in retrospect that I found it extremely hard to really look at those feelings and behavior. Dealing with my own anxiety, I dodged Roberta's giddy efforts to share lurid details of her assaultive behavior. Consequently, it became even more difficult to help Roberta overcome her own reluctance to wonder openly and expansively about what such behavior and feelings meant and how they felt for her.

To the extent that I oriented toward Roberta as a vulnerable victim, I failed to fully integrate aspects of her personality that were more external, aggressive, and reactive. This failure had several consequences. First, it communicated to Roberta that those aspects of herself were not speakable or knowable: It "stranded" Roberta "with a violent part of herself" and only exacerbated her tendency toward fragmentation (Hunter, 2001, p. 116). At the same time, it actually undermined my ability to help her find her own sense of agency. As Horne wrote,

> Young people, defending against the memory of helplessness in the absence of [an internal] protective object, find aggression paradoxically difficult. It emerges in an uncontrollable fashion in their lives, overwhelming others and themselves. . . . Identifying with the adolescent's victim role can result in the therapist missing the aggression: it is important to have it in mind as a constant undercurrent, and to connote aggression and agency as necessary and, where it is problematic, to perceive the roots in an early defence [sic] against intolerable feelings. (2001, p. 10)

Second, it caused me to retaliate when my own fantasy crashed in on itself. For example, Roberta arrived for a session after I learned that she had stolen a young woman's pair of dirty underwear. She did not bring up the incident and launched into a breathless monologue about boys. Consciously, I brought up the incident because it felt unfair not to let Roberta know that I had information about which she would have strong feelings. Yet, the awkward way in which I brought up the incident indicated that my motives were far more complicated. I summarized in my notes, "I then told Roberta that I wanted her to know that I knew about some of her conduct at the group home—and that she was likeable regardless, but that I thought it was mean, but that I thought she did those things to express feelings. . . ." Even before the session was over, I realized that I had been like all of the other adults in her life: preachy, shaming, and "super-egoish" (Horne, 2001). My focus had shifted away from Roberta and onto my own bruised therapeutic ego. Just as her social worker had been disappointed by Roberta's failure to succeed in her out-of-county placement, perhaps I really meant that she had disappointed and embarrassed me by not behaving like the vulnerable victim of my rescue fantasy.

Forgetting that my role was not to rescue, to stop, or to preach—but to help Roberta find meaning, psychic integration, and agency—Roberta's acting out made me anxious and afraid. Her behavior challenged the basis of my own grandiose rescue fantasy and made me feel helpless and naïve. I worried that in my incompetence, I would not be able to reign in her rage (Fingert-Chusad, 1990). If I could not or did not protect Roberta, if I could not or did not stop her behavior, what did that say about me?

Helplessness and Systemic Devaluation

Of course, helplessness hides behind grandiosity—precisely what I felt when confronted with Roberta's aggression and the social worker's defensive detachment. Lacking sufficient confidence in my capacity to hold and contain as a psychotherapist, I often wondered whether I had gotten in over my head. While these feelings were partially an expression of my inexperience, they were principally rooted in my interactions with the foster care agency and in my work with Roberta. Because psychotherapy and, more fundamentally, relationship continuity were not trusted or valued by the foster care system, a great deal of my energy actually went toward logistically ensuring the continuity of my work with Roberta. I engaged in a total of 170 contacts with various professionals involved in the foster care system (e.g., transport workers, social workers, supervisors, foster parents, school personnel); 68 were just to facilitate treatment—about twice the number of sessions I had with Roberta.

Boy Talk and Roberta's Alienation

Roberta talked about boys to avoid feeling. Breathless, insistent, and eager, Roberta's boy talk was oddly ritualistic, undifferentiated and vaguely disembodied: "Did I tell you about Antonio? I'm in love with Andre, but Antonio.... De'Marcus is so fine, but he's only after booty.... Oh, Robert. Did you know he likes me? He and Tyler are...." There were so many boys in her life that no one boy ever stood out for long. In the beginning of our work, I believed that the actual person mattered to Roberta. But over time, I noticed that the talk never seemed to change—no matter whom Roberta was talking about. Roberta also mentioned that she could talk with me like she did with her girlfriends and after one boy talk monologue, even asked if she could bring a friend to one of her therapy sessions. (Given Roberta's triangulated relationships with girls and her struggles with gender identity, this comment had many potential meanings—including that she was consciously giving me a compliment.)

I was annoyed by her comparison to girlfriends and I found the boy talk depressing. It took over my "thinking space" (Hunter, 2001, p. 72). I felt as though I had nothing to say, nothing to offer that would be of consequence. As I listened to Roberta, struggling to remain focused, I realized why I felt so annoyed and depressed. It was not just the boys who were interchangeable or those relationships that were lifeless. I too felt alone—unable to connect to Roberta, reduced to a passive and admiring girlfriend. In the end, I believe that Roberta's boy talk was communicating precisely that: Relationships come and go; they are not to be trusted; keep your distance.

Defending the continuity of treatment to the foster care agency, struggling with endless providers to logistically sustain our relationship, and feeling inconsequential in the face of Roberta's boy talk, it is not hard to understand why I devalued my work. Grandiosity feels much better than worthlessness. Only dimly aware of it at the time, I tried to run from my own devaluation. Thinking about my experience with Roberta, the relationship between devaluation and grandiosity is apparent: one being the manic flight from the other. Given the extreme levels of deprivation that

Roberta (like most foster children) endured at school, in the community, and at home, there was no shortage of crucial things to do. So I did those things often. I met or talked on the phone with Roberta 38 times. In contrast, out of a total of 170 substantial interactions with service providers, 102 were unrelated to our psychotherapy sessions: I advocated for her school to provide Roberta with an appropriate education plan; I explored day treatment options and obtained a neuropsychological evaluation. I connected Roberta with a music/drama program, pressured her social worker to establish a visitation plan for Roberta and Mrs. Harrison, and discussed Ruby's sexual abuse disclosure with various social workers.

These were all good things. The point is not that they should have gone undone, or even that they should have been done by someone other than me. Instead, these nonpsychotherapeutic activities needed to be brought into the scope of psychoanalytic inquiry (Altman, 1995). From this perspective, it is clear that I did much of this work as a furious defense against my own feelings of helplessness and rage at the system's inertia. That I engaged in such numerous social work activities while I had weekly support from my supervisor and from the Children's Psychotherapy Project (CPP) consultation group indicates the magnitude of the pull to act, fix, and feel productive. The consequence was that rather than facilitate my psychotherapeutic work, these activities distracted me from thinking about Roberta and what I could uniquely offer: a space for reflection, for thought, for going on feeling. As Hunter wrote, "In the eye of the storm, as it often seems, there is a child whose distress needs to be considered . . ." (2001, p. 22). Running from feelings of helplessness, I also ran from Roberta.

CONCLUSION

At all levels, the foster care system desperately needs space, a symbolic fuzzy green pillow, to go on feeling, to go on thinking, and to not act. Internally, Roberta had no chance to develop her own safe space for thinking; within our therapeutic relationship, both Roberta and I colluded in doing more than feeling; and for social workers, detachment is one of the only options when they have no room to breathe. Ideally, I would have stayed put to avoid my own fragmentation and to help Roberta cohere hers. However, the counter-transference that arises in working with children such as Roberta within the foster care system can be exceptionally disorientating and painful. Without the time, safety, or supportive context to explore and integrate these feelings—indeed, without sustained supervision and the CPP consultation group that is at the core of CPP program—it would have been impossible to even sometimes strike the right balance for Roberta. Specifically, the consultation group was my container—it gave me the chance (or forced me) to slow down, gain perspective on what was possible to achieve, and remain attuned to the psychological complexities and relational dynamics present in my work with Roberta. Indeed, it functioned as my fuzzy green pillow.

Finally, fuzzy green pillows are not all that is needed. As Horne noted in her comments about aggression, not all action is bad. Living in a world with so much inequity means that rage is appropriate and "appropriately assertive" action is crucial (2001, p. 9). So once we get the space, we also must use it to radically and structurally change the broader conditions of our external world: for the children with whom we work, for social workers, and for ourselves.

REFERENCES

Altman, N. (1995). *The analyst in the inner city: Race, class, and culture through a psychoanalytic lens.* Hillsdale, NJ: The Analytic Press.

Anastasopoulos, D. (1997). Shame in psychotherapy with adolescents. *Journal of Child Psychotherapy, 23*(1), 103–123.

Bendarsky, M., Gambini, G., Lastella, A., Bennett, D., & Lewis, M. (2003). Inhibitory motor control at five years as a function of prenatal cocaine exposure. *Journal of Developmental Behavioral Pediatrics, 24*(5), 345–351.

Bennett, D., Bendarsky, M., & Lewis, M. (2002). Children's intellectual and emotional-behavioral adjustment at 4 years as a function of cocaine exposure, maternal characteristics, and environmental risk. *Developmental Psychology, 38*(5), 648–658.

Black, M., Schuler, M., & Nair, P. (1993). Prenatal drug exposure: Neurodevelopmental outcome and parenting environment. *Journal of Pediatric Psychology, 18*(5), 605–620.

Campbell, D. (1994). Breaching the shame shield: Thoughts on the assessment of adolescent child sexual abusers. *Journal of Child Psychotherapy, 20*(3), 309–326.

Dowling, S. (1977). Seven infants with esophageal atresia: A developmental study. *Psychoanalytic Study of the Child, 32*, 215–256.

Emanuel, L. (2002). Deprivation x 3: The contribution of organizational dynamics to the "triple deprivation" of looked-after children. *Journal of Child Psychotherapy, 28*(2), 163–179.

Fingert-Chusad, J. (1990). Neutrality in the analysis of action-prone adolescents. *Journal of the American Psychoanalytic Association, 38*, 679–704.

Fonagy, P. (2001). *Attachment theory and psychoanalysis.* New York: Other Press.

Frank, D., Augustyn, M., Knight, W., Pell, T., & Zuckerman, B. (2001). Growth, development, and behavior in early childhood following prenatal cocaine exposure: A systematic review. *Journal of the American Medical Association, 285*(12), 1613–1625.

Frank, D., Jacobs, R., Beeghly, M., Augustyn, M., Bellinger, D., Cabral, H., & Heeren, T. (2002). Level of prenatal cocaine exposure and scores on Bayley Scales of Infant Development: Modifying effects of caregiver, early intervention, and birth weight. *Pediatrics, 110*(6), 1143–1152.

Heineman, T. (1998). *The abused child: Psychodynamic understanding and treatment.* New York: The Guilford Press.

Heineman, T. (1999). In search of the romantic family: Unconscious contributions to problems in foster and adoptive placement. *Journal for the Psychoanalysis of Culture and Society, 4*(2), 250–264.

Hickman, S. (2004). The holding environment in adoption. *Journal of Infant, Child, and Adolescent Psychotherapy, 3*(3), 329–341.

Horne, A. (2001). Brief communications from the edge: Psychotherapy with challenging adolescents. *Journal of Child Psychology, 27*(1), 3–18.

Hunter, M. (2001). *Psychotherapy with young people in care: Lost and found.* New York: Bruner-Routledge.

Kenrick, J. (2000). "Be a kid": The traumatic impact of repeated separations on children who are fostered and adopted. *Journal of Child Psychotherapy, 26*(3), 393–412.

Kenrick, J. (2004). Remembering and forgetting: Working with memories of trauma with fostered and adopted children. *Journal of Infant, Child, and Adolescent Psychotherapy, 3*(3), 356–368.

Kleinerman, L. (2004). Being lost, being found, being alone. *Journal of Infant, Child, and Adolescent Psychotherapy, 3*(3), 406–414.

Lanyado, M. (2001). The symbolism of the story of Lot and his wife: The function of the "present relationship" and non-interpretive aspects of the therapeutic relationship in facilitating change. *Journal of Child Psychotherapy, 27*(1), 19–33.

Lester, B., Tronick, E.Z., Lagasse, L., Seifer, R., Bauer, C., Shankaran, S., Bada, H., Wright, L., Smeriglio, V., Lu, J., Finnegan, L., & Maza, P. (2002). The maternal lifestyle study: Effects of substance exposure during pregnancy on neurodevelopmental outcome in 1-month-old infants. *Pediatrics, 110*(6), 1182–1192.

Levy-Warren, M. (1996). *The adolescent journey: Development, identity formation, and psychotherapy.* Lanham, MD: Jason Aronson.

Mawson, C. (1994). Containing anxiety in work with damaged children. In A. Obholzer & V. Zagier-Roberts (Eds.), *The unconscious at work: Individual and organizational stress in the human services* (pp. 67–74). New York: Routledge.

Menzies Lyth, I. (1988). The functioning of social systems as a defence against anxiety: A report on a study of the nursing service of a general hospital. In *Containing anxiety in institutions: Selected essays: Vol. 1* (pp. 43–85). London: Free Association Books. (Original work published 1959)

Messinger, D., Bauer, C., Das, A., Seifer, R., Lester, B., Lagasse, L., Wright, L., Shankaran, S., Bada, H., Smeriglio, V., Langer, J., Beeghly, M., & Poole, W.K. (2004). The maternal lifestyle study: Cognitive, motor, and behavioral outcomes of cocaine-exposed and opiate-exposed infants through three years of age. *Pediatrics, 113*(6), 1677–1685.

Rustin, M. (2001). The therapist with her back against the wall. *Journal of Child Psychotherapy, 27*(3), 273–284.

Schore, A. (2003). *Affect dysregulation and disorders of the self.* New York: W.W. Norton.

Sutton, A. (1991). Deprivation entangled and disentangled. *Journal of Child Psychotherapy, 17*(1), 61–77.

Waddell, M. (1985). *Living in two worlds: Psychodynamic theory and social work practice.* Retrieved January 18, 2005, from http://human-nature.com/free-associations/waddell%20-%20living_in_two_worlds.htm

Winnicott, D.W. (1965a). The capacity to be alone. In *The maturational processes and the facilitating environment: Studies in the theory of emotional development* (pp. 29–36).Guilford, CT: International Universities Press. (Original work published 1958)

Winnicott, D.W. (1965b). Ego integration in child development. In *The maturational processes and the facilitating environment: Studies in the theory of emotional development* (pp. 56–63). Guilford, CT: International Universities Press. (Original work published 1962)

Winnicott, D.W. (1992). The antisocial tendency. In *Through paediatrics to psychoanalysis: Collected papers.* New York: Brunner-Routledge. (Original work published 1956)

Winnicott, D.W. (1996). Adopted children in adolescence. In R. Shepard, J. Johns, & H. Robinson (Eds.), *Thinking about children* (pp. 128–148). Boston: Addison Wesley. (Original work published 1955)

Zagier-Roberts., V. (1994). The self-assigned impossible task. In A. Obholzer & V. Zagier-Roberts (Eds.), *The unconscious at work: Individual and organizational stress in the human services* (pp. 110–118). New York: Routledge.

CHAPTER 4

Seeing and Thinking

Bringing Theory to Practice

Julie Stone

Psychodynamic theory takes the importance of developmental experience as its starting point. It seeks to explain the ways in which a person's unique life experiences influence and shape his or her habitual ways of relating and behaving. This chapter explores some of the concepts from psychodynamic theory. Having such background will aid in understanding the chaos of past experiences and present expectations, thoughts, feelings, challenging or puzzling behaviors, and demands that may influence our work with a child or adolescent living in foster care.

Children or adolescents live in foster care placements because, for whatever reasons, their birth families are unable to respond to or meet their needs in an appropriate and sustained manner. Psychodynamic concepts offer a lens with which to see these children more clearly. At their best, these concepts do not distance us from the children's experience; rather, they offer scaffolding and support for our thinking about and understanding of the children and young people we meet. This understanding can inform and prompt us to relate to foster children in a way that may open new possibilities.

INSIDE/OUTSIDE: CONCEPT OF THE INNER WORLD

Imagine two gifts. The first is beautifully wrapped in vibrant, shining paper with carefully applied tape and perhaps a bow of color-coordinated ribbon. The other is in a battered box that has torn edges, and is stained with coffee. How does one know what is in either box? What clues, if any, does the wrapping give to what is inside?

The *inner world* concept is central to psychodynamic theory. The inner world is the realm of feelings, fears, beliefs, longings, and losses. These are not easily ascertained from looking at a child's or an adolescent's outer shell of appearance and behavior. The internal world is the wellspring of the *self*—and is the hiding place for what is precious and important and for what is feared to be damaged and destructive. For most children receiving foster care, early experiences will have left poisonous and toxic traces in the internal world of their beliefs about and expectations of self and others (Eigen, 1999).

The inner world of a child will influence and shape ways of behaving and relating to others. When working with children receiving out-of-home care, it is important to keep in mind this interplay of inner and outer realities. When we consider behavior meaningful and a way of communicating about the inner world, we have an opportunity of connecting with and relating to children in a more hopeful and meaningful manner.

The purpose of offering psychotherapy sessions to children in foster care is to strive to make sense of certain issues—both with, and sometimes for, the children and those who care for them—in an effort to relieve suffering. In particular, it is important to make sense of a child's past experiences, to determine how these experiences have left their mark on his or her inside world, and to understand how these experiences continue to influence the way the child behaves and makes choices. We must help bring the disparate and incoherent pieces together. The goal is to bring some coherence to the child's journey in the world: past with present, inside with outside, feelings with behavior.

Unlike a diagnostic manual or a knitting pattern, no one unified psychodynamic theory can be learned and applied to make the incoherent coherent or to bring order to chaos. Training, reading, practice, and reflective supervision help us hone our thinking and incorporate the concepts and ideas that improve clinical practice. Only the concepts and ideas that make sense to us will help us in our efforts to help the children and young people we meet in our work.

The concept of *the unconscious* is now commonplace. It is vital to understand that everyone's thoughts, feelings, and actions will, from time to time, be influenced by unconscious forces that arise unbidden from a place to which they have no rational access. Interest in the unconscious and the inner world of the psyche, or *the intrapsychic experience*, has always held a central place in psychoanalytic thinking. The place for interpersonal aspects of experience, the world of external reality and of relationships, and how these influence the internal world arise and yet depart from Freud's original drive theories (Tyson, 2002). This chapter primarily explores concepts and ideas from object relations theory, in its various formulations, and from attachment theory. Hypotheses, propositions, and truths from these theories are chosen because they can enhance our understanding of the failures in family relationships that may lead to a child or young person living in foster care. Furthermore, they best explain how these failures may have influenced, and may continue to influence, an individual's way of being with and relating to others.

THE IMPORTANCE OF BEING
LOVED AND FEELING LOVABLE

Donald Fairbairn was a Scottish psychiatrist, psychoanalyst, and theoretician writing in the mid-20th century. He made an important contribution to the development of object relations theory and was one of the first theorists to claim the centrality of an infant's early relationships to the development of personality. He wrote,

> The greatest need of a child is to obtain conclusive assurance (a) that he is genuinely loved as a person by his parents, and (b) that his parents genuinely accept his love. . . . Frustration of this desire to be loved as a person and to have his love accepted is the greatest trauma that a child can experience. (1952, pp. 39–40)

For many children, the severance of day-to-day contact with their birth family, and the events that led to this separation and the move into foster care, provide them with conclusive evidence that they are not genuinely loved and that their love is neither accepted nor acceptable. As made clear by Fairbairn, this is "the greatest trauma that a child can experience."

In our work as consultants or psychotherapists for children and young people who live apart from their birth families, it is important to allow the impact of this "greatest trauma" to resonate within the heart and mind. In other contexts, the language of placement or placement breakdown, permanency planning, or reunification invites us to distance ourselves from children's emotional experiences. This language invites us to forget that we are working in the world of hurt feelings and fractured human relationships. It is important that we do not confuse the tasks and language of management with our task of psychological understanding and being aware of the child's need to love and to be loved.

Peter Fonagy holds the Freud Memorial Chair in Psychoanalysis and is Director of Clinical Health Psychology, University College London. In writing about the impact of childhood abuse and neglect on a child's capacity to think clearly, he echoed Fairbairn when he stated, "The child who recognizes the hatred and murderousness implied by the parent's acts of abuse is forced to see himself as worthless or unlovable" (1999, p. 2). Not seeing and not thinking may be necessary for a child to survive this intolerable emotional dilemma. However, when ways of not seeing and not knowing become entrenched patterns or habitual ways of being and relating, they can hinder the development of other potentially more positive and nourishing relationships.

Sometimes these habitual ways of relating to other people are considered maladaptive or defensive. It is important for us to recognize that these ways of being and relating arose from the child's need for emotional survival. It is only when this survival behavior generalizes to other situations, where defending against malice and hate is not necessary, can it be said that it is maladaptive.

A frequent consequence of neglect and abuse—and of feeling neither loved as a person nor having one's love accepted—is that children or adolescents become, and remain, "muddled." They are confused about the interrelatedness of intention and action, who or what is good or bad, and what is right or wrong (Lanyado, 2004).

So often in therapy children say or do something that speaks to seeing themselves as worthless and unlovable. However, in their next breath they may boast of parental superpower and ability, which is completely at odds with the evidence. For example, they may share a snippet of how frightened they were when a parent tried to hurt them and then soon afterward tell an heroic story that idealizes the parent and completely denies any past hurts or ruptures in the relationship. The therapist may be sought as a source of comfort or support one minute and then derided and denigrated as useless the next. This switch between two different ways of seeing oneself and others is sometimes called *splitting*. Splitting is a way of managing contradictory and confusing experiences. It is an unconscious process, a way of not seeing and not thinking. When two or more opposing fragments of experience cannot be brought together in a way that makes sense and can be tolerated, then the psyche keeps them split and apart. Integration is not possible.

SEEING AND THINKING: EMPATHY AND COLLABORATIVE COMMUNICATION

Mary Ainsworth is a pioneer of attachment theory. She is perhaps most well known for developing the Strange Situation, an observation and research tool designed to measure and describe young child–caregiver interactions (Ainsworth, Blehar, Waters, & Wall, 1978). Her work has spawned an enormous amount of research worldwide. Karen stated, "[Alan] Sroufe [Professor of Psychology, University of Minnesota] credits Ainsworth with enabling developmental psychology to recognize and measure the qualitative aspects of behavior" (1994, p. 165). Karen also noted Sroufe's belief that this move facilitated a paradigm shift "from studies of individuals as units, to thinking of relationships as units to study . . . [and that Ainsworth gave the field] a way of conceptualizing and assessing relationships" (p, 165).

Ainsworth's Strange Situation consists of a series of 2-minute separations of the child from the parent or familiar caregiver. It is a procedure devised to mildly stress the child. During some separations the child is introduced to a stranger, who stays with the child during the known caregiver's brief absence. It is interesting to note that there has been some debate within the clinical and research community about whether this procedure is ethical because some children become acutely distressed upon separation from their caregivers. However, within the foster care system, children's distress upon separation from known caregivers is often completely ignored.

For many infants, toddlers, children, and adolescents living in foster care, not just brief, 2-minute separations, but life-changing separations are often made without prior discussion, preparation, or planning. These children are moved from one placement to another, from a home and routine that is familiar and known to a strange situation to which no one familiar is going to return. Then, they are expected to settle therein and behave "appropriately," accepting this new placement without showing any distress. Sometimes when a child fails to settle down, he or she is moved again to yet another strange situation. This is a clear and painful example of the confusion between the tasks and language of management and our task of psychological understanding. This all-too-common practice supports a split within the system that allows not seeing and not knowing about the children's and young people's distress, that fails to recognize the children's and adolescents' hurt and humanness. Ainsworth argued that the mother, or primary caregiver, must be able to

> Empathize with her baby's feelings and wishes before she can respond with sensitivity. That is, a mother might be quite aware of and understand accurately the baby's behavior, but because she is unable to empathize with him—unable to see things from the child's point of view—she may tease him back in good humor, mock him, laugh at him, or just ignore him. (1969, p. 2)

Many things may impinge on a caregiver's capacity and opportunity to see and interpret the world of the baby's experience from the baby's point of view. An article by Fraiberg, Adelson, and Shapiro (1987) shared compelling details from families' histories to illuminate why and how child–parent relationship difficulties can persist across generations. An inability to see and feel the world from the child's point of view is at the heart of this difficulty. Parents who did not experience empathic, attuned, and sensitive care as children, or in later intimate relationships, can find it profoundly difficult to offer empathic, sensitive care to their children. This is particularly true if they have never had an opportunity to think about and make sense of their childhood experience and its possible effects on their parenting relationships.

Karlen Lyons-Ruth examined the complexity of the task of being a sensitive and empathic caregiver. She stated, "Empathy should not be viewed as a simple apprehension of one person's state by another but as a complex outcome of a number of skilled communicative procedures for querying and decoding another's subjective reality" (1999, p. 584). This complex communication is built within a relationship and over time. The "querying and decoding" of the caregiver who is striving to see the world from the infant's point of view will be "approximate at best, fraught with error, and subject to constant revision" (Lyons-Ruth, 1999, p. 584). It is a challenging and difficult task. Perfect attunement is not required. What is required is an interest in and a willingness and intention to understand the child, an openness to the child's communication and to getting it right some of the time.

A caregiver needs to have some capacity to put aside his or her own needs to meet the infant's needs and to facilitate collaborative communication with the infant. This in turn allows the infant to develop a sense of being someone who can engage with life, who can influence what happens to him or her, and who can enjoy a sense of mastery and accomplishment. When the primary caregiver is unable to put aside her or his own needs for those of the infant, and is thereby unable to see the world from the infant's point of view, then what Winnicott (1958) called *a false self* may be created. This false self serves to hide and protect the true self. Children without a robust true self often feel empty and look to others to fill them with their feelings. The distinction between self and other becomes blurred. As a result, there can be no true sense of mastery, accomplishment, or self-esteem.

Collaboration is a two-person activity; it involves the caregiver doing something together with the child, not the caregiver doing something to the child. Lyons-Ruth stated, "Collaborative dialogue, then, is about getting to know another's mind and taking it into account in constructing and regulating interactions" (1999, p. 583). The empathic and sensitive caregiver recognizes that the child has a mind and is open to and is interested in the child's state of mind. All of the child's feelings and expressions are of interest. The child is not left alone with messy, confused, and overwhelming feelings. Instead, the caregiver helps bring order and meaning to the child's world. Tyson noted the result of this interaction:

> The consciously aware self . . . emerges from the coherence of the infant–caregiver system as the agent of activity. As extended consciousness brings a constant subjective sense of self over time, the self-as-agent becomes increasingly competent in self-control, self-organization, and self-regulation. (2002, p. 37)

The caregiver's thinking about the child's communications and about how to communicate with the child builds the possibility and creative potential for two-way communication. This collaborative communication enables the child to develop a capacity to think, and later to speak, for him- or herself. Hobson said,

> A person needs a self in order to think. At the same time, a person needs to think if she is to acquire a developed sense of self. And if one

cannot think straight, then this is likely to affect one's self-awareness. If one's thinking becomes muddled or one's mind seizes up altogether, then one becomes disoriented and lost. It seems that we can maintain a clear sense of ourselves only when we can think properly. (2002, pp. 206–207).

Mounting clinical and research evidence suggests that abuse and neglect impair a child's capacity for thinking and reflection. Abuse and neglect thus also inevitably impair the child's sense of self. Children who have been maltreated tend to withdraw from the mental world, the world of thinking (Fonagy, 1999). It seems that one can only think properly when one has been thought about and cared for appropriately—that is, with interest, empathy, sensitivity, and developmentally appropriate responsiveness.

THE SECURE BASE ELEMENT
FROM ATTACHMENT THEORY

John Bowlby, the father of attachment theory, was a British child psychiatrist and psychoanalyst working from the mid-1940s until his death in 1990. At the commencement of his work, Bowlby's interest in attachment, separation, and loss was stimulated and encouraged by his wish to make sense of his "observations of the ill effects on personality development of prolonged institutional care and/or frequent changes of mother-figure during the early years" (1988, pp. 20–21). Bowlby was not alone in this endeavor. In "The Origins of Attachment Theory," Bowlby cited and acknowledged the interest and contribution of his colleagues working "on both sides of the Atlantic" (p. 20). Throughout his work, Bowlby continued to be guided by his wish to help clinicians understand the impact of disrupted early relationships in ways that might inform and direct their clinical practice.

Ainsworth, who wrote her doctoral thesis on security theory at the University of Toronto in the mid-1930s, met Bowlby in London in the early 1950s. The two embarked on a long, productive collaborative relationship (Karen, 1994). Ainsworth introduced Bowlby to the concept of the parent as a secure base. Bowlby adopted the metaphor and elaborated it, incorporating the notion of a secure base as the foundation of attachment theory. In attachment theory, a secure base is a feature central to effective parenting. Bowlby likened the parents' role to that of an "officer commanding a military base." He saw a secure home base as essential to equip a child with the skills necessary to creatively engage with life and to meet its many challenges. For children or adolescents, a home base is secure when it provides a safe haven to which they can return to receive physical and emotional support and encouragement. They return to base confident those receiving them will be welcoming and interested in their experiences. When their needs are appropriately responded to, children and adolescents can continue to explore the world around them with increasing confidence and independence. Bowlby wrote,

> Those who are most stable emotionally and making the most of their opportunities are those who have parents who, whilst always encouraging their children's autonomy, are none the less available and responsive when called upon. Unfortunately, of course, the reverse is also true. (1988, pp. 11–12)

Because of his involvement in World War II, Bowlby's military elaboration of the secure base metaphor is not surprising—and for many children living in foster care, the metaphor of a world at war is perhaps an apt one. The notion of a secure base is important as well because it illuminates for us the great loss for many children living in foster care. Some children who find themselves in a stable and settled foster home may, over time, develop a sense that their foster home provides a secure base. However, many children are not settled within their foster placement; they often do not know how long they will stay in one place. Nor are they confident, knowing that when they return to the foster home they will be welcomed, nourished, comforted, and reassured. Many of the children we meet in our work have no expectation that an adult will be there to support them if and when they need this. All too often, their experience is of being alone with no one they can depend on and trust and with no safe base to which they can retreat to when they encounter a setback.

Erik Erikson, one of America's first child analysts, highlighted the importance of the social context together with the psychological context as key influences on a child's development and forming identity. Trust is the bedrock foundation of Erikson's exposition of the eight stages of psychosocial and emotional development; the foundation on which all other achievements are built. He explained that an infant's trust in the world grows steadily as his or her caregivers respond in a manner that can be depended on. Feeding and sleeping routines are established as caregivers help the child find ways to manage the discomforts of hunger, tiredness, and being alone. With time, these seemingly threatening and overwhelming feelings become increasingly familiar to the infant. When he or she has been responded to appropriately, comforting and reassuring responses to these experiences also become familiar and associated with what Erikson called "a feeling of inner goodness." He argued that an infant begins to trust when his or her caregiver "has become an inner certainty as well as an outer predictability" (1963, p. 247). With predictability in the outer world, an infant becomes settled, with an inner certainty that he or she will be responded to in a manner that appropriately meets his or her need. Such infants learn to trust their caregivers and, in turn, themselves.

Bowlby's conceptual framework of attachment theory was built over his life's work. His theory, supported and strengthened by his collaboration with Ainsworth, has led to widespread familiarity with the notion of secure and insecure attachments. Researchers and clinicians from many disciplines are aware of the patterns of attachment that have been described and that have led to insights into human behavior across the life span. (See Karen [1994, pp. 443–445] for a clear description of secure, avoidant, and ambivalent attachment patterns and Fonagy [2001, pp. 36–44] for a discussion of disorganized attachment.) In Bowlby's theory, a secure base is founded on trust.

Beyond the Secure Base

Sroufe emphatically noted Bowlby's contribution to psychodynamic theory and developmental psychology. He praised Bowlby's contribution to the field by saying,

> Bowlby retains and elaborates . . . [Freud's] idea of the critical importance or early experiences especially early relationships. He also builds upon the idea of unconscious processes being the key to the ongoing power of early experiences and the role of relationships in reworking such experience. (1986, p. 841)

By compiling data and supporting evidence, proponents of attachment theory set out to elucidate the processes and ways in which infants' experiences with their caregivers become internalized within the self. The work of Bowlby, Ainsworth, and others also has sought to explain how this internalized sense of self and other from early relationships influences an individual's way of relating to the world and creating relationships throughout life (Fonagy, 2001; Karen, 1994).

Historically, Bowlby attested, "[Attachment] theory was developed out of the object relations tradition in psychoanalysis; but it has drawn from evolution theory, ethology, control theory, and cognitive psychology" (1988, p. 120). In object relations theory, the internalized concept of one's parent or caregiver is referred to as the *internal object*. Attachment theory has adopted the term *internal working model* for referring to this concept.

When considering Bowlby's contribution to the understanding of children and their emotional experience, it is extremely important to remember and honor the psychoanalytic roots of his conceptual framework. Bowlby was aware that some clinicians, without being familiar with the conceptual framework, viewed the theory as a type of behaviorism (Bowlby, 1988). He also recognized that his use of terms such as *information*, *communication*, and *working models*, might cause some people to believe his theory was "concerned only with cognition and one bereft of feeling and action" (Bowlby, 1988, p. 156). Musing on this misapprehension of attachment theory, Bowlby cited his failure to distinguish attachment behavior and attachment clearly enough as contributing to the confusion. Attachment behavior can be observed; it belongs to the outside world. To know about and understand the meaning of a behavior, one must reflect on attachment—that is, the longing to be safely and lovingly connected to others, which stirs within all human hearts. To understand a foster child or adolescent's experience, we must look beyond the behavior and wonder what the behavior communicates about the child or adolescent's inner world.

As stated at the beginning of the chapter, the internal world is the wellspring of the self, the hiding place for what is precious and important and for what is feared to be damaged and destructive. Thoughts, feelings, and beliefs are encoded within the inner world. The internal working models of self and other drive behavior and shape the way that one behaves and expects (and often provokes) others to behave in response. Bretherton and Munholland remarked,

> The internal model of self and other in relationship . . . regulates an individual's relationship adaptation through interpretive/attributional processes that are at the same time reality-reflecting and reality-

creating—not only for the individual himself or herself, but for relationship partners as well . . . (1999, p. 107).

Bowlby (1988) did not forsake the unconscious. When writing about psychotherapy, he gave emotional and unconscious communication between a patient and psychotherapist the place of highest importance. He wrote that it was the emotional communication experienced in the relationship built in the psychotherapy that facilitated the restructuring of a patient's internal working models.

One of the limitations of attachment theory, however, is that despite the place given to emotional communication, it does little to help us understand the challenges of individuation, assertion, aggression, sexual curiosity, perversion, or the momentum of development in all spheres. Karen stated, "In focusing so much on experience Bowlby eventually lost touch with the child's fantasy life and its inevitably irrational components" (1994, p. 437). When we work with distressed, confused, unhappy, and very hurt and angry children and adolescents, it is vitally important we remain open and receptive to all the aspects of the client's inner life: the rational and the irrational, the perverse and the aggressive, the fearful and the ferocious.

EMOTIONAL COMMUNICATION IN PSYCHOTHERAPY

According to Hopkins, "Freud wrote in 1909 that 'a thing which has not been understood inevitably reappears; like an unlaid ghost it cannot rest until the mystery has been solved and the spell broken'" (2004, p. 155). Through the relationship established between the client and the therapist, psychodynamic psychotherapy creates an opportunity to revisit past experiences and to think about current circumstances. For foster children, the treatment, which occurs within the therapeutic relationship established over time, offers a space where all things can be thought about and talked about. The therapist takes in and thinks about the child's communications—conscious and unconscious—and provides a scaffolding on which the child can begin to think about him- or herself and others in new ways. This thinking together opens the possibility to make links between past and present, feelings and behavior, inside and outside. Through these links and discoveries, choices and options for the future widen.

With the therapist, the child or adolescent has an opportunity for collaborative communication—that is, the interfacing of two minds. Fragmented, diverse, confusing, and contradictory thoughts, feelings, and experiences can be gathered together and woven into a more integrated whole. Splits can be healed, ambivalence tolerated, mysteries solved, and traumatic and projected ghosts laid to rest. Kernberg stated, "There are many patients whose 'true self' . . . exists only as a potential, fragmented structure. This potential structure may become actual only after efforts at integration in the course of a psychotherapeutic relationship" (1976, p. 121).

Many of the metaphors or images used to describe the therapeutic relationship are the same ones used to describe an infant's relationship with his or her primary caregiver. One of the most important is the idea of the therapist as *container* for the client's muddled and often chaotic thoughts, feelings, and behaviors. In writing a postscript to a paper first published in 1986, Hopkins brought attention to the increased recognition of the vital importance of containment in psychotherapy with children who have been traumatized. Hopkins believed that in this context, psychotherapy "can free children from the worst effects of trauma by enabling them to accept both the reality of the traumatic event and of the feelings which it aroused" (2004, p. 155).

The therapist must be available to take in children's thoughts and feelings, to contain them, and then to reflect on them in what Lanyado called "therapeutic reverie" (2004, p. 11). In this process, the therapist thinks about the thoughts and feelings and their possible meanings, then offers back to the client the understanding that is wrought. Often, however, the therapist must wait, because understanding is only shared if and when the client is ready to hear the words spoken.

It also is important to offer insight and understanding in such a way that the foster child or adolescent remains sure that his or her experience is being thought about. The therapist must not eschew the child or adolescent's chaos in a desire to understand or in a hurry for the child to understand. In her book *The Abused Child: Psychodynamic Understanding and Treatment*, Toni Heineman included an illuminating chapter on the paradox of language. She noted, "Before language can be successfully brought to treatment, the therapist is obliged to recognize and withstand the wordless, chaotic terror in which abused children live" (1998, p. 134).

So often, children and adolescents living in foster care are left alone with their wordless, chaotic terror. They are often overwhelmed with anxieties about which they have little or no awareness or understanding. Their bizarre or challenging behavior is often their best effort to attempt to manage their inner chaotic terror and to communicate to others that they are struggling.

If and when a child or adolescent who lives in a foster care placement comes to therapy, he or she usually has a glimmer of awareness that something potentially good may be available. Yet, very often he or she is also wary and fearful that another disappointment or loss awaits. As with a sensitive and attuned caregiver, the therapist is interested in the child or adolescent and this fear, along with all aspects of his or her experience. The therapist is available and open to the child or adolescent's communication. Much of the communication with the therapist is emotional. Feelings that are communicated to the therapist are reflected on and responded to thoughtfully. The consistency, continuity, and sameness of the therapeutic contact offer the possibility that over time the child or adolescent will become familiar with the responses and will begin to trust the therapist and the therapeutic relationship. The boundaries around and defining the therapeutic relationship help to build trust. Trust is built on experience.

The therapist's thinking is at the center of the therapeutic relationship. The therapist contains the child's or adolescent's feelings; in turn, the therapist's supportive networks contain and support him or her and the therapeutic work. This containment, supporting the therapist and the therapeutic relationship, enables the therapist to bring an open heart and mind to each therapy session. This is important because the therapist must be able to think about and consider the possible horror of the child's or adolescent's experiences. A Home Within, the parent organization of the Children's Psychotherapy Project, contains and supports our work with children in foster care. Other supports include consultation, supervision, and peer review.

Getting rid of an intolerable or uncomfortable feeling state by giving it or attributing it to another—an action that is sometimes called *projection*—is another area encountered during therapy. Taking in the feeling states of another is termed *projective identification*. Both of these unconscious processes are part of every infant–caregiver relationship. Menzies Lyth remarked, "Young children and disturbed children are likely to project . . . into caretakers. . . . It is to some extent a normal method of communication telling the other what the child is feeling or what for the moment he cannot tolerate in himself" (2004, p. 203). Fonagy (1999) noted that some infants receive projections from frightening and/or frightened caregivers. It is likely that projections will again be played out within a therapeutic relationship.

The relationship between the client and therapist is complex, and in therapy, what is projected on the therapist and what the therapist feels in response form an important aspect of the therapeutic dialogue. The relationship consists of the present relationship as well as echoes and reverberations of relationships from the past. The internal objects or models of self and others that were built from relationships in the past are brought to therapy. As noted, Bretherton and Munholland (1999) proposed that these models influence and shape present relationships through processes that reflect and create reality for both the individual and those with whom he or she has relationships. In working with foster children, a therapist's commitment is to resist entering into a familiar dance pattern but, rather, to find new ways to dance with the child. Through this type of relationship, it is hoped that the child or adolescent will come to recognize his or her potential to be more free and joyful in future relationships.

The new relationship dance between therapist and child is learned and choreographed in collaborative communication, by reflecting on the feelings and thoughts that are passed between them. The therapist thinks about the feelings stirred within and reflects on the child's attributions and interpretations, as declared and played out unconsciously in therapy sessions. The unconscious enacting and emotional reexperiencing of past relationships within therapy is sometimes called a *transference relationship*. Transference is what the child or adolescent brings from the past and attributes to, projects on, or transfers to the therapist. Through the transference, the therapist builds a picture of the child or adolescent's internal world. The therapist begins to understand and contain the conflicts and splits that, in the past, the child needed to keep separate in order to survive (Rosenbluth, 2004).

Of course, a therapist will have feelings in response to situations encountered in his or her work, and these feelings are sometimes termed *counter-transference*. Training to become a psychotherapist includes one's own participation in psychoanalysis or psychotherapy. This is an important component of training because the therapist must know enough about his or her own personality and needs to remain mindful and reflective. A therapist must do all that is necessary to ensure that his or her needs do not disrupt the capacity to think. The therapist also must ensure that his or her own needs do not impinge on the client's needs and thereby disrupt the therapeutic process. When working with foster children, it is vitally important that those who are disturbed and in distress meet a therapist who is open and available to them and who is committed to thinking about them and their needs. We, as psychotherapists, offer ourselves as witnesses to the children's or adolescents' pain and suffering, in service of their healing and creative development.

CONCLUSION

Hunter's book *Psychotherapy with Young People in Care: Lost and Found* begins, "In wanting to help children whose faith in adults is slim, whose experience of adults is dire and whose cynicism is often entrenched and well founded, therapists have to communicate in a way that might reach these individuals" (2001, p. 1). The task is profoundly difficult. Nonetheless, the work described in Hunter's book and throughout this book confirm for us that the task is not impossible.

As therapists working with foster children, we embrace the totality of the children and their experiences. In offering ourselves as witnesses and in opening our hearts and minds to the experiences of children and young people who have often been deeply hurt by their caregivers, we can revisit their greatest traumas with them. Yet, within the vessel of the therapeutic relationship lies the possibility of transformation. A child or young person who receives therapy may not just survive but may emerge knowing him- or herself as someone who is genuinely loved and as someone whose love is genuinely accepted.

REFERENCES

Ainsworth, M.D.S. (1969). *Maternal Sensitivity Scales*. Retrieved July 1, 2004, from http://www.psychology.sunysb.edu/ewaters/552/senscoop.htm

Ainsworth, M.D.S., Blehar, M.C., Waters, E., & Wall, S. (1978). *Patterns of attachment: A psychological study of the strange situation*. Mahawh, NJ: Lawrence Erlbaum Associates.

Bowlby, J. (1988). *A secure base: Clinical applications of attachment theory*. New York: Routledge.

Bretherton, I., & Munholland, K.A. (1999). Internal working models in attachment relationships: A construct revisited. In J. Cassidy & P.R. Shaver (Eds.), *Handbook of attachment: Theory, research and clinical applications* (pp. 89–101). New York: The Guilford Press.

Eigen, M. (1999). *Toxic nourishment.* London: Karnac.

Erikson, E.H. (1963). Eight ages of man. In *Childhood and society* (pp. 247–274). New York: W.W. Norton.

Fairbairn, W.R.D. (1952). *Psychoanalytic studies of the personality.* New York: Brunner-Routledge.

Fonagy, P. (1999). *Pathological attachments and therapeutic action.* Retrieved July 19, 2004, from http://psychematters.com/papers/fonagy3.htm

Fonagy, P. (2001). *Attachment theory and psychoanalysis.* New York: Other Press.

Fraiberg, S.H., Adelson, E., & Shapiro, V. (1987). Ghosts in the nursery: A psychoanalytic approach to the problems of impaired infant–mother relationships. In L. Fraiberg (Ed.), *Selected writings of Selma Fraiberg* (pp. 100–136). Columbus: Ohio State University Press.

Heineman, T.V. (1998). *The abused child: Psychodynamic understanding and treatment.* New York: The Guildford Press.

Hobson, P. (2002). *The cradle of thought.* New York: Macmillan.

Hopkins, J. (2004). Solving the mystery of monsters: Steps towards the recovery from trauma. In P.S. Barrows (Ed.), *Key papers from the Journal of Child Psychotherapy* (pp. 155–167). New York: Brunner-Routledge.

Hunter, M. (2001). *Psychotherapy with young people in care: Lost and found.* New York: Brunner-Routledge.

Karen, R. (1994). *Becoming attached: First relationships and how they shape our capacity to love.* New York: Oxford University Press.

Kernberg, O. (1976). *Object relations theory and clinical psychoanalysis.* Lanham, MD: Jason Aronson.

Lanyado, M. (2004). *The presence of the therapist: Treating childhood trauma.* New York: Brunner-Routledge.

Lyons-Ruth, K. (1999). The two-person unconscious: Intersubjective dialogue, enactive relational representation, and the emergence of new forms of relational organization. *Psychoanalytic Inquiry, 19*(4), 576–617.

Menzies Lyth, I. (2004). Development of self in institutions. In P.S. Barrows (Ed.), *Key papers from the Journal of Child Psychotherapy* (pp. 195–211). New York: Brunner-Routledge.

Rosenbluth, D. (2004). Transference in child psychotherapy. In P.S. Barrows (Ed.), *Key papers from the Journal of Child Psychotherapy* (p. 59). New York: Brunner-Routledge.

Sroufe, L.A. (1986). Appraisal: Bowlby's contribution to psychoanalytic theory and developmental psychology—attachment, separation, loss. *Journal of Child Psychology and Psychiatry, 27*(6), 841–849.

Tyson, P. (2002). The challenges of psychoanalytic developmental theory. *Journal of the American Psychoanalytic Association, 50,* 19–52.

Winnicott, D.W. (1958). Primary maternal preoccupation. *Through paediatrics to psychoanalysis* (pp. 300–305). London: Karnac.

RECOMMENDED FURTHER READING

Some items in the reference list may be helpful for those who want to learn more about the theoretical and clinical aspects of practice. Bowlby (1988), Fonagy (2001), and Karen (1994) are useful regarding theory; and Heineman (1998), Hunter (2001), and Lanyado (2004) are good resources for clinical issues.

Therapists at Work

The Children's Psychotherapy Project in Practice

The work described in this section resembles a memorable jazz performance. The clinicians in the Children's Psychotherapy Project (CPP) are akin to a group of talented and skilled musicians who have come together to create new music. Like jazz, CPP provides the containing structure that allows for improvisation within certain rules that have connections to a long and rich tradition.

Each chapter tells a different story and each story is sung to a different tune—one created by therapist and child. You will quickly see that CPP clinicians do not work from a particular technique or formula. Each clinician brings a unique therapeutic voice—one that he or she has developed over years of experience as a child, adolescent, and adult and as a student, client, and therapist. These voices create the melodies of the therapeutic work in CPP.

However, CPP clinicians do speak a common language. It is a language that resonates deeply with unconscious processes and has profound connections to the relationships that bind human experience. It captures the unique external matrix in which each individual lives and grows. This common language provides recognizable harmonic relationships for individual melodies.

In the background of these songs with their particular melodies and familiar harmonies you will also hear the rhythm of the consultation groups. The consultation groups, with their predictable meeting times and consistent members, offer a unifying beat to the work of CPP clinicians. They provide measured and consistent reference points. As you will hear in the stories ahead, the rhythm of the consultation groups guides the CPP therapists as they try to sing on key while learning to conterpose new melodies against familiar harmonies.

CHAPTER 5

Doctor Forever

Acute Loss in the Context of Chronic Loss

Norman Zukowsky

Severe, unpreventable psychological blows to children who have already been injured seem commonplace among foster children. Although it is reassuring to think that the presence of a skilled therapist and long-term treatment will disrupt the pattern of children in a war zone—to think, "Now, at least *this* child is safe"—it is not true. In the case this chapter discusses, my long-term, attachment theory–based, psychodynamic therapy could not erase old traumas nor prevent new injuries to the child in my care. However, such treatment can go some way to repair or restore essential emotional functioning, buffer the effects of new traumas, and assist in long-term healing, and it did so for this child.

About 2 years into the successful weekly treatment of a school-age boy with a history of neglect, abuse, and abandonment, his foster parents died suddenly and violently. The loss was very difficult for him and reverberated painfully through the families, social agencies, and clinicians that were involved. It was very trying for me as his therapist and for my consultation group.

Work with high-risk foster children is challenging on a number of counts. It can require advocacy with government agencies and other out-of-the-office activities. It elicits stressful experiences for the therapist such as feelings of incompetence and failure, the blurring of boundaries, and the risk of indirect and direct traumatization. In my experience, a developmentally-informed, relational clinical method and a parallel structure of consultation and support, a circle around the therapist, can help the therapist help the child through the stormiest of waters. Both can stay safe.

WILLIAM'S BACKGROUND

Accepting a Children's Psychotherapy Project (CPP) case, I began working once a week with William, a 6½-year-old boy who had been with his foster parents, the Smiths, for approximately 1 year. I also participated in a 1-hour weekly CPP consultation group led by a senior clinician. William's sister, older by two years, also lived with the Smiths and received treatment from a CPP therapist. A younger sister, their biological half-sibling, was placed in another foster home.

Mrs. Smith was an excellent foster parent. In my observations of her and my conversations with her, she displayed firm limit setting; common sense; and abundant, consistent affection. During my first year of working with William, she informed me with a mixture of reticence and pride that she had won an award for foster parent of the year from the agency supervising the case. Mr. Smith was little involved although apparently supportive of his wife's project. *She* was the parent.

William's birth parents had histories of long-term drug abuse and criminal convictions; he was exposed to drugs and alcohol in utero. William's father was uninvolved in the care of William and his sister. The father of their younger half sibling was untraceable. Their mother led a chaotic, reckless life; she often left her children with relatives and did not return. There had been five child protective services (CPS) referrals in one 12-month period. Reports cited physical abuse, lack of food and clothing, and other maltreatment. There were suspicions the children had been exposed to adult sexual behavior. William's older sister protected, dominated, and picked on him. She also displayed sexualized behavior: She sucked on William's ear, which annoyed William. At the same time, they were devoted to each other, clinging together like shipwrecked sailors.

At the time William and his sisters were last removed by CPS, they were living with their mother in an unheated garage with no cooking or bathroom facilities. William's father repeatedly failed to make good on his promise to provide a home for them. The children were placed with a relative but were removed when she beat William with a belt—an incident that left scars on his chest.

The Smith home seemed like an ideal foster placement. Mr. Smith was semi-retired, and Mrs. Smith had a part time job as well. Mrs. Smith had time and enthusiasm for foster parenting. The Smith's well-kept blue house was in a quiet, lower middle class neighborhood next to the freeway. Mrs. Smith's brother and his family lived in a house a half a block away. Her grown children lived within an hour's drive.

Mrs. Smith told me that when the children were first placed with her they were "wild," and "getting them to settle down and behave" had been a full-time job for the first 6 months. She succeeded spectacularly since by the time I began work with William, both children were calm, obedient, and doing well in school. His sister's bossiness toward William had decreased, and the sexualized behavior had stopped. William had at first picked away at his clothing continually with his fingers, slowly destroying it, and his sister had picked at her own skin, but those actions too had disappeared.

The children followed Mrs. Smith's rules and met her expectations. She had old-fashioned values and ran a tight ship, but it was lightened with flexibility, cheery humor, and love. My primary task with her was to validate her parenting, reassure her about what she was doing and the positive effect it was having on the children, and put in psychological context for her their past and present behavior. It was hard for her to believe what they had been through; it was shocking to her.

INITIAL TREATMENT

I began by visiting William at his home each week for several months. Then I saw him at my office weekly, although I continued home visits approximately once a month. Because William was receiving such good care at home, I did very little work related to parenting, but home visits inevitably resulted in regular brief consultations—talks on the stairs or at the front door—and a growing, warm professional relationship with Mrs. Smith. Occasionally we had extended discussions. I met Mr. Smith but rarely saw him.

My clinical work with children consists of psychodynamic play therapy. I use attachment theory (e.g., Bowlby, 1988; Main, 1996) and related notions from developmental psychology (e.g., Siegel, 1999; Sroufe, 1996). For example, I understand persistent negative emotions and behavior as typical features of disorganized attachment (Solomon & George, 1999)— that is, a pattern of distortions in development due to an earlier pattern of caregiving that in important respects was far from what a child needs.

Also, I focus on maintaining an attuned relational stance (Ainsworth, Blehar, Waters, & Wall, 1978), following closely and moving in step with the affective, verbal, and physical dance of the child (cf. Stern, 2004). Within practical and ethical constraints I always follow the child's lead. Of course, such work with children can be challenging. They can be angry, morose, clingy, distant, and unpredictable. The dance can be a difficult one.

Work with William was a pleasure. I found him friendly and charming. He was also anxiously compliant, emotionally needy and dependent, and hungry for what I could provide as his therapist. At once I noted that he resisted talking about the past, even about events of the day or anything outside the room. In one telling incident, my single mention of abuse from his aunt precipitated a brief, anxious stillness. He became very quiet, his eyes wide, and he stared straight ahead looking at nothing until my voice brought him back.

Instead of "talk," he always wanted to play, *now*, and he talked readily enough as part of *that*. I saw his urge to play in part as an expression of his anxiety; it was almost compulsive. My understanding as well was that William wanted—in a spontaneous, unconscious way—to work at a very basic emotional and cognitive level.

Like a much younger child, he was focused almost completely on the immediate moment in the room, and, appropriate to that developmental stage, he wanted to play, or rather, he wanted *me* to play with *him*. My consistent participation, cooperation, and approval seemed enormously useful to him. It appeared that he was using the opportunity that I provided to secure missing experiences of warm, attuned and attentive, adult-child interaction—the necessary relational nutrition that infants and young children obtain via their caregivers (Ainsworth et al, 1978; Stern 1985). Those repeated synchronized experiences of shared positive feelings (Sroufe, 1996) and repairs of missteps (Tronick, 1989) serve myriad important functions in children's inner growth. So rather than addressing traumas, we had bigger fish to fry. William was playing developmental catch-up; through his activity, he was asking me to nourish him in a very vital way.

My therapeutic approach was a good fit with William's implicit need. He seemed to melt and warm in response to my closely coordinated attention. He never showed overt anger and rarely expressed negative feelings; instead, he was always happily and anxiously in charge, determining our activities and winning every game we played by changing rules shamelessly. I cooperated. He set the activity, its form, and its outcome, and I accompanied him where he went, for the most part holding my adult prerogatives in reserve. Once in a while he would ask me to decide or choose something. When I did he was reassured, and he would very quickly and happily reassert his leadership. Controlling or coercive behavior is a common outcome of disorganized attachment (George, West, & Pettem, 1999).

When I began treatment with home visits, I brought with me only paper, pencils, and a clipboard. (I eventually expanded my travel kit a bit, and drawings went into a folder.) William was very creative in using the basic materials I brought to fashion improvised, competitive games. We rolled paper up into baseballs and pencils became bats. Endless variations of baseball were given other names. The common element was that he made the rules, he went first, he changed the rules and violated them, he kept score, and he always won. Drawings, races, card games, and board games had the same basic pattern: He taught me, he showed me, he led me, and he "won" me; repeatedly, inevitably, and—in my clinical view—necessarily.

Mild gloating emerged, tempered by his not wanting to offend me. He did not want to risk another loss, especially of such an intensely rewarding relationship. I joined his celebrations of victory and tolerated his narcissism and my defeats. Occasionally he made drawings of vampires, Frankenstein, and Superman. When I inevitably made a solid hit and the ball flew across the room or I did something else better than he did, William was very impressed—giving a wide-eyed "wow"—and a bit chagrined, as if *he* had failed or as if I might reject him for being inadequate. It was clear that inside he felt very small and weak. With me he was a star, he was somebody. He saw to it.

Eventually—when I thought his anxiety had quieted a bit—and I gently questioned his always winning, his explanation was assertive, simple, and correct: "I'm the kid." (Later we would formalize the principle as "kid rules.") At the same time, due to my consistent attunement and my allowing his self-inflating victories, William was almost always somewhere between happy excitement and joy in our sessions. As Mrs. Smith and my consultation group observed, he adored me.

Developmentally, I believe that William was re-regulating his affective processes (Schore, 1994) to allow strong internal options of happiness and joy, a solid sense of self, loving relationships, and trust in a safe and positive world. In other words, through experiencing these elements, William gained new, constructive possibilities in addition to the hard and mean lessons he had absorbed earlier. Mrs. Smith told me that once when she was scolding him, he asked, "Do you still love me when you're mad at me?" Her anger instantly dissolved, she said softly, "Yes, William, I still love you." Fitting his new life and experiences together with his old ones was a formidable task.

William gradually and reluctantly accepted that I saw other children, that his sister could not join us, that our sessions had to stop a bit short of an hour, and that I could not join him in family social activities. I learned gradually that he did not want reminders of our sessions drawing to a close: 10 minutes to go, 5 minutes, and so on. "You don't have to do that," he protested mildly. Under low-key questioning, he revealed that he did not want to think about the time almost being over; he preferred to find out when it happened.

During a session approximately 1 year into treatment, William's open expression of connection and the nature of our growing relationship was strikingly expressed. He entered my office slowly, all aglow, with a warm, broad smile that seemed permanent. He gazed at me throughout the session with a wide-eyed look of love. His eye contact was almost constant. I have seen and experienced such overt devotion in healthy infants and toddlers madly in love with their caretakers and freely, trustingly, expressing it. However, William was 7½ years old.

We put marbles in the sand tray and played with Matchbox cars, but his focus on me was unavoidable. Brandishing the sizeable toy rake that I kept to smooth the sand at the end of sessions, he asked if he could comb my hair. He asked repeatedly, with an unerasable grin. I hesitated on several counts: the crude instrument; the variable fine motor control of young boys; the rarely expressed anger; as well as my own concerns regarding my hair, being touched by clients, and so on. A litany of considerations fit for a long rehash in my professional circle.

Meanwhile he stood before me with rake in hand and love in his eyes. I followed my instincts, my sense of him and us, and the feel of the session, the moment. I nodded, closed my eyes, and braced myself. He very slowly combed and arranged my hair and then attempted to braid it, all in the interest of making me "look real good," as he assured me I did when he was done. It took a long time, and ended with a quick touch to my eyebrows. He stepped back and beamed, proud of his work.

I saw his activity as many things, including devotion, a gift, and his continuing need for dominance, as well as, of course, addressing the need for improvement in my appearance. It also felt like an act of reluctant trust on my part. To my surprise, this anxious and controlling child was amazingly careful and delicate in his ministrations; he had a calm and gentle touch. It was a rich experience of discovery for both of us, a communion of intimacy and surprise from taking a chance on our relationship, from trusting in what we had grown together.

We went on to do other things, including an exciting car race with a track we had improvised. Near the end of the session, bursting with intense feeling, he blurted out loudly to the room, "I'm glad I'm your doctor."

I assumed the error was a cognitive slip due to overwhelming emotion and risk-taking, but I pretended not to notice and I responded in kind: "I'm glad you're my doctor, too."

"Hey," he said, "How can I be your *doctor*? I'm your friend."

I replied in similar tone, "Yeah, I'm glad you're my friend."

He paused for a few seconds as if gathering himself. "I wish," he exclaimed enthusiastically, again to the room, "I wish you could be my doctor forever."

"Yeah," I said, "wouldn't that be nice?"

It was a poignant moment in a magical session. He had internalized our interactions, was aware of their value, and was trying to integrate them cognitively—to put labels on who we were for each other—enabling the expression of his love in words as it had been earlier in action (i.e., the beauty treatment). Furthermore, he imagined a positive future—permanent, connected.

William and his sister continued to do well in school and at home. They both were popular with peers and got good reports from their teachers. William's sessions with me were quite consistent: He beat me decisively at something—"kid rules"—and we both had a great time. Occasionally sessions were rich with symbolism and meaning, but usually they were not; we just played. He made good use of my office. He found a crawl space between the couch and a wall; he enlisted my collaboration in constructing a clubhouse of furniture, pillows, and a rug; and he found a small rocking chair to sit in while he batted in game after game of baseball. We were much noisier in my office than was tolerated at his home. His overt anxiety slowly waned, although his need for control loosened only a little.

Nonetheless, his development seemed on track, especially considering his history. I often felt guilty that compared with my peers in CPP I had this easy case of a charming, resilient child who had luckily landed in a great foster home.

A NEW TRAUMATIC LOSS

More than 3 years after taking them in (and a little more than 2 years into my treatment), Mrs. Smith had found herself happily and irreversibly committed to the children. William referred to the Smiths as "Mom and Dad." He also spoke of his "real mom," but such mentions were rare and it was clear that "real mom" was a label he had learned, not a statement of priority or preference. As part of legal proceedings the children had been asked to speak their minds, and both of them were very clear on their wish to live with the Smiths until they were 18 years old. Mrs. Smith had completed the requirements and signed all the papers; she was the legal guardian for William and his sister, foster children no more. Adoption lay ahead, a happy ending for a difficult start in life. It was an occasion to celebrate, and I had a good, long session with Mrs. Smith on the stairs, reviewing her decision, the children's history with her, and their future together.

A few days later I found a message on my machine from William's former social worker. I could not comprehend it at first. The gist was that the children were with some relatives because their parents were dead. It did not make sense to me. If their parents had died, why were they not with the Smiths? I replayed the message and this time I heard every word. Mr. and Mrs. Smith were dead. Last night he had shot and killed her, then himself. Mrs. Smith's brother had found the bodies early this morning. The children were safe and were "all right."

I was plunged into a morass of denial, sorrow, helplessness, and confused concerns about William. My phone contacts with him were dulled and numb on both sides. When I told him vaguely that I would see him soon, he advised me, "Don't go to the blue house; I won't be there." I found myself grieving for Mrs. Smith and stunned by the strength of my feelings, and also curious about the inexplicable, impossible events. But those reactions had to be put on hold—as much as they could be—as I scrambled to contact all of the relevant people and agencies and tried to influence whatever happened next. From a secure, first-rate placement to chaos, his life had crumbled. William and his sister had no home, no family. They went back into the foster care system.

A friend contacted me who was a consultant for the city and who happened to take the lead in what was that day's big emergency case for several departments. She had interviewed William and his sister not knowing that I was William's therapist—she found out later as all the pieces came together. She told me that she had assumed at once that he must have had a lot of therapy as he was coherent and very clear about his feelings: sad, scared, and not wanting "to go back there." William and I had rarely talked about emotions; he had avoided expressing negative feelings with me.

I dreaded telling my consultation group about the disaster because I knew they would go through what I was going through. They had followed this case with me for 2 years, giving support and advice, and delighting with me in William's progress and the satisfactions of successful treatment: a lost child getting on track. They were thrown into shock, sorrow, and anger. We felt it all together. Dumbfounded, we mourned.

In my first session with William after the deaths, he was distracted and wanted only to play. The life in the room, in him, was reassuring, and there was also a profound gloom. I forced myself to comment on what neither of us could talk about. I talked about feelings: my being sad, feeling very bad about what had happened, and not knowing what to do or say. He listened. We returned to play. My understanding was that the continuity of our play, of our relationship, was sustaining for him. Other than his sister—who was also a child adrift—I was now the only person he could rely on.

Awkward phone calls and offers of assistance bounced between a few colleagues and CPP staff and found me. There were confusion, mixed signals, advice, and heart-felt expressions of support. I collaborated with William's sister's therapist. We plotted strategy about the critical issue of placement for the children. Where would they go? What would happen to them? Would they be split up? Would I be able to continue working with William? My role had gone from useful to critical, and the ground beneath my feet was shaky. William, too, was fearful of his future and of losing me. I spoke of it when he could not, although not as much as I should have, I think, because it was my fear as well, and it was hard for me to face, hard to say.

I began arduous, frustrating phone calls and tense meetings trying to influence the foster care system to find a new foster home, a good one. I was unaccountably angry at the social workers, the system, and at potential placements. Reminders of Mrs. Smith resonated painfully with memories of my own personal losses. Acute loss seemed to be a cold lake that could be entered from many points to find the same familiar waters. She had within the last year purchased a used but sporty-looking car from her modest earnings; she had been enjoying it immensely. Those cars now seemed everywhere, making my heart sink when I saw one. I had intended to go by the blue house to gain some of the mythical closure, but I could not make myself do it.

The children had first thought their parents had been murdered in a robbery and they clung to that belief. The police had seen otherwise at once. Slowly I learned things. Mr. Smith had been on psychiatric medications. The couple had been engaged in a disagreement for some time regarding a hitherto-unknown son of Mr. Smith, conceived just before the Smiths got together. The boy's home had dissolved and Mr. Smith wanted his son, now a teen, to come live with him—with them. Mrs. Smith had been shocked, angry, and adamantly opposed. She had told no one in her family about the standoff, and no one knew that Mr. Smith owned a gun.

Skipping details, I told William my best understanding was that there had been no robbery. His dad had been sick, taking strong medicine, was confused, and had made a terrible mistake. He listened respectfully but skeptically. I learned from him that neither he nor his sister had heard gunshots. Late the next morning, with their parents not rising, they had investigated and had actually found the bodies. They thought at first they were asleep, concluded they were dead, and went out to summon Mrs. Smith's brother. William's shock, sorrow, and fear showed briefly on his face as he relived the sequence. It was hard for us both.

I was troubled by second-guessing my previous actions and playing what-if. Why had I not done more parent work? Why had I not met with both Mr. and Mrs. Smith? Mrs. Smith had become increasingly receptive and open in our conversations, more interested in understanding what psychotherapy was about. If only. . . . The thought occurred to me more than once that I had failed William in the most fundamental way: I had not kept him safe. The children, their legal guardianship, and eventual adoption, were by implication a critical part of the quarrel. Mr. Smith's biological child versus Mrs. Smith's foster children. Things could have happened that I did not want to think about.

I was sustained by the emotional sharing of CPP members and by my certainty that they were there, even the senior clinicians, if I needed them. In addition, I had the feeling that they knew—somehow—what I was going through. My consultation group was a sanctuary; the weekly meetings were islands of concern, connection, and useful opinion. I was also sustained by my work with William, difficult though it was. Surprising to me at first, he was superficially much the same with me as he had been previously. He was not joyous, but we played; we had fun. I knew that I was now his only consistent adult, although my vital role contained its own inherent failure. I knew what was coming but that did not make it easier.

Finally, during the often disappointing search for a new home, William asked to live with me. He lit up as if it had just occurred to him—what a clever idea, a great solution—but there was also an undertone of expected rejection. "Ahh," I sighed and said sadly, "Wouldn't that be nice?" before I explained awkwardly that I could not take him in. His face fell, then recovered, and he was all smiles again. Part of me—the professional, explaining part, the sensible part—knew better, but the part of me that was engaged with William in a real relationship of feelings and caring felt deep regret. In a sense I was failing him again, a kid who keeps being abandoned. I tried to be with him from both the sensible, caring adult part as well as the hurting and worried part—the sense of failure, loss, and fear that we both felt.

A NEW PLACEMENT
AND SUBSEQUENT TREATMENT

After many disappointments and false leads, a stable foster placement was found. William and his sister were taken in by a young woman, their biological half-sister. She had known the children for many years, before the Smiths, but at that time she was too young and financially unsettled to step in. Now she was mature, responsible, and apparently committed. There were some practical problems with the placement, mostly geographical, but it seemed a good home with a solid woman who was family in every sense. There was the added possibility that the children's younger sister might be reunited eventually with them in the new placement.

My treatment with William continued. Although pragmatic factors made attendance somewhat reduced, we made do. William had to cope with not only a devastating loss but also a period of uncertainty, of having no home and no future, and then to living in quite another world. He went from the conservative structures of the Smiths' home to rap music, theme parks, late night movies, and a young foster mother with boyfriends.

William's overt happiness in our sessions returned within months. I was a bit startled the first time he picked up a toy gun. The symbolic and practical implications were rich and almost overwhelming for me, but he acted concretely, without direct reference to the deaths of his parents. We played out endless fantasies in which he was a cop, a good guy, and I was a robber. He delighted in catching me and shooting me, often many times, often without cause, often by whim and casual impulse. He was assertive, aggressive, almost angry. I died often, dramatically, in pain. He also taught me—as if I did not know how—to shoot rubber bands, and to power folded paper bullets by rubber band slingshots. He grumbled but accepted my limits about targeting and safety. Inevitably our contests were evenly divided. We both shot, we both got hit, we both—sometimes—felt the sting of pain.

In board games and card games his winning seemed preordained as always. His sand tray activity usually involved battles between monstrous action figures. His won. Alternately, cars or figures were buried and searched for. We sometimes played Hide-and-Seek. In a single room, real hiding places were soon exhausted and our play took on a surreal and silly quality of hiding in plain sight under pillows or crouched behind a coat or a cloth throw. To make such fictions workable I started pretending and he followed at once. The seeker had to be very obtuse, leading to absurd, verbally explicit "not-findings"—that is, not recognizing the poorly disguised other person for what he was but insisting that "it" must be something else, such as a pillow. As before, his affect tended to be strongly positive. He was focused on play, avoiding talk of anything external to our activity or outside of our sessions.

At my instigation, we very occasionally talked about our mutual loss of his mom and our sad feelings. Such discussions were sometimes matter of fact and fleeting and sometimes brought a sinking chill into the room for both of us. Despite my clinical faith in such things, I had never tried to construct a narrative, his history, with him (Engel, 1995). One day, extending one of William's comments, I mentioned that he had lived in two homes. He startled me by breaking out of his usual demeanor and articulately rattling off all of his placements from birth to the present, with appropriate details. He used direct eye contact, a sober face, and a strong, hard-edged voice. My sense was that because we had been regularly working at a deep relational/emotional level, he was able to do such important cognitive level work on his own.

Also, although William was consistently operating at a younger developmental age in his sessions with me, there were occasionally times, as when he spoke of his mom, when he seemed distinctly older, with a resonant sorrow and depth. From the beginning, from the first time I had entered the blue house, he had chosen, or we had collaborated, to consistently bring in his joyous, looking-for-a-closely-synchronized-dance self. Yet, a much sadder, weaker William was always just beyond the emotional horizon, carefully watching and, I hoped, learning and healing. If so, that William had expanded enormously since the death of his parents. If my work, and Mrs. Smith's work, had produced significant healing, her murder and his effective abandonment had enlarged his wound, his burden of pain and unimportance.

AFTERMATH

Approximately a year before the deaths, I had moved to a new office that enabled the use of a small basketball hoop that mounted over the closet door. "Real" basketball became our frequent and favorite activity. There were a number of practical problems and limits to be negotiated and solutions created. Ordinary balls bounced too much, endangering office fixtures, so we made "papier-mâché" balls (William taught me how): hard, light, no bounce.

There were obvious inequalities. I was tall; he was small. I could easily block and dunk; he was fast, could dive to the floor and scramble around furniture. Over a period of time in the year after the deaths, without any discussion we reached an accommodation led by me. I would block him from the basket with impunity, but he could shoot over me. If I got the rebound—often easy—I would not dunk it but would take it out and shoot from the field. If the ball went far or on the floor, I let him get it—I could seldom beat him there. Thus, we evened things up. He kept score loosely and always won.

Our physical exertion and close body contact led to a mix of competitiveness, high spirits, and aggressive physical affection—a sort of rough-housing—such as when he would climb on me if I were so foolish as to attempt to go to the floor for a ball. In those long bouts of rivalry, tacit co-operation, and intense fun, keeping score and winning and losing sometimes slipped away from his attention. As time passed, the complex interpersonal satisfactions of our games seemed to eclipse his need to always win.

William settled into the routine of his new life during the year after the tragedy, and our sessions became even more important for him—something to be protected by him, something he feared could be lost. He resisted any interest by me in intervening with his home, school, or after-school program. It took a long time for me to elicit his explanation for his caution. In essence, his concern was that if I got involved and complained about anything, I might rock the boat and he might lose his home, have to live somewhere else or have to go to another school. The final event in the hypothetical chain was he might not be able to come to see me any more. We agreed on a highest priority, that nothing I did would endanger our meetings.

William's school and other activities had proceeded without major disruption. He began to talk occasionally about his life. I heard about scary movies, funny songs, and the frustrations of run-ins with teachers, school rules, and annoying peers. Through his stories I learned of William's world where he noticed that some girls were nice and fun and others were not nice. I bore witness to the heady gratification of being liked by a girl or several girls, and the shimmer of a boy's first ephemeral romances. Sometimes, but very seldom, we spoke of missing his mom.

William often came into my office with a strong, glowing smile. I could see it emerge as he walked down the hall from the waiting room to my door. He was often joyous from the session's start to its finish, and sometimes he left without any concern about the session being over. When I accidentally gave William a 10-minute warning and caught my error, he reassured me: "That's okay, doesn't matter." He was changing, getting older. A few times he surprised me with the loudness of his voice. At times it seemed much deeper than I had heard before. His extra-loud burps would shock us both, before the requisite laughter.

His need to win all of the time, every time, seems less these days. In board games and basketball games he sometimes ignores it, or catches himself and seems to weigh alternate motivations. He was recently able to ask my help, albeit gingerly, with complaints about his after-school program. My sense was that three tracks were converging. Maturation was doing its unstoppable developmental work. His growing maturity, his life outside our sessions, and our work in therapy were coming together in new ways. As I write this chapter, William is almost 10. We meet nearly every week; the arrangement seems secure for now, although when we look more than a few months ahead, it seems less certain. He continues to absorb what he needs from our relationship, and he has some trust that his present home and our meetings will continue.

CONCLUSION

Spontaneous play and a clinically sophisticated close relationship can be very effective therapeutically, as they were in this case of a boy with an anxious need for control. My 3 years of work with William were a good fit of clinical method with a resilient foster child who had earlier suffered abuse, neglect, and abandonment. He also benefited from having very good remedial parenting for more than 3 years. Therapy plus a good home is a powerful combination. The deaths of his foster parents also demonstrate the continual risks for foster children. There is no way to protect them absolutely; there are no guarantees. Yet, something very useful can be done for them.

It is clear to me that my treatment of William would have been much harder without Mrs. Smith's parenting and without my CPP consultation group and my circle of support. My loss of Mrs. Smith was painful but bearable; my clinical work doable and very rewarding. I also think that the work of Mrs. Smith enabled William to survive his loss of her and that despite that pain, he is much better off for having had a good and loving mother, for knowing what that is like.

In retrospect, my task in part was to elicit the growth of internal structures that would also help William to endure a new severe loss and continue his forward movement. It occurs to me now that I will be his doctor forever, because with me he has grown something strong inside himself and it will be part of him always. Just like his mom. She is slowly fading into the past, as I will eventually, but something important of us will remain. Forever is inside.

REFERENCES

Ainsworth, M.D.S., Blehar, M.C., Waters, E., & Wall, S. (1978). *Patterns of attachment: A psychological study of the strange situation.* Mahwah, NJ: Lawrence Erlbaum Associates.

Bowlby, J. (1988). *A secure base.* New York: Basic Books.

Engel, S. (1995). *The stories that children tell: Making sense of the narratives of childhood.* New York: W.H. Freeman.

George, C., West, M., & Pettem, O. (1999). The adult attachment projective: Disorganization of attachment at the level of representation. In J. Solomon & C. George (Eds.), *Attachment disorganization* (pp. 318–346). New York: The Guilford Press.

Main, M. (1996). Introduction to the special section on attachment and psychopathology: 2. Overview of the field of attachment. *Journal of Clinical and Consulting Psychology, 2,* 237–243.

Schore, A.N. (1994). *Affect regulation and the origin of the self: The neurobiology of emotional development.* Mahwah, NJ: Lawrence Erlbaum Associates.

Siegel, D.J. (1999). *The developing mind: Toward a neurobiology of interpersonal experience.* New York: The Guilford Press.

Solomon, J., & George, C. (Eds.). (1999). *Attachment disorganization.* New York: The Guilford Press.

Sroufe, L.A. (1996). *Emotional development: The organization of emotional life in the early years.* New York: Cambridge University Press.

Stern, D.N. (1985). *The interpersonal world of the infant: A view from psychoanalysis and developmental psychology.* New York: Basic Books.

Stern, D.N. (2004). *The present moment in psychotherapy and everyday life.* New York: W.W. Norton.

Tronick, E. (1989). Emotions and emotional communication in infants. *American Psychologist, 44,* 112–119.

CHAPTER 6

Beyond the 50-Minute Hour

A Continuum of Care for a Foster Child

Martha P. Harris

Working with children in therapy is a challenging undertaking at best. It requires forming a relationship with a child, gaining trust, and creating a level of comfort so that the child can freely play, talk, do, and be. It also requires an ability to make a connection with the parents or caregiver in a way that is supportive and nurturing but not intrusive and overpowering. Essentially, the goal of the child therapist is to help create the conditions to allow the child to recover from whatever trauma or issue has led to his or her development going awry and to find the way to get back "on track." The path to reaching this goal is varied and unique to each child. It involves working with the child to understand his or her story. It involves translating one's understanding of the child's strengths and challenges in a comprehensible way to the parent or caregiver. It requires helping caregivers to create an environment that takes into account the child's particular temperament, learning style, and challenges. It requires that the therapist be creative and find new ways to reach out and gather together resources that will benefit the child. It demands much more than the traditional "50-minute hour" allotted for therapy sessions. My work as a Children's Psychotherapy Project (CPP) therapist with a little girl in kinship foster care illustrates how therapy happens both inside and outside the office.

MONIQUE'S BACKGROUND

It is usually best to start a story at the beginning, but I was not there at the beginning, when Monique was born to a 14-year-old girl who was not prepared to take care of a baby independently. Fortunately she had a family who supported her, giving her a place to live and raise her little girl surrounded by people who cared. There is much I do not know about Monique's first 2 years, but clearly there was love and warmth even in the face of hardship and tragedy. I do know that when she was only 2½ years old, just starting to talk and understand the world in a toddler way, she mysteriously fell from the second-story window of the family home while in her mother's care. A neighbor apparently witnessed the event and said that Monique "tried to get up" after landing on the ground.

Monique was taken to the hospital for observation for several days. The doctors told the family that "everything seemed okay," and Monique went home with only bumps, bruises, and a slight limp. Within weeks of this trauma, Monique suffered a more profound loss: Her young mother died suddenly and unexpectedly. The family was left to grieve their loss and raise Monique as best they could.

Vera, the grandmother, and her extended family were fortunate to live near a specialized child trauma unit at a large hospital. The family was referred for therapy and began treatment around the time of Monique's third birthday. Vera and Monique received regular home visits for approximately 1 year. The therapist, who was specially trained in infant–parent psychotherapy, focused on helping the grandmother with the many challenges she faced in raising Monique. In addition, the therapist helped to address Vera's own personal difficulties and issues. During the course of treatment, one of the suggestions made by the therapist was that the grandmother consider moving to a different community to make a fresh start with her new husband and Monique, for whom she was now the primary caregiver. The child trauma unit was instrumental in helping the three of them find an apartment in a nearby community. Once that was accomplished, a number of things improved. Vera started taking classes at the local community college, and subsidized child care was arranged for Monique. It was at this point, when Monique was about 4½ years old, that the family was referred to CPP. This would be my first case with CPP, and I was excited to meet the family.

Initially, it was difficult to establish a meeting with Vera for an intake appointment. She had a busy class schedule, her husband sometimes worked two shifts, and it was challenging for Vera to find child care for Monique outside of her regular program. When we did finally meet, Vera was forthcoming with information about Monique and the family situation. The grandmother herself had grown up in an abusive environment and had struggled with drug and alcohol problems for many years. She was still grieving over the sudden death of the youngest of her three children 2 years earlier, but she stated that she was determined to work hard to provide Monique with "everything she needed." It became clear during the first session that I would be working not only with Monique and her various issues but also with Vera, especially around parenting issues involving her granddaughter. In time, it seemed that Vera began to think of me as her therapist as well, relying on contacts with me in lieu of seeing her own therapist, with whom she no longer had sessions due to lack of funding. Vera sought my advice not only about Monique and her needs but also regarding her community college classes. It became the routine for Vera to bring Monique for her Friday afternoon appointment with me and to set up a small table in the waiting room with her books, papers, and so forth, thereby using the time as a study hall while I was seeing Monique. As the school semester progressed, Vera proudly gave me—"for Monique's file"—copies of papers that she had written for her community college classes. I learned more details about Vera and her childhood from these autobiographical pieces.

THERAPY SESSIONS WITH MONIQUE

At the start of therapy, I felt almost overwhelmed with all of the family history and the series of losses that were experienced by Monique and her grandmother. As I continued to work with them and to appreciate the strengths that they both brought to the relationship, I became more hopeful that with time and support, they would be able to overcome the challenges that they faced. Vera had many dreams and plans for her own future as well as for her granddaughter. She was starting out by taking courses at the community college but hoped to transfer to a university program and complete her bachelor's degree in either business or social welfare. She had a lot of energy and a way of making things happen. However, it became apparent over the years that I worked with this family that some plans never got off the launching pad and there were disappointments and setbacks that might have discouraged a less-determined person. Vera was able to manage somehow and never let go of her belief that she could provide a good and supportive home for her granddaughter. It soon became apparent that I was to be the stable, grounded reference point to which Vera turned when she needed advice about parenting.

One of the presenting problems that Vera described early on in our work together was that Monique was a strong-willed child who had some behavioral issues at child care as well as at home. For instance, if Monique was not tired when it was naptime at the child care program, she would stay awake and disrupt the quiet atmosphere that was necessary for the other children to sleep. In consultation with the child care providers, a plan was developed to give Monique some responsibility to "take care of" the younger children (she was the oldest in the group at the time) and help the teachers when they needed assistance. Monique rose to the status of being the teacher's helper, and the disruptive behavior subsided.

Temperament Issues

In an attempt to help Vera better understand Monique's behavior, I suggested that Vera complete a temperament questionnaire (Kristal, 2005) on Monique's typical behavior (this is something I often do in the initial phase of working with a child and family). Vera found this experience to be very interesting and informative, and it gave us a new way to discuss and understand Monique's individuality. The temperament profile that was generated from a questionnaire (Cameron & Rice, 1999) indicated that Monique was high in intensity, somewhat slow in adapting, and quite persistent in pursuing what she wanted. These traits were creating a challenge for Vera, who had not parented a young child in many years. Together, we talked about effective ways to approach parenting issues, especially discipline. For instance, children who are highly intense tend to be loud and dramatic and to overreact both positively and negatively. Children who are slow to adapt basically do not like change and have difficulty making transitions from one activity to another. These children need time to adjust to new rules, routines, and different situations. They need to know what to expect and to be prepared in advance of changes about to happen. Children who are high in persistence are often stubborn but, on the positive side, can work at a task until it is completed. However, highly persistent children sometimes get locked into certain behaviors and ideas and lack flexibility. This way of understanding Monique's behavior was very useful to Vera and helped her avoid taking the behavior as a personal affront or an indication that Monique was "bad."

An understanding of Monique's unique temperament and how it interacted with Vera's parenting style proved to be a useful tool when there was friction between Monique and her grandmother. One Friday afternoon as they were arriving at my office, I could hear Monique crying and Vera berating her as they walked into the waiting room. When I asked Vera what the problem was, she angrily described how Monique had lost her brand new (expensive) jacket at school, and she carried on about how thoughtless, careless, and "bad" Monique was for having lost it. Vera was clearly upset, not thinking about how her angry tone of voice and hurtful words were affecting Monique, who was crying uncontrollably. I had observed how, when Vera got upset, she often lost her ability to think clearly about how to solve the problem at hand. I immediately asked Monique a few questions about when she last had her jacket, where it might have been left, and then suggested to Vera that a phone call to the preschool might result in finding the jacket. She settled herself enough to dial the number, spoke to the teacher, and was relieved to hear that they had found the jacket on the playground and that Monique would be able to pick it up on Monday. After both Monique and Vera had calmed down a bit, I suggested to Vera that Monique was usually good about taking care of her things, that 4½-year-olds often get carried away with their play, and that it was not unusual for items such as jackets to get left behind. I mentioned that Monique was a sensitive girl and often responded with tears and distress when Vera spoke harshly to her. I suggested that when these things happen, that Vera might take a deep breath, remind herself of Monique's age, and then think about the best way to address the problem. In this way, difficult situations could be transformed from shameful experiences into learning opportunities.

General Applications Regarding Temperament

My experience with Vera around understanding temperament issues suggests the potential usefulness for this kind of approach and information for foster parents in general, especially those who have not known the child's individual characteristics from birth. By using a temperament profile approach, foster parents can be helped to understand the children in their care as unique individuals with certain inborn characteristics that may be more or less than those of "average" children. This, in turn, would help foster parents adjust their parenting styles to better fit individual children, potentially avoiding behavioral problems from developing. This strategy is based on the temperament research by Chess and Thomas (1986, 1999) and their concept of "goodness of fit" between child temperament and parenting style.

Mother Identification Issues

In addition to working on temperament issues with Vera, I learned from Monique that she felt "misunderstood" at her child care program. During one session just after Monique's fifth birthday, I mentioned that I had spoken to her preschool teacher about Monique's crying at school. Monique responded, "I cry 'cause I miss my mommy. . . . " I asked Monique if she meant her grandmother, thinking that she was confusing her mother with her grandmother (who had been her primary caregiver since age 2 ½). Monique immediately replied, "No, my mommy who's in heaven." She then added that her teachers did not understand her and told her to go to sleep when she said she missed her mother. When I asked her what she thought might help, Monique could not think of anything at first but then said, "Well, I can tell my grammy. . . . but I can't tell my teachers, 'cause they don't know my mom." I suggested that perhaps Monique could tell her teachers about her mother, maybe even show them a picture of her. I then asked Monique if she had a picture of her mother and what she looked like. Monique answered, "She's white. She had a tie up on her head. She had a red shirt. . . ." She then added, "There's a picture of her and me too—in my room." I told Monique that I would like to see that picture one day, but Monique abruptly changed the subject, saying that she wanted to play a game and started searching in the playroom cupboard. It is interesting to note that this was one of only a few times that Monique's mother came up in sessions, despite my attempts to invite the topic either through play themes or conversation. After I had been working with Monique for approximately a year, she began routinely to refer to her grandmother as "Mommy." For a while, I was confused and several times corrected her, continuing to refer to Vera as "Grammy." However, after a while, I too resorted to "Mommy" for Vera, as Monique seemed most comfortable with this term. I wondered how Monique's ability to think about her biological mother would be affected by her calling Vera "Mommy." For all intents and purposes, Vera was Monique's mommy at that point. On one occasion, I did get to see a picture of Monique's birth mother at age 14 or 15 years. I was struck with the amazing resemblance between Monique and her mother, imagining that I was seeing a younger version of the girl in the picture when I looked at Monique.

Monique's Early Play Style

Early therapy sessions involved much exploration of the playroom space and investigation of the toys and games. Monique initially showed great interest in the baby dolls and various doll equipment, engaging in much nurturing, cleaning, dressing, feeding, and soothing of the babies. On a number of occasions, she created families out of dolls, animals, or sand tray items. She was delighted when she discovered that the little bears in the sand tray cupboard "could be a bear *family* . . . a dad, a mom, and two kids!" Monique was clearly trying to work out what the word *family* meant and of what her family now consisted. When I referred to Vera as her grandmother at one point during the first year of our work together, Monique corrected me, saying, "She's not my grandmother anymore. . . . she's my mommy now." After I replied, "She's your mommy 'cause she takes care of you and you live with her, " Monique said, "My other mommy's in heaven . . . but we don't need to talk about it. " This was one of a number of times that we touched on a sensitive issue and Monique veered away in no uncertain terms.

After a period of time when Monique explored the playroom and played with the dolls and other toys, she subsequently turned her attention to board games. Even though she was often confused about the rules, she ventured forth, managing the best she could. She showed good resilience in the face of setbacks, such as when she would draw negative cards or was losing. I modified the rules of several more difficult games and generally tried to steer her toward games that were appropriate for her age. However, she often would insist that she knew how to play a particular game (e.g., Battleship), but when it came to actually playing the game, she did not have a clue. She would try for a few minutes and then say that she wanted to play something else. She loved it when she finally won a game; she would shriek and clap and sometimes do a "victory dance." If she did not win, she would usually insist on playing again, with the intention of winning. After several weeks of choosing to play a board game each session, Monique announced to me, "I want to do *all* of them," indicating the whole cupboard of board games stored in the playroom. One week Monique chose the Talking, Feeling, Doing Game, a therapeutic game in which the child picks a card and then responds to the directions by answering a talking, feeling, or doing question. This is a game often used in therapy with children ages 8 and older. I pointed out that this was really a game for older kids, but Monique insisted. One of her cards asked, "What was the most frightening thing that ever happened to you?" to which Monique matter-of-factly replied, "Nothing—I've never been scared." After playing this game for a while, she tired of the questions (but liked that I had to answer questions, too), so we switched to another game. This particular game was based purely on luck, and Monique believed she could win. Near the end of the game, Monique threw a 7 on the dice, zoomed ahead 25 spaces to reach the finish line, and excitedly exclaimed, "I WON! I WON!" This was one determined little girl. It seemed as if her choice of board games and attempting to do that which was a little beyond her reach was an example of her striving, or her "achievement motivation."

Limit Testing

During this time of fairly regular attendance at therapy sessions (usually averaging three times a month), Monique tested many limits with me. A small room off of the playroom was used by the therapists as a kitchen area, with a water cooler, teakettle, and microwave oven. Monique was intrigued when she saw all of the equipment and promptly announced that she was thirsty. I found a cup and poured some water for her, at which point she said that she liked her water warm. Sensing that she was pushing the boundaries, I said that she would have to drink her water cold because we could not use the microwave oven; it belonged to the other therapists. As I was walking out of the kitchen area to go back into the playroom, Monique quickly sneaked the cup into the microwave and turned it on, looking pleased that she had gotten her way. I was annoyed (but tried to remain neutral) and said that we would need to leave the kitchen door closed from now on because Monique had a hard time following the rules. This was a glimpse into the limit testing that I was hearing about from her grandmother as well as from the teachers at her preschool. It is interesting to note that the next week when Monique came for her therapy appointment, we entered the playroom together and she announced, "Oh, we need to shut this door," walking over to the kitchen door and closing it. She had remembered the episode from last week and was now able to provide the boundary for herself.

Another session that was quite instructive to me as a therapist came after I had been working with Monique for several months. She had been testing limits in various ways, but this instance took me by surprise. After a brief discussion with Vera in the waiting room, Monique indicated that she was anxious to get started and instructed me to set up the dollhouse (we had played with it last session) while she looked for rocks in the sand tray. After putting all of the furniture in the second floor of the dollhouse, Monique stated that she needed more dolls from the cupboard. She discovered that it was locked, although the key was in the lock. She played with locking and unlocking the doors, interested in the whole concept. She then started to play with the pretend food, naming each item and feeding the dolls. Abruptly, she stopped, and announced, "I want to put this up now; I'm done." We then played checkers and Connect Four. When the session was almost over, she asked, "Can I do a little picture?" Trying to remain patient and understanding, I explained that we were already over time, saying, "I know it's hard when we are out of time and you still have more things to do, but we have to stop now." After a few more delaying tactics involving my helping Monique with various things, we finally left the playroom.

We met Vera in the waiting room, and I exchanged a few words with her. Monique apparently got bored (or angry, because I had just told her that we had to stop for today) and wandered out of the waiting room. Vera called for Monique to leave. I heard the door to my office slam, and Monique appeared in the waiting room door. Only after the two of them left did I discover that Monique had closed and locked the door to my office with my keys inside. Because this was late Friday afternoon and everyone else had already left, I had to call a fellow therapist who lived nearby and was able to let me back into my office.

Once inside my office, I looked for the keys where I thought I had left them on my desk, but they were nowhere to be found. I did an exhaustive search of my office, finally finding the keys in the wastebasket. I racked my brain to figure out how they had gotten there and assumed that I had carelessly dropped them while throwing something else away. Next week at my consultation group meeting, I recounted the story; all of the assembled therapists immediately thought Monique probably threw away the keys. I was shocked, surprised, and not convinced that a 5-year-old would do such a thing, still clinging to my belief that I had probably been the culprit. It was clear that we would need to discuss the incident in our next session together. In my experience as a child therapist, this was a first in the annals of limit testing!

When Monique arrived for her next appointment, I told her that we needed to talk about something in my office before we went into the playroom. She sat on the sofa and looked up at me. I told her that the last time she was here, my keys got lost, and I looked all over the room—behind the desk, under the sofa, behind the cushions—but I could not find them anywhere. Monique asked, "Did you look in here?" pointing to the wastebasket. I said that, yes, I finally did look there and found the keys. Trying not to sound accusatory, I then said, "I think that you were feeling mad at me when you did that because I was paying attention to your grandmother and not to you; you didn't know what to do about that feeling so you decided to hide my keys. That's something I want to help you with." With that, Monique got up from the sofa and headed for the playroom. At first, she could not decide what she wanted to do, but she then settled on painting with watercolors. We painted together. Monique wanted to have a paintbrush exactly like the one I was using. Next, we switched to playing doctor, with me being assigned the role of patient. Monique ended the session by constructing an elaborate train track with my help and then running the train around the track, singing "The Train Song." We had reconnected. We were "back on track." I hoped that she was learning through her experience with me that relationships could withstand ruptures and repairs.

Initiating Monique's School Transition

Later that year, the topic of kindergarten became an issue. Vera was considering the advantages of public schools and a parochial school in their community. Realizing that Monique was a particularly bright and verbal child caused me to think in terms of a school placement where she would be academically challenged. I discussed this idea with members of my CPP consultation group, who encouraged me to contact a particular private school that prided itself in a diverse student body and offered scholarships to students whose families had limited financial resources.

Vera was very excited about the prospect of a private school education for her granddaughter and immediately called the school from my office to make an appointment. Several months later—after applications, interviews, and testing—we were happy to learn that Monique had been accepted as a scholarship student.

I had some concerns about Monique's transition from a public preschool setting into the new academically oriented private school. Not only would the requirements for attention, focus, and academic work be higher but also the culture of the school itself would be very different from Monique's and Vera's previous school experiences. I had little doubt that Monique was up to the challenge of the academic work: She was bright and verbal and genuinely liked school. My worries were more in the realm of social-emotional development, Monique's ability to get along with her classmates, and Vera's ability to switch into the private school mode as Monique's primary caregiver. I attempted to address these issues during the summer months, but between Vera's summer term classes at the community college and summer camp for Monique, Vera was unable to keep regular appointments. In fact, from May through August, they were only able to come for seven sessions.

Shortly before kindergarten started, the school arranged several orientation experiences. One involved current students and their families inviting a new student to their homes to welcome them into the school community. Monique came to one of her therapy appointments in August before school started and announced to me that she had visited a first-grade student's house and had organic strawberries for a treat! What a different culture she was about to experience!

Consultation Group's Assistance Regarding Parenting and Family Issues

The CPP consultation group to which I belong meets weekly at the office of our senior clinician, who volunteers her expertise and time to the project as we volunteer our time as clinicians to our individual CPP clients. Across the 3 ½ years that I worked with Monique and her family, the consultation group was supportive and immensely helpful in crafting my understanding of Monique and Vera, the challenges they faced, and the ways that I might be helpful to them. The group encouraged me when I believed that I was not effective enough in my therapy sessions with Monique, helped me to support the family in constructive but not dependency-fostering ways, and provided four more clinically attuned and experienced minds to focus on this challenging case. The group gave me specific ideas about and interpretations of the case material but also acted as a holding environment where I could express my concerns, worries, and hopes about this little girl and her future. For that I am very grateful. I believe that the consultation group provides the nourishment that keeps the CPP clinicians going, in both good times and bad.

One instance in which the consultation group came to my aid was during a period when things started falling apart for Vera and she was having a hard time coping. She was having financial troubles, her community college classes were extra challenging, and she was trying to find a full-day summer camp program for Monique that would be fun and educational. I did a little research and found a few programs that fit the criteria and were within range, both geographically and financially. Vera chose a program, registered Monique, and told me about it when she brought Monique to one of her therapy appointments. Upon hearing about the summer camp, Monique started demanding that her grandmother take her there immediately; she was pleading and crying. I tried to explain to Monique that summer camp sounded great but did not start for another month; at that time, she would get to go every day. Vera just rolled her eyes at Monique's dramatics and said angrily, "This is how she gets!" It would have been useful to have a collateral meeting around these issues, a time when Vera and I could talk about the things that made Monique especially challenging to parent; unfortunately, scheduling any sessions with Vera alone proved to be almost impossible. It was difficult for her to plan ahead and keep appointments on any other day than Friday, and we needed that time for Monique's appointments. The result was that I would try to squeeze in a few minutes before or after Monique's appointments to talk to Vera about pressing issues. Monique seemed fairly content to go into the playroom and entertain herself at the start of one of her sessions but, as noted previously, got annoyed when I told her that time was up and then proceeded to talk to Vera for 5–10 minutes longer. In fact, Monique locked my office again, but fortunately I had my keys with me this time. To address this issue, my consultation group suggested phoning Vera in lieu of having a face-to-face appointment. I was able to do this on several occasions and avoided the before- or after-session scene with Monique and Vera.

The consultation group was instrumental in providing the support and information necessary for me to strongly encourage Vera to apply for legal guardianship of Monique during the first year of our work together. Monique's biological father essentially disappeared after the tragic month when Monique fell from the window and her mother died. Vera did not know where Monique's father was; she noted that he knew how to get in touch with them but did not make the effort.

There were a number a reasons why it was important for Vera to obtain legal guardian status, one of which was access to Monique's medical records. Vera made contact with a legal aid society, which guided her through the process of becoming Monique's legal guardian. As Monique's therapist, I offered to be the person to nominate Vera on the application as someone who knew Monique and could vouch for the appropriateness of this petition. It was satisfying to know that I had been a part of Vera's quest to become her granddaughter's legal guardian and thereby formalize the relationship.

Transportation Issues

At one point, Vera suffered some serious financial setbacks and found herself without a car. This worried us both because she had to drive approximately 15 miles to bring Monique to my office. Vera was determined to get Monique to her therapy appointments, so the two of them decided to travel by rapid transit. This entailed not only getting to the station near their home but also walking about 15–20 minutes once they arrived in the town where my office was located. The first time they attempted taking public transportation, they had not arrived by 15 minutes after their scheduled appointment time. Vera's husband called to say that they were on the way but had taken a wrong turn from the station and had initially headed away from the office. They finally arrived, almost 35 minutes late but resolved to get here again. They made several more round trips by rapid transit, but it was difficult for Vera to keep regular appointments during this time. Eventually, Vera was able to obtain another car, which made transportation much easier.

Not Having Enough and Wanting More

The themes of not having enough and wanting more surfaced many times during my work with Monique. Although Monique's extended family provided her with many material things (toys, books, after-school classes, and trendy clothes), Monique often wanted to have something from the playroom or my office to take home with her. Sometimes she would be satisfied with a picture or craft project that she had made or my offer of a few sheets of colored construction paper from the playroom. Other times she would ask if she could have a particular toy or item. One day after Monique had discovered the Slinky, she asked if she could take it home with her. I explained that the playroom toys needed to stay in the playroom but that she could play with it next week. Our session ended, but Monique continued to hold on to the Slinky as we walked back to the waiting room to meet Vera. I talked with Vera briefly and then the two of them left. A few minutes later, Vera and Monique reappeared at my door, with Vera angry and Monique contrite. Apparently the Slinky had made it all the way to the car before Vera discovered it and made Monique bring it back to me. After relinquishing the "borrowed" item, Monique asked if she could have a hug from me before she went out the door. The following week, the Slinky came up in the course of the session. Monique explained, in great detail, exactly what happened by speaking into a play phone while I listened on another play phone (Monique's idea). When I said, "Sometimes you just want something so badly that you just take it, but then you realize that you should give it back—and you did." Monique nodded, said, "Let's have tea now!", and got two pink plastic glasses, which we clinked together while saying, "Cheers!"

Kindergarten in a New School Environment

The school year began, and I heard glowing reports from both Vera and Monique about how much they liked the private school, the kindergarten teacher, and the new friends and new contacts with other families. Despite the fact that both Vera and Monique claimed that everything was going fine at the new school, I heard differently from the kindergarten teacher. As early as the second month of school, I had a phone conversation with her regarding Monique's problematic interactions with her classmates, including one incident of hitting and twisting someone's arm. In our sessions together, I tried to make openings for Monique to talk about school, her classmates, and her teacher, but she managed to brush me off, saying that everything was okay, and then quickly moved toward playing a game or engaging in an arts and crafts project. Yet, the kindergarten teacher's concerns persisted, and I was invited (by both Vera and the teacher) to attend the first parent–teacher conference. In addition to the teacher and me, Vera and her older daughter (Monique's aunt) were present. The teacher stated that Monique seemed to lack emotional boundaries and often got angry and acted impulsively if she did not get her way. The teacher also saw in Monique a pattern of "whining and manipulation," rather than an ability to ask in a normal tone, when she wanted something. Fortunately, the teacher stated that Monique had begun to accept some limits at school; however, she had a particularly hard time making the transition back into the school's culture after weekends. The teacher also noted that Monique did better in structured than free play or unstructured activities. This observation was interesting in light of the fact that Monique often chose board games or specific arts and crafts activities, such as stringing beads or making pipe-cleaner animals, rather than other imaginative types of play in our therapy sessions together. This clearly was her comfort zone, where she felt in control of herself as well as the situation. One interesting question that the teacher posed to Vera was, "Which family members parent Monique?" This was a particularly timely question, as Vera had been taking Monique to stay at a relative's home on weekends so that Vera could get a break from the constant demands of having an active, curious, talkative 5-year-old in the home. Perhaps this was one of the reasons why Monique found it so difficult to reenter school after a weekend away. This initial parent–teacher conference was the beginning of my ongoing collaborative effort with the school to help address challenging issues for Monique's family.

I was concerned about how to broach the subject of school behavior problems with Monique herself because she consistently maintained that everything was fine at school. Finally, at the end of a session throughout which I had been hoping for an opening to bring up the subject, I told Monique that we needed to talk a bit about school. I said that I had spoken to her teacher, which surprised Monique, and that although Monique was doing well with the work at school, she seemed to be having trouble with the other children. I then said that I thought that this school had some different rules and expectations from her previous school and that we would work together so that she could be successful at her new school regarding both her schoolwork and her classmates. Monique nodded in agreement. After the session was over, I visited with Vera in the waiting room briefly and loaned her my copy of the book *Boundaries with Kids* (Cloud & Townsend, 1998), which the teacher had recommended Vera read.

I stayed in contact with Monique's teacher during the school year. She believed that Monique's behavior had improved slowly but steadily as she learned the school rules and expectations. She said that Monique had fewer outbursts, was generally happier, and was better able to take constructive criticism. However, she remained concerned about Monique's continued bossiness and manipulation, particularly with one student whom Monique sometimes reduced to tears. The teacher believed that Monique had a strong need to be seen as number one, along with a need to be in control of situations, in order to feel safe. As Monique's therapist, I could understand why this was the case, given her early losses, but I was concerned that she continued to have these behavioral issues at school.

While Monique was adjusting to life in kindergarten, Vera was having challenges of her own as a community college student. She was taking several demanding classes and feeling exhausted by the combined effort of raising a 5-year-old, attending classes, studying for tests, and writing papers. As noted, she proudly brought copies of her own papers "for Monique's file," demonstrating a need to tell me about what was going on in *her* life as well as what was happening in Monique's. Often, I found that the few collateral sessions that we were able to schedule ended up focusing almost entirely on Vera. Being interested in and concerned about Vera's problems and issues was an important aspect of being Monique's therapist, as Vera was trying her best to be a good parent to her granddaughter without the advantage of having good role models from her parents. I was her sounding board regarding decisions she had to make about Monique, such as what after-school activities to pursue, how to create a sense of family with the extended family living nearby, how to arrange play dates with other children from Monique's school, how to balance Monique's needs with Vera's need for quiet (e.g., for studying), how Vera could meet her need for couple time with her husband, and so forth. It seemed that my attending to Vera's needs and questions about parenting allowed Vera to better attend to Monique's needs. We endured many ups and downs during the more than 3 years that I worked with Monique, but I always tried to be a stable presence in their lives.

END OF THERAPY

Toward the end of the time that I was seeing Monique in therapy, the frequency of sessions dropped off dramatically. In the first few months of our work together, Vera was able to bring Monique for appointments usually two or three times a month. During that time, Vera was generally able to comply with my office policy of calling if she needed to cancel an appointment. However, as we came to the end of the first year of treatment, the sessions started to become more erratic, usually only once or twice a month. On several occasions, I questioned Vera about her inability to keep weekly appointments. She always had legitimate-sounding reasons: illness in one or both parents or Monique herself, too much schoolwork, pressing demands of dealing with her two grown children or extended family, transportation problems, or other doctor's appointments. In consultation with my CPP group, I realized that every-other-week appointments (i.e., twice a month) were fairly typical and that I should not be overly concerned, as long as appointments were regular. Usually after I discussed the problem with Vera, she would make a concerted effort to get Monique to her appointments every week; however, their attendance would then drop off again. At one point, I wrote a letter stating the importance of regular therapy appointments to Monique's continued healthy development. Vera responded with renewed efforts to get Monique to our sessions more frequently.

During the final year of therapy, things became much more erratic. Vera had dropped out of school, had been trying to find a job, had separated from her husband, and was having a hard time getting Monique to school on time. The school was particularly concerned about the late arrivals, and Monique's teacher and I had discussed the situation by phone on several occasions. I talked with Vera about the problem, both by phone and in person when she was able to bring Monique in for her therapy sessions. Vera said that she would try to get Monique to school on time, but sometimes she had trouble falling asleep herself and then would oversleep in the morning.

Eventually, Vera stopped responding to my phone messages about rescheduling appointments for Monique, and I became increasingly concerned about their welfare. I finally wrote a letter to her saying that perhaps it was time to end treatment, as she no longer seemed able to get Monique to my office for appointments. Vera did finally call me and informed me that she was looking for a larger house in a community about 40 minutes away so that she could become registered as a foster parent and care for a number of children in her home. It was clear that continuing therapy with me through CPP would not be possible, and I reluctantly faced the fact that we indeed needed to terminate treatment. Together, we scheduled a final session so that Monique and I could say good-bye after all the years of work together. Vera was unable to bring Monique to the scheduled appointment and did not call to cancel or reschedule the session. I was frustrated and concerned at the same time. The consultation group suggested that if I was not able to see Monique in my office, perhaps I could arrange to see her at school. I phoned Vera and offered this as an option, and she agreed, saying it would probably be the best solution because they were planning to move to the new community as soon as the school year was over. I got a release of information and permission from Vera so that I could visit Monique in her after-school program. I made the arrangements with the school to reserve a space where the two of us could say our good-byes.

I arrived at the school at the appointed time, but Monique was initially reluctant to meet with me. It had been months since I had seen her, and she probably thought it strange to see me on her turf rather than at my office. After an awkward start to the meeting, Monique warmed up as I showed her several pictures she had made over the years that we had worked together and that I had saved in her file. We had some fun remembering the things that we had done together. I had made a collage of photos that I had taken of Monique over the years, and she was surprised at how young she looked when we had started therapy together. I told her that I thought it was important to have a chance to say good-bye to someone you have known for a long time, rather than just having them disappear from your life. I gave Monique a little address book as a good-bye present, with one of my business cards enclosed, saying that I would be happy to hear from her after she moved and started her new school. We talked about where the card should go in the book (i.e., under "M" or under "H"). Once Monique had decided, she carefully printed my entire name, work address, and office phone number in her best grade-school penmanship on the appropriate page. She thanked me for the address book, saying she had "always wanted one," gave me a quick hug, and ran off to rejoin her friends on the playground. It was hard for me to realize that I probably would not see Monique again, but at the same time, I felt gratified that I had been a part of her life for 3 ½ years. Although additional therapy would have undoubtedly been beneficial both to Monique and to Vera, I believed that they were in a better place than when they first came to CPP. I had seen Monique and Vera for a total of 82 sessions. Perhaps I will have the opportunity to hear from them in the future. I would be very happy to know how things are in both of their lives.

CONCLUSION

Monique was very fond of a little set of nesting dolls, or Matreshkas, that I had in my office. She would play with them, opening first the biggest doll, which revealed a medium-size doll, then a smaller doll, then the smallest of all, neatly nestled inside one another. She would line them up, play with them, and then carefully reassemble them one inside the other. It seemed that this play was another way of her working out what it means to be a family, to have people who care about and for you—people who stay the same but also change and grow. Thinking back on my experience with Monique and her family, I realized that the set of Matreshka dolls had another meaning: It represented the continuum of care within CPP. First there was Monique. Next came her grandmother, Vera, the primary caregiver and the new "mommy," holding Monique the best she knew how. Then came me, Monique's therapist, who tried in various ways to hold both Vera and Monique and to help these family members nurture each other and thrive. Finally, there was my consultation group, which provided the container within which I was able to feel supported and nurtured in my work with this family. As the saying goes, "it takes a village" to successfully respond to all the needs of a child who has suffered early loss. I am grateful for the set of nesting dolls created to provide the holding environment needed for Monique and me as we did our work together.

REFERENCES

Cameron, J., & Rice, D. (1999). *Cameron-Rice Temperament Questionnaires.* Retrieved June 1, 2005, from http://www.perventiveoz.org

Chess, S., & Thomas, A. (1986). *Temperament in clinical practice.* New York: The Guilford Press.

Chess, S., & Thomas, A. (1999). *Goodness of fit: Clinical applications from infancy through adult life.* New York: Brunner/Mazel.

Cloud, H., & Townsend, J. (1998). *Boundaries with kids.* Grand Rapids, MI: Zondervan Publishing House.

Kristal, J. (2005). *The temperament perspective: Working with children's behavioral styles.* Baltimore: Paul H. Brookes Publishing Co.

CHAPTER 7

Falling Through the Cracks

The Complications of
Reunification for an Adolescent in Foster Care

Christopher Bonovitz

This chapter addresses issues surrounding the reunification of foster children with their birth parents. At the time this chapter was written, I had worked with Pedro, age 15, for more than 4 years. During the course of working with him, there were two failed reunification attempts with his birth mother[1], with a brief stint at a residential group home in between each. The chapter focuses on the time that he spent in a residential group home prior to the second trial discharge attempt, in which he would return to live with his mother on a permanent basis.

For children such as Pedro, treatment in the context of the Children's Psychotherapy Project (CPP) runs counter to everything the child knows. It offers a therapeutic relationship that extends "for as long as it takes"—that is, a promise of sorts that may hold many meanings for clients and therapists, meanings that may shift and evolve during the course of treatment. Although this sounds ideal in theory, I think that all of us who have done this work have been humbled by the limitations imposed, despite wishes for magical solutions. First, there is the whole element of time. For children whose histories are littered with separation, loss, and abandonment, time with a past, present, and future is anything but coherent or linear.

Many of these children have little sense of self through time. Past trauma has been dissociated in order to survive, and the future often ap-

---

An earlier version of this chapter was presented as a paper at the Washington School of Psychiatry in October 2003. Edited parts of this chapter grew out of a presentation given in February 2005 at the Manhattan Institute for Psychoanalysis with Neil Altman, Ph.D., Kate Dunn, Psy.D., and Elizabeth Kandall, Ph.D.

[1]In this chapter, the term *birth mother* and *mother* are used interchangeably.

pears precarious at best. Regardless of the conditions of the therapy arrangement, one cannot escape the trauma of loss and separation that makes the potential of an attachment with a new parental figure terrifying. In addition, although some people might consider private practice a more ideal setup that may provide greater continuity, this kind of insulation does not protect the treatment from the ills of the foster care system itself and the high risks that these children live with on a daily basis. All of these things pervade the therapy room. In short, there are no magical solutions. Rather, CPP offers a sustained sense of hope and commitment over time. Moreover, the project affords much needed support to its therapists through its weekly consultation groups and the CPP community as a whole: a communal structure necessary to hold together the treatment during times of crises and prolonged disruptions and to contain the powerful feelings or numbness that comes with the territory.

This chapter raises questions about adolescents in foster care and attachment, particularly how adolescent development works against the process of reattaching with one's birth parent. Furthermore, the chapter addresses the denial of loss that pervades the individuals within the foster care system. It examines how the foster care system as a whole acts as a surrogate parent, then disowns this function upon discharging children to their birth parents or primary caregivers.

PEDRO'S STORY

Pedro was first taken away from his 40-year-old mother, Maria, when he was 3 years old because Maria suffered from long-standing bipolar disorder and was too volatile to care for him. Before placement in foster care, he had been severely neglected by his mother, often left unattended for long periods of time. Pedro did not remember his father. He had an older brother who was being raised in the Dominican Republic by relatives. Maria regarded Pedro's brother as her favorite and was prone to idealizing him when problems arose with Pedro.

Just before Pedro was first removed from his home at the age of 3, his father, who was separated from his mother at the time, was killed in an automobile accident. Maria was traumatized by the loss. She experienced frequent breakdowns, during which she would cry uncontrollably and find herself completely unable to care for Pedro. From the ages of 3–5 years, Pedro lived with a foster parent who, according to Pedro, held his face down in a steaming hot plate of food. Pedro returned to live with Maria at age 5 and remained with her until the age of 8, at which time he was removed from her home for a second time after running away during one of her breakdowns. Pedro ran to the home of his mother's boyfriend, Manny, who had become a surrogate father to him. Manny called the police, alleging that Maria was neglecting Pedro, and Pedro was brought back into foster care. The details of this account, like much of Pedro's history, were vague. Pedro would not return to his mother for 5 years. In the meantime, he lived with his foster mother, Jennifer, with whom he had a relationship that initially was fairly stable but progressively became more problematic.

Maria's own history is mostly unknown to me. She spoke very little English, and I spoke even less Spanish; at times, I had to use an English/Spanish dictionary during our sessions. Furthermore, Maria described (through Spanish-speaking professionals) her own childhood as very positive, discounting or minimizing negative events. Her narrative lacked substance and a sense of cohesion, and instead was jumbled and filled with generalities. She was an only child of parents who divorced when she was a young child. She was raised by her father and stepmother. She was married to Pedro's father at the time that he died, and she later immigrated to the United States when she was 25 years old. Since coming to the United States, she had been hospitalized eight times for psychiatric reasons and diagnosed with bipolar disorder, for which she took medication. Through her local clinic, she had four different individual therapists during a 2-year span.

When Pedro began therapy with me at the age of 11, Jennifer expressed her concern about the severity of what she considered depression. He had had recent bouts of encopresis, was unresponsive with her, and had very few friends. He spent the majority of his time sitting numbly in front of the television. In school, he was reported to be a bright student who did not present behavior problems but was unfocused and rarely performed to his potential. Through the 4 years that I worked with Pedro, various people came in and out of his life: one foster mother, four case workers, two law guardians, two intensive case managers, and two therapists before me. Although this may sound like a lot of people, compared with other children in foster care, it is actually a rather low number.

Jennifer, a proud foster parent, was a key figure in Pedro's life. She was strong willed, sharp edged, and stubborn, and she believed in tough love. She was a long-time foster parent with a history of trauma and loss in her own background. Her husband had committed suicide, and her oldest son was killed in a gang fight. Jennifer relied on caring for neglected and abused children as a means of treating her own scars and working through her tragic losses. Twenty-seven foster children had passed through Jennifer's home before Pedro.

ADOLESCENCE AND ATTACHMENT: FAILING THE TEST

Similar to the first failed trial discharge, in which Pedro's behavior communicated his intense ambivalence in returning to live with Maria, a month prior to the start of a second trial discharge Pedro began lashing out at Jennifer. Between threatening to break her windows and hitting her on one occasion, he managed to provoke what he most feared in response to his feelings about losing her. Jennifer rejected him by kicking him out of her home before he had a chance to leave.

Although Jennifer had been his primary caregiver for 6 years, more time than Pedro spent with Maria, he was determined to destroy his relationship with her before leaving, as the loss of Jennifer was too much to bear. Pedro, similar to the parental figures in his life, had been unable to mourn the losses that accumulated over the course of his short life. As a result, more than the loss, it was really the denial of the loss and the inability to mourn it that stood in the way of his development. Without mourning, new attachments were that much more difficult to form, let alone internalize.

GROUP HOME

With Pedro's second trial discharge imminent, the foster care agency determined that Maria was not quite yet prepared to handle him, as she had recently been hospitalized following a breakdown and could barely support herself on the welfare money she was receiving at the time. It was decided that Pedro would be moved to a group home facility until more supportive interventions were put in place for his mother. To my surprise, the 5 months that Pedro had spent in the group home proved to be one of the more meaningful experiences for him that I had witnessed since I had started working with him. In retrospect, it symbolized the birth of the psychological self in him—that is, a capacity to reflect on and make meaning of his own experiences. Although the situation with Maria continued to remain unstable, he came to life for the first time, as though the bundle of feelings, especially his rage, that had been stored up unraveled in the form of words, thoughts, and expressed feelings. Pedro showed signs of developing the capacity to reflect on his own feeling states as well as on the thoughts and feelings of others.

Fortunately, the all-boys group home in which Pedro was placed happened to be a few blocks away from where I lived at the time. In my first trip to this new setting, I was immediately struck by the army-like inculcations that adorned the walls. For instance, one poster read, "Where boys will learn to become men"; another read, "Without education, you're nothing." Next to these were pictures of famous men—such as Tiger Woods, Michael Jordan, Muhammad Ali, and Colin Powell—who came from minority ethnic backgrounds. The group home was run by a young, tall, somewhat intimidating Caucasian man who looked fresh out of the military. The staff was mainly composed of African American and Latino men and women.

Our first meeting in the group home took place inside the weight room due to the lack of available office space; this room became the space in which we would convene once a week for the next 5 months. As we sat down to talk amid the stacks of weights and the Nautilus machines, Pedro picked up a pair of 20-pound dumbbells and proceeded to complete a set with each arm as though he were merely performing his morning workout routine. I was surprised and intrigued with Pedro's introduction, and I immediately had the sense that he was feeling stronger and more hopeful. He appeared significantly more engaged than I had ever seen him; he was more talkative and spirited. When I commented on this observation, Pedro gave me the adolescent grunt indicating agreement and then proceeded to exaggerate the movements and sounds that one associates with weightlifting. He told me of two movies he had seen recently, both of which dealt with themes of men cheating on women and of sons in need of their fathers. As he spoke, he moved onto the punching bag; the slight smile out of the corner of his mouth seemed to indicate that he enjoyed the sound of the thump when his fist hit the leather and the jingling of the bag's chains. As Pedro hit the bag, I thought of his own father, a former amateur boxer who probably spent a lot of time in the weight room.

I also recalled Manny, who was now Maria's ex-boyfriend and with whom Pedro spent a great deal of time with between the ages of 4 and 8 years. He had become a surrogate father to Pedro and had continued to visit him even after Pedro had been taken into foster care. However, Pedro had not seen him for several years. When I asked Pedro about Manny, Pedro grew sad and quiet and mentioned that he did not think about him much anymore.

In our subsequent sessions, Pedro's words sometimes contradicted the communication conveyed through his behavior. Although he professed to dislike the group home and was never short on complaints, he enjoyed the privileges with which he was rewarded for his stellar behavior, and he performed at an exceptionally high level in school. Although he was quick to add that he was on good behavior in order to ensure he was discharged as soon as possible, Pedro could not hide the fact that he actually liked where he was living. To admit this would mean also admitting to himself that returning to live with Maria may not be what he needed or even wanted on an unconscious level. This thought was too frightening to approach. He dealt with the ambivalence he felt toward his mother by fantasizing that his case manager, the group home staff, and I were in a conspiracy against him. In our sessions, Pedro accused all of us of deliberately holding him back from his mother and of harboring the unstated plan of sending him to another residential placement rather than the stated plan of returning him to his mother. This fear was grounded in his early experience of being taken from Maria when he was 3 years old and then again when he was 8. During one of our sessions, Pedro recalled the event that precipitated the removal from his mother when he was 8 years old. When Pedro was picked up by the police following Manny's report of abuse, the police had told Pedro that he would be brought back home later on that evening. Instead, he was taken to what he described as the police station and then to a holding area; later the next day, he was taken to Jennifer's home, where he would remain for the next 6 years. How could Pedro really trust that this was not happening to him once again? He told me, "I don't trust leaving places, because it usually means I won't return, and I don't know how long I will stay anywhere."

For the first time in our work, Pedro spoke about his mother's severe depression, when she was unable to get out of bed, and her manic episodes, which on occasion resulted in hospitalization. Pedro expressed feeling the need to take care of her, and he worried about what might happen to her if he were to be placed in a more permanent residential setting. In his reflections, Pedro conjured up the idealized mother in his mind who loved him and needed him. Yet, when Pedro was actually with her, he was unresponsive or cruel, testing her loyalty to him through his rejection of her or requiring some sort of compensation for her past neglect and abandonment through his demands for money or clothes. These two maternal objects, the psychic one in his mind and the actual one, were most difficult for him to bring together into a whole person who was good and bad. Pedro's denial of any sort of positive feelings towards other adults—including Jennifer, his case manager, or me—was an attempt to preserve the idealized mother. To relinquish this mother was equivalent to nonexistence, as it would leave him with nothing.

While in the group home, Pedro also made efforts to begin constructing a narrative about his life that had a past, present, and future. He was apprehending pieces of himself, reclaiming them, and, in turn, building a psychological self as a replacement for the stick figure who appeared in his early drawings—the figure who stood with his elbows shrugged, repeating, "I don't know," and floated in the wind. I noticed that at the end of our sessions at the group home, Pedro sometimes stopped by the bathroom mirror to look at himself, as though he were really beginning to see himself.

Whereas before Pedro's rage had been turned inward, the group home provided a stable enough environment to allow for the expression of aggressive feelings. Expressing these feelings allowed him to discover his own, separate self through his aggression but in the context of a highly structured setting with strict rules, consistency, and predictability. There were walls for him to bump up against, which made him feel safer with his own emotions. Unlike Maria, who had relinquished her parental reins, or Jennifer, who retaliated, the staff allowed space for his anger to breathe.

Pedro's aggression manifested itself through several different avenues. First, there were his articulated fantasies of retaliating against the system, which was responsible for taking him away from his mother and continued to hold him captive. Second, it was sublimated into his accelerated performance in school and into competition with his peers for rewards incorporated into the behavioral point system. Third, most important, his aggression found a creative outlet as he began to write rap songs. Pedro was turning to the norms and language of the rap culture to begin imagining a place for himself in the world. Our sessions sometimes began with Pedro pulling a crumpled piece of paper out of his pocket or fetching one from his room. Unraveling the paper, a smirk crossed his face as he either read the words himself or asked me to do so. With my slightly off, monotone voice, my renditions quickly lost any sort of rhythm, evoking chuckles from Pedro and some embarrassment on my part. These rap songs not only brought to light Pedro's creativity but also the outlines of an ego-ideal, one organized around the image of himself as a future musician like some of his idols. It seemed that in not having a father figure in his life at that time, Pedro formed an image of himself based on cultural stereotypes of the male gender role and on some of the male staff at the group home. To some extent, the group home itself, with its rules and authority, came to represent a father figure that could contain Pedro and function as another source of identification.

Pedro's rap songs also put into focus some of the differences between us. Pedro voiced his perceptions of me as a much older white man who was out of touch with Pedro's culture. In commenting on my "whiteness," Pedro gradually spoke of his own skin color and identity. Specifically, he noted how he was often mistaken as being Puerto Rican, not Dominican. As Pedro's curiosity about himself deepened, so did his interest in me. This was a contrast with the past, when he had tried so hard to avoid my presence.

After 5 months, when Pedro's stay at the group home was ending and his destination was still uncertain, he stridently tried to deny his attachment to anyone, including me. If he sabotaged his relationships before he left the group home, he would leave empty, without enduring the pain of loss and without feeling his intense yearnings. This manifested itself with me in his denial of his needs and in his questioning my motivations.

Pedro protested the length of his stay at the group home, complaining that no one, including me, was doing enough to help him. He said that no one really understood him. This situation is demonstrated by a snippet from one of our sessions around this time.

Pedro turned to me and said, "You don't understand, you weren't in the system, and so you have no idea the hell that I have been through—my father died, my mother is going through hell, and I'm going through hell. I don't want to have anything to do with anyone once I leave. Therapy has not been helpful, and what's the use? You don't have any power anyway to do anything for me. It's useless talking about my feelings, I don't need that."

I responded, "So you feel you can do it all for yourself and that you don't need help from me or anyone else. You don't want to know that others care for you and you care about them. You try so hard not to allow people to be important to you."

"You get paid anyway; this is just a job for you."

I asked, "How do you know I get paid?"

Pedro replied, "There's a boss' name on my card [the business card I gave him], so you're paid by someone. And, if you're doing it for free, you're dumb, retarded, and stupid. You think you can help, but you can't."

"I think you would rather think of me as doing this just because it's a job or because I am dumb and stupid, instead of someone who cares about you."

"Even if you do care for me, there's not much you can do for me anyway," Pedro said. "What, help me get the stuff inside of me out?"

Thus we have a glimpse of Pedro's attempt to reduce or deny my significance to monetary or self-serving motivations only. In addition, there is a part of me that wanted him to know that I do *not* get paid for my work with foster children. Let us consider Pedro's point for a moment at face value, putting aside seeing it as a defense against closeness. Was there some part of Pedro that wanted to be reassured that, in fact, I was receiving monetary compensation for my efforts (like meeting with him in the group home). Maybe he was not that far off base when he accused me of being "dumb, stupid, and retarded" for doing this for free. Is there something masochistic in providing pro bono psychotherapy to which Pedro was responding in his devaluation of me?

He asked a very good question, albeit in a critical and disparaging manner. Why was I seeing him in therapy for free? What were my motivations? If I was not getting paid, what would I be seeking as compensation if not money? Perhaps it made him a bit uneasy, a bit uncomfortable, knowing that I was doing this for no money. What kind of relational currency did I expect of him in the absence of money? Did he want to believe that, indeed, I was getting paid in order for him not to feel so guilty about how he used, took, or received from me? Also, how much could he dish out knowing that I was doing this on a pro bono basis? Without money as a form of compensation or even a safe buffer, to what extent was Pedro's aggression inhibited or, conversely, fueled?

Although I briefly explained to Pedro at the start of treatment that the project and the therapists work on a pro bono basis, this of course was packed with meanings for him that shifted and changed over time. If all good partnerships are in part exploitative, and I would argue that this is especially true of analytic relationships, what did it mean for Pedro that we do not accept monetary compensation for our work? Did my feelings, or *care*, become that much more dangerous and threatening to Pedro in the absence of money?

Pedro's protests about the point of therapy, such as the one illustrated in the dialogue, led to a discharge planning meeting among the group home staff to determine whether Pedro should return to his mother on a trial discharge basis or move to a more permanent residential placement. On my way to the meeting, I decided to buy a box of doughnuts to share. When I arrived at the group home, I was informed that there had been a miscommunication and that the meeting was already in progress. Feeling excluded, I sidled into the meeting late. Following a short series of presentations, including one by me, the director of the group home asked Pedro's case manager, who had been leading the meeting, for his opinion. The case manager, George, was a young, Latino man who had worked with Pedro when he entered the foster care system 5 years previously. George spoke on behalf of Maria's and Pedro's wishes to have at least one more opportunity to make this work between them, before going ahead with what is referred to as an *independent living plan*. When my opinion was solicited, I agreed with the case manager, yet at the same time I could see how both George and I had come to see ourselves, in part, as rescuers of this family. In retrospect, it seems that we were enacting a romanticized role of the father figure reunifying this mother and child. We held onto the image of the "good" mother, as Pedro did, while others in the group could see the "bad" one or the problematic relationship that did not bode well for the future. We both felt hard pressed to find reasons that would warrant depriving Pedro and his mother of one last chance, as she had done everything asked of her. Yet, Pedro had clearly undergone a dramatic change during his stay in the group home. He had demonstrated remarkable change in this highly structured home with clear rules, boundaries, and a sense that there were caregivers in charge—something his mother had trouble providing.

After arriving at the decision to move toward a trial discharge period between Pedro and Maria, both were brought into the room to be informed of the decision as well as of the guidelines for Pedro's return. Pedro at first smiled along with his mother but then suddenly grew quiet, sitting in silence for several minutes. A few moments later, tears started to stream down Pedro's face; it was the first time I had ever seen him cry. The room was filled with sadness, and I could feel in myself the weight of everything that he had been through over the course of his short life; it became just too much to hold it all together. His mother had trouble tolerating Pedro's tears. As I had witnessed many times before, Maria tried to coax Pedro out of crying—his feelings were too much for Maria to bear because they recharged her own overwhelming feelings. Pedro alluded to the tremendous pressure he felt in moving back with his mother on a trial basis, as he could blow it with one misstep. Yet, part of him clearly knew that he might be better off not living with Maria—but admitting to that thought was too painful.

With all of the meeting's decisions and emotions, I realized that I had forgotten about the doughnuts. It was not until Pedro and I spoke alone together briefly after the meeting that we finally indulged ourselves. Pedro chose his favorite kind of doughnut, only to find a hair on it. When Pedro requested a replacement doughnut, I felt the need to only allow him one doughnut. My initial impulse was again to withhold the doughnuts in the face of his hunger, suggesting that I was somehow afraid of the depth of his hunger or that he would want more than I could supply. Not only had I deprived everyone in the group of food but also the food I offered Pedro was spoiled.

Similar to other occasions during the course of our treatment sessions, it seemed as though what I had to offer, or feed, Pedro—whether therapy for "as long as it takes" or the kind of power he had mentioned wanting during his group home stay—did not always taste so good or was even rotten. In a way, although we had formed a relationship that differed from others in his life, I could still not avoid failing him, not giving him what he really needed; what I had to give was not enough. In addition, Pedro had tremendous difficulty in accepting what I had to offer, as if accepting what I had to give would then mean coming into contact with absence, intense yearning, and desire. For him to deny or detach himself from these feelings required sabotaging his relationships with those he cared about. As a result, he did not allow anything in or, as Pedro put it, kept the inside stuff inside.

As Pedro prepared to leave the group home and return to his mother around Christmastime, he reported during our sessions that he would not miss anyone and disavowed any sort of connection with the people he was leaving. In fact, what did emerge was greedy, hoarding behavior. He took the Christmas gifts given to him by the staff with a sense that they were owed to him. The gifts became a tangible symbol of the attachments he had formed, which he could take with him. Pedro clearly felt bereft, but he was determined not to show any signs of attachment to someone or something—thereby engendering feelings of being used or rejected in those who had grown fond of him. He barely said good-bye to the other foster children and the staff when he left the group home, sneaking out the door unnoticed and into his mother's car. The second trial discharge had now begun.

RETURNING HOME: A SETUP FOR FAILURE?

The foster care agency requires a trial of just 3 months to determine whether child and mother (or primary caregiver) are able to live with each other on a permanent basis. In some cases, this time frame is extended. A time frame of 3 months to reattach, especially for an adolescent who is in the throes of developmentally appropriate attempts at separation and individuation, is not only unrealistic but also a setup for failure for all parties involved. For the first 2 months or so, Pedro and his mother managed to live together without much trouble, although they spent much of their time in separate rooms of their apartment—not so far from what one might expect with most parents and their teenagers.

During this time, sessions with Pedro, or with Pedro and his mother, revealed feelings he had about leaving the group home; he even shared a story of having returned for a visit. As time went on, Pedro began spending more time away from home, coming home late or not at all, and not attending school. Maria was unable to embrace her parental authority, partially out of guilt for her past neglect. This behavior left Pedro with a sense of having too much power and led him to interpret his mother's lack of action as failing the test, one designed to gauge her commitment to him. As Maria lost faith in her own ability to parent Pedro, he further sabotaged the relationship. He also seemed to be losing whatever reflective capacity he had developed while at the group home; "I don't know" reappeared as the default response to my questions. It occurred to me that Pedro did not want to know or believed there was too much to know—that to survive, he needed to drain his emotions of their knowledge.

The representations of self that Pedro had developed at the group home eventually eroded. For Pedro and other adolescents in foster care, it can feel like a lose-lose situation. He was placed in the situation of having to reconnect with his mother after being separated from her for 6 years, returning to her during a time when most children his age are symbolically leaving home. For Pedro, there was not enough of a foundation from which to spring. If separation is contingent on the parent's recognition of the child's autonomous strivings, separation in Pedro's case was equivalent to being dropped.

As the situation worsened, Pedro began missing his sessions, requiring me to chase after him a bit. Although he enjoyed being found, this effort on my part did not work to reel him back into treatment. In the few sessions we did have together during this time, he associated me with the system—the system that had been a surrogate parent in his life but was responsible for meddling in the relationship with his mother. Whatever fury Pedro held toward his mother was displaced onto the larger system; seeing that as the cause of his problems helped Pedro preserve the tenuous tie to his mother. When waiting for Pedro to arrive for appointments, I was brought into contact with feelings of despair and exasperation—feelings I imagine Pedro had lived with for most of his life. To address these moments, I relied on my weekly consultation group to sustain my own hope and sense of being alive.

With Pedro's behavior communicating his ambivalence toward living with his mother and the knowledge that living in a residential placement might have been something he needed, Maria for the first time was also admitting her own limitations in being unable to parent him. Following a joint decision by the professionals involved to extend his foster care placement and place him in a residential facility, Pedro was struck with another blow. I received a call from his long-time case manager, George, who informed me that he was choosing to take Pedro off his caseload. I was shocked, as this was happening just before preparations were being made for Pedro to be placed in a residential facility. George explained that he had to do this for his own well-being and that he felt unable to continue working with Pedro. Although George was well aware of Pedro's fondness for him, he had become unable to see past Pedro's recent devaluing treatment of him. During George's home visits, Pedro refused to speak with him and on one occasion told him, "F— off." As George explained all of this to me, I could hear George's feeling of being used by and fed up with Pedro. Despite my efforts to help George see his importance to Pedro and to offer other ways of interpreting Pedro's hostility, George had become yet another casualty. That afternoon, George visited Pedro, told him he would not be working with him anymore, and then introduced Pedro to his new case manager. In retrospect, it seemed that George had bought into Pedro's devaluing of him, resulting in George's attempting to turn their significant, personal relationship into a more anonymous one.

What I had witnessed in George mirrored a frequent outcome for the workers in this system. The pain and anguish of experiencing a child's despair, hopelessness, contempt, and rage becomes too much to feel, so one detaches, or dissociates, oneself to survive—that is, to function within the system. The system has its own norms and culture that one adapts to in order to contend with the surrounding deprivation and impoverishment. This translates into turning the child into a case or adopting a language that takes the humanity out of the individual or group of people. For instance, words such as *worker, agency, intervention,* or *supervisor* form a language of anonymity that distances one from psychological pain and bolster one's own, and the system's, defense network.

Another example of this kind of defense is demonstrated by Pedro's story. Pedro was several weeks away from being placed in a residential facility when a court hearing took place. A new judge on the case decided that the problems between Pedro and Maria could no longer be attributed to Maria. The judge ruled that because Pedro was 15 years old, he—not his mother—was responsible for his behavior. Therefore, the judge ruled that Pedro should not be sent to a placement but instead issued a final discharge returning Pedro to his mother on a permanent basis. All of the reports that had been submitted by the various professionals advocating for placement were briefly scanned prior to this ruling and, despite Maria's plea, in which she stated that she could not sufficiently care for her son, the judge ruled that Pedro should be removed from the foster care system and placed back with his mother. Afterward, one of the attorneys informed me that the judge was known for finding reasons to keep children out of foster care, often making decisions without much direct input. This was an emerging trend within the foster care agency.

This ruling shocked and angered me. It seemed that all of the work done by those close to Pedro had been ignored. The place of the foster care system in this family's life, namely the foster care agency that had worked with this family for more than 8 years, promptly exited the picture, leaving Pedro and his mother to fend for themselves with very little support. The system that had twice taken Pedro away from his mother in order to protect him was now sending him back without any regard for this family's institutional relationships and without proper support and preparation to manage the obstacles facing them in their attempt at reunification. In trying to find out more about this situation, I found myself feeling furious at times, anxious about the fate of Pedro and his mother and dismissed by those I had been working closely with during the previous 4 years. The agency and its workers stopped returning my calls; I was told that the case was no longer in their hands. The foster care agency informed me that the case would be closed with them as well. This judge's decision, which was made in a matter of minutes, sealed the door shut between Pedro and the foster care system in its role as surrogate parent.

The relationship between Pedro and the people within the system had been severed, ripping away all that he had known for his latency and pre-adolescent life. The foster care system as the surrogate parent was now abandoning Pedro, a reenactment of earlier abandonments in Pedro's short life. It seemed that Pedro's needs came into conflict with the mechanics of the foster care system, as though his situation was made to fit into one of the prefabricated categories. The decision by the judge appeared to be made according to these categorical rules—rules in place to address the overwhelming number of children in the system.

During the next few months, as the various people and agencies divested themselves of their involvement with Pedro and his mother, the situation became progressively worse. Maria refused to apply for intensive in-home services, and Pedro continued to be truant from school and to stay out all night. After being unable to reach Maria for more than a week, I called their home once again and spoke to Pedro. Receiving either a grunt, a groan, or an "I don't know" in response to my questions about himself and his mother's whereabouts, I became increasingly concerned. My hunch was that he knew where she was but was hiding it from me for fear of her being found out and him possibly taken away once again. The "I don't know" response that I repeatedly heard seemed to be a communication about Pedro's not being able to know, not wanting to know himself, or perhaps even not being able to think about what was happening in his life.

I called Pedro a couple of days later and, to my surprise, his tone of voice sounded more alive and engaged. I again asked him about his mother, and he told me that she was in the Dominican Republic. He had just found this out from a relative, after being left alone for 2 weeks and not knowing where she had gone or what had happened to her. Pedro said Maria had gone to collect his older brother and would not be returning for another week. I was stunned. Yet, I felt an uncanny, dissociated experience in our conversation. On the one hand, Pedro sounded relieved, possibly because he knew where Maria was. On the other hand, he seemed unfazed by what he discovered. I could feel my own sense of relief, yet what was dissociated from both of us was the shock, rage, and sadness in Maria's abandonment of Pedro, leaving him alone in order to collect her other, favored son.

Pedro refused to come to see me, and I felt obligated to report to child protective services (CPS) what had happened. After much discussion with my consultation group, I was reminded of how Pedro had come into the foster care system the second time. At that point, his mother had been neglecting him and Manny, who had become a father figure to Pedro, called the police. This resulted in Pedro's 5-year separation from Maria. Was this type of situation happening once again? I felt conflicted. On the one hand, it seemed that I was betraying Pedro and Maria by reporting them; on the other hand, I felt the need to protect Pedro, seeing his telling me the details of the story as a plea for help.

Upon returning, Maria explained that there was a complete misunderstanding and, in fact, she had arranged for Pedro to stay with relatives. When I asked why she had not told me she was leaving, she claimed that she had mentioned it several months before. It is interesting to note that, for the moment, Maria did not seem disturbed or bothered by what had occurred and, similarly, seemed to feel relieved by my having called CPS, as it had resulted in the provision of an intensive case manager—much-needed support. Rather than remove Pedro from his mother, the foster care agency had decided to provide the family with preventive services to aid Maria in parenting.

What did occur here between Pedro, his mother, and me? Was this the inevitability of enactment—enacting the role of the bad object that we as therapists cannot avoid? Was this a repetition of what had happened previously—Manny's call to the foster care agency many years ago? Was my calling the agency a compensatory rescue operation, using or maybe even exploiting the opportunity of Pedro being "abandoned" by his mother to assert my goodness and make her the bad, neglectful one? What about Pedro's and Maria's roles in all of this? Why didn't Maria tell me that she was leaving for the Dominican Republic? Was Maria setting me up to be the one who enlists the agency, perhaps something she unconsciously or consciously wanted but was unable to do so because of feeling inadequate as a mother? Why didn't Pedro tell me that he had been left in the care of his relatives? What were his motivations for suggesting that he had been left alone by his mother? Then, there is my own guilt and resentment, which I felt later when finding out that Maria left Pedro with her relatives.

Although Pedro had been refusing to come to therapy even before my report to the agency, this became further reason for him to refuse therapy with me or anyone else. It seemed that for the time being, I was associated with the "bad foster care system" that was trying to take him away from his mother. He needed to make me the bad one as a means of negotiating his own ambivalent feelings toward his mother and me as well. To protect and even preserve the idealized mother in his mind required distancing himself from me.

As sometimes is the case in the treatment of children in foster care, Pedro's therapy has led to an ambiguous ending, an unresolved one leaving in its trail more questions than answers. I have not seen him for approximately 2 years at the time of writing this, and my meetings with his mother stopped upon referring her to a bilingual therapist from within CPP.

CONCLUSION

This chapter shows the course that my thinking took in my work with Pedro. Looking back, I see the tension that exists between social responsibility and family autonomy. Whereas earlier on I was invested in reuniting Pedro and his family, sharing in Pedro's wish for some sort of magical union and trying to restore his mother's parental authority without the intrusion of others, I moved closer to seeing the social network's need to take on more responsibility for this family. In becoming more familiar with the complications inherent to the treatment of children in foster care, I began to construct an image of concentric circles that is like the arrangement of the planets in the solar system. These interlocking dynamic systems exist within the same sphere, beginning with the analytic dyad of the child and therapist and moving out, through the foster care network, through the culture, and to the edges of society.

Amid all of this, what does psychoanalysis have to offer to a child such as Pedro? First and foremost, there is the relationship. No longer is insight and interpretation the key to therapeutic success; the current consensus is that the actual relationship between therapist and child is what results in change. Although it required a leap of faith at times in the face of Pedro's retreats, perhaps Pedro's relationship with me is the only one that has survived through time. I have the luxury of not being forced to go away; I wait and, in the meantime, remind him of my presence. In the words of Alvarez (1992), I consider myself "live company" with Pedro, restoring flickers of light, or inner vitality, which I hope will make a difference in bolstering his own resiliency and psychic survival.

Second, for someone like Pedro, the mind's capacity to make meaning and the sense of oneself as an agent, or intentional being, has been severely compromised. An analytically oriented therapist working with a child who has suffered profound disruptions has the challenge of holding onto an image of the child while experiencing his or her own feelings through the cancelled sessions, innumerable losses, chronic instability, constant change, and prolonged breaks that occur during the course of treatment. It is this kind of experience that enables the child to discover him- or herself in the mind of the other, a kind of psychological birth.

Through Pedro's many disappearances and my contact with the foster care agency, it is astounding to see how the child who reenters the foster care system is an unknown entity or a blank slate. All continuity, all history, is ruptured. There are some facts, but the people previously involved are sometimes long gone. It can feel like the child's history has been erased or forgotten—an all too common reaction to trauma. In this kind of situation, the therapist has the essential task of collecting "pieces" of the child and his or her history; the therapist stores these inside and transports them.

The therapist is in some ways an embodiment of the child's living history, someone who can connect all of the splintered pieces and offer a coherent narrative about a life—one that, in an ideal world, is transmitted to the child over time.

REFERENCE

Alvarez, A. (1992). *Live company.* New York: Tavistock/Routledge.

CHAPTER 8

Sunset in December

Working with Young
Adults in Foster Care

Isabelle Reiniger

oates pointed out, "Case reports are enormously important for studying the intricacies of meaning-making in the individual child" (1998, p. 117). This chapter is written in the hope that the following case report of work with a late adolescent helps those working with adolescents in foster care. The adolescent's history, the treatment history, and a treatment update are followed by a discussion of multiple issues that arose in thinking about this case.

RHANA'S BACKGROUND

From the start, working with Rhana had a different feel to it. Maybe it was because she had been born in the Middle East and spent the first 10 years of her life there before coming to the United States. However, disruptions in her attachment experience, similar to those of most children in foster care, are evident from the start of her story. Her parents separated early in her life, and shortly after, her father emigrated to the United States. Her mother worked as an entertainer and had irregular contact with Rhana, who was raised by her paternal grandmother until she was 5 years old. Rhana's memories of her grandmother were fond, and she felt that her grandmother truly cared for her. After Rhana's grandmother died when Rhana was 5, her paternal aunt took over the care of Rhana and her 4-year-old brother. In contrast to the grandmother, Rhana's aunt was erratic in her care, at times hostile and abusive and at other times adoring and supportive. It is doubtful that Rhana and her brother were allowed to fully mourn the loss of their primary caregiver.

Although Rhana had erratic contact with her mother, her older half-sister lived with their mother. Thus, Rhana was faced with feelings of envy and rejection. In addition, Rhana was not adequately protected while visiting her mother. Rhana reported several incidences of having been molested by her mother's boyfriend when she was 7 and 8 years old. One incident was brought to court, but rather than provide Rhana with justice and relief, this seems to have added feelings of shame. Her aunt went as far as accusing Rhana of seducing Rhana's uncle, which indicates some belief that Rhana brought the molestation on herself.

At age 9, Rhana and her brother were brought to the United States by their father, who had been working here as a truck driver. No provisions had been made for Rhana and her brother to have any contact with their mother. The three of them lived in a one-room apartment, and Rhana's father apparently worked hard to take care of his children. When the children were at the playground, he would drop by with his truck as much as possible. Rhana describes herself as being very shy around her father.

Once Rhana entered puberty, conflicts around her budding sexuality as well as her assimilation into American youth culture began to arise. She was friends with an ethnically mixed group of children at school and had some of them over on one occasion. By the time her father arrived home, one of the boys (in whom Rhana was not romantically interested) was still in their apartment. Rhana's father kicked him out and beat Rhana. The tension between father and daughter escalated when her father found out that Rhana, at age 16, had a boyfriend. Although Rhana says that she was not sexually intimate with Ray, the discovery of the relationship was followed by another incidence of physical and verbal abuse, after which Rhana ran away from home. She briefly stayed with a friend, then entered the child welfare system. Parallel to Rhana's running away, Ray and his mother moved to another state. Once she was in the foster care system Rhana started seeing Juan, whose brother was exposing him to and possibly involving him in dealing drugs. Eventually, Juan began physically and verbally abusing Rhana. Her performance in school began plummeting. Her initial placement in a group home was changed after approximately a year, when racial tensions in the home made it impossible for her to continue living there. She moved to a second home. The goal of placement was to prepare Rhana for independent living, even though reconciliation with her father was also considered and attempted.

TREATMENT WITH RHANA

It was at this point that I started seeing Rhana, when she was 17 years old. She reported depressive symptoms (e.g., sadness, overeating, nightmares) and was in an abusive relationship. I saw Rhana once a week for psychoanalytically oriented psychotherapy. I want to share material from my first session with Rhana to give a sense of how we got started in our work. She was brought to my office by her case worker, Ms. Adam, who joined us for the first part of the session. Ms. Adam said that Rhana had not wanted to come that day. She also told me that the group home would need to know whether Rhana was attending therapy.

Once Ms. Adam left the room, I turned to Rhana and said, "It sounds like you weren't too excited about coming here today."

Rhana replied, "No, why should I be? I don't know what good it will be to come to you. I'll tell you everything, and then what is that good for?" When I encouraged her to tell me more about her fantasy around this, Rhana shared, "Well, you get paid to listen to me and then you go home to your own life."

Rather than delve into a discussion of the structure of the Children's Psychotherapy Project (CPP), which might have seemed defensive on my part at this time, I wanted to explore her fantasy more. So instead I asked, "Do you think it would be hard for me to really care about you because I get paid?"

"Yeah, why should you? Anyway, what good is it for me to tell you everything? I have told people stuff and it didn't change anything. How does therapy help anyway?"

I started explaining therapy, but I felt myself getting lost in intellectual explanations that I was having a hard time following myself. Therefore, I stopped and said, "Maybe what is more important than how therapy helps is that you need to make sure that you can trust the person you talk to."

Rhana explained, "I don't have a problem trusting people. I can tell them everything—it just doesn't seem to change anything."

"I guess what I was trying to say was that sometimes we need to test whether we feel comfortable with somebody."

"Anyway, maybe this isn't so important."

"I think the questions you have brought up are very important, and I am glad you brought up your concerns."

"I don't know, I have just been through so many changes over the past 2 years, and there have been so many different people."

Rhana then talked about Juan, who also went through several group homes. From here she began sharing her history. Although her initial comments about therapy conveyed a sense of futility, she seemed eager to spill everything. In fact, she seemed to be signaling poor boundaries and an inability to protect herself in a situation that she had just described as untrustworthy.

I was struck by the intensity of our early sessions. It felt as if we had been working together for much longer than a couple of weeks. Rhana was sharing very intimate details of her life. The initial phase of our work was dominated by themes of loss, starting with one of the group home's case workers suddenly dying and Juan's cousin being murdered. Also of importance was the onset of the loss of her relationship with Juan due to his physical and verbal abuse. The theme of loss continued with her case worker, Ms. Adam, who left the job abruptly $3\frac{1}{2}$ months after Rhana and I started working together. Ms. Adam had been somewhat of a mother figure to Rhana, and losing her was very difficult. Rhana was given a temporary case worker. Only after 2 months did she have a new permanent case worker, Ms. Bozell, but Rhana clearly had lost some trust in the permanence of a relationship with her case worker. I certainly had gotten the sense that Rhana had little stability in her life, as well as an indication that she was experiencing the kind of disruption within the foster care system that Kenrick (2000) mentioned.

Approximately 3 months into treatment, Rhana commented on our work for the first time. From her point of view, it was weird that we never had an introductory or "getting to know each other" phase. We had briefly introduced each other by name and then I had asked for her history. She shared that she had met with her legal guardian the day of that session and 3 months into treatment had talked about her relationship with me. The lawyer apparently had said maybe it was better that we did not have much of an introductory phase. Rhana concluded that she experienced me as neutral, and she seemed to appreciate that neutrality.

During this early phase, Rhana also turned 18. Turning 18 represented loss of her childhood in the sense that she now was responsible for herself. If she decided to leave the group home and the child welfare system, nobody would hold her back. Although her caseworker was still pursuing reconciliation between Rhana and her father, Rhana's birthday was a milestone toward independent living and never returning to his home. This milestone seemed to intensify her feelings around losing her family. In addition she could not graduate from high school because she was missing credits and had not passed a standardized test. This meant that she was not going to move on with her classmates and would not be able to start college in September. I think this was very depressing to Rhana because it symbolized failure. Her father had predicted that she would never amount to anything because she had gone off the proper path. Was he right? Would this become a self-fulfilling prophecy? Also, was this something that I, as Rhana's therapist, might have to face later during Rhana's treatment as transference or as a prognosis for treatment outcome (e.g., Rhana repeating the dynamic in failing me)?

This treatment phase ended with my going on two vacations during the summer. Hence I was proving to be "unreliable," and my absence meant that Rhana had to deal with another loss. During a session in between my two breaks, Rhana for the second time reflected on our work and its usefulness to her. She said that it was unfortunate that I did not see her that often and did not know the people in her life. Yet, she liked that I was less involved with the day-to-day details of her life and did not get angry easily. She also said that it was helpful to talk to me, even though I was not like a doctor who dispensed pills to remove pain.

However, following my second vacation, Rhana frequently missed appointments, including an absence of several weeks in a row. She blamed it on being in summer school. I suggested that we start meeting twice a week because perhaps doubling our sessions would help Rhana develop a more trusting relationship with me. I had the feeling that making this change would help her attend sessions more consistently.

Rhana and I began meeting twice a week in September, and we continued doing so for 3 months. During this time we finally seemed to be able to develop a working relationship. Early during this phase, Rhana revealed the molestation she had experienced. She also shared intense feelings of loss with me after she heard that a Middle Eastern family with which she had become friendly would be moving to another state. Ms. Abahd had become a mother figure in Rhana's life. Losing her was devastating; Rhana sobbed and was very angry with Mr. Abahd for initiating the move. During this session, we were able to make the link to losing her own mother.

Rhana said, "It seems that everybody in my life seems to end up leaving." I replied that it might feel like she is not important enough to others for them to stay. She continued sobbing through the end of the session despite my attempts to get her out of this state by raising practical issues—for example, by asking questions about her plans for the rest of the day. I had to let her go still sobbing. In the evening I chose to call the group home to make sure she had returned home safely. She sounded more composed and thanked me for my concern. I wondered whether I had overstepped a boundary; however, I also believed that without calling her, there was a risk of Rhana's missing the next few sessions.

During this period, Rhana continued going to school part time and working toward her exams. She got a job in a coffee bar. She worked very hard to end her relationship with Juan and began reestablishing her relationship with her first boyfriend, Ray, through numerous phone calls. He was with the military and stationed abroad. The theme of relationships was very important during this period. Rhana raised the question of what kind of man she should date. Should he share her nationality? Should he be a Muslim? Her first two boyfriends had been Latino. The Abahds, especially Ms. Abahd, had helped support Rhana during this period. Yet the family was part of a larger community that held traditional views on how a young woman should live. Wedding a Muslim was a must.

During this phase, Rhana seemed to be using her therapy sessions very well. She was thoughtful and insightful. On one occasion, we discussed her treatment goals together, and she immediately dictated them for the quarterly progress form in a lucid and articulate manner: "Reduction of depressive symptoms" and "Realize the abusive nature of her relationship and begin to realize that behavior is repetition of childhood history."

One time she called to say she could not make it to our session and expressed concern that I would not get paid. I suggested we talk about her concern the following session. However, the next time we met Rhana had many things to share and did not return to her worry about my compensation. I wondered whether I should have been frank with her, as Levy-Warren (1996) suggested when working with adolescents, and started the session off by discussing the pro bono structure of CPP and explaining the nature of the consultation groups. We could have then used the remaining time to explore her thoughts and feelings around the meaning of my compensation to Rhana and the value of our work. Her concern for me clearly seemed to be in line with her general tendency to assume the role of a care-giver for others.

Rhana introduced the term *mold* (as in a cast) into our work, and it became a recurring theme. To her, *mold* meant that one's destiny is determined by one's childhood. In addition, she raised the question as to whether she had changed since we had started working together. I asked, "Do you think you have changed?" and she answered, "I don't know." I said that I believed she had changed. In hindsight, I think that I wanted to infuse some hope. I said that she appeared to trust the therapeutic process more and to be less impulsive, weighing things more carefully.

"Sometimes you seem to feel that the process with me is not helpful, and then we miss a couple of sessions," I said.

Rhana replied, "It is not that I don't want to come in. It is that my feelings are too strong." She continued to ask whether she had changed while further discussing her fear of molds.

This time I did not reply with an affirmative answer but said, "It sounds like you are asking whether there is hope that your life can be lived without having to follow the mold—whether there is a chance of change."

She replied, "Yes, that is how I feel."

Rhana went on to talk about how proving herself academically was part of her mold. She was referring to her father's expectations.

I responded, "But it isn't just your father's voice in you telling you what to do. You also have this baggage of pain and suffering; this suitcase that is so heavy that you aren't able to move forward."

Again Rhana replied, "That is exactly how I feel." Then, she became tearful and said, "You are the only person who understands me completely."

She grabbed some tissues and then apologized. When I asked what made her apologize, she said that I had seen how much it meant to her that I understand. I asked if it made her feel vulnerable. After her affirmative reply, I asked what she thought I might do with this information, and Rhana said that I might hurt her. She then talked about her fear of becoming attached and her fear of my leaving.

The new year seemed to usher in a new phase for us, during which our treatment relationship seemed rockier than it had been during the previous 3 months. At the same time, the material we discussed continued to have more depth. We cut back to meeting once a week. Rhana initiated this change on the basis of her schedule. Perhaps there was another factor: The

New Year break was the first 2-week gap in treatment since we had started meeting twice a week in September.

During this phase, Rhana found out that her father had a girlfriend and her brother was drifting into using drugs. She got attacked by a girl in the group home, opened a bank account, and started talking about the possibility of getting herself a subsidized apartment. She also discussed applying to colleges, then finding out that she was missing yet another high school credit in order to graduate. Finally, it appeared that her seemingly near-perfect image of me was cracking a little. We had a couple of sessions in which Rhana brought up some friends from high school and was sure that she had mentioned them to me before. She had in fact talked about them about 6 months earlier but never by name. She seemed startled when I could not place them immediately. She had been so accustomed to my seeming to remember every detail.

At one session that took place a year into treatment, Rhana shared that she had been through a psychiatric and psychological evaluation that day. Both were reportedly needed for the records at the group home. She enjoyed mapping out stories in response to the pictures of the Thematic Apperception Test (TAT; Murray, 1943). However, when she was asked how the stories ended, she said that she did not feel like supplying endings. Rhana then said that her own story had no ending. Her inability to end the stories seemed to symbolize that endings were too painful to consider. Anna Freud (1958) compared adolescence to a state of mourning. The adolescent gradually lets go of his or her family as he or she loses some parental idealization and turns more intensely to peers and a life outside of the family. In cases of foster care, it can be complicated to sort out which experience and resulting behavior originates from normal adolescent development and which results from loss and trauma (Garber, 2000). With Rhana, who lost her grandmother at age 5 and lost contact with her mother at age 9, we can speculate that the mere thought of loss and separation—and even the concept of finality itself—was too painful to consciously feel.

During the following months, we often discussed Rhana's anticipation of an impending several-week visit by Ray. She began searching for an identity to present to him. This was revealed by questions regarding what she was going to wear for his arrival at the airport. The relationship seemed positive overall, and I could not detect any abusive elements. If there was any difficulty in this relationship, it was caused by Ray's mother, with whom Rhana was spending quite a bit of time. His mother had a history of substance abuse and had reportedly been in several abusive relationships. Her relationship with Rhana was erratic: Sometimes she would treat Rhana like a daughter; at other times, she sounded somewhat paranoid and expressed concern that Rhana might seduce her own boyfriend. Despite Rhana's tendency to experience older women in her life as mother figures, she never seemed to develop that kind of relationship with Ray's mother, who may have resembled Rhana's aunt too closely.

In one of the last sessions during this phase, Rhana had shared the pain of not having any supportive family members and the fear of not being able to master her future. By the end of this particular session, I had a strong feeling of wanting to protect her. The following week, she explained that she literally could not see me. She had been to the eye doctor, who had given her drops that made her vision blurry. Nevertheless, she seemed to be in one of her bubbly, cheerful moods. She had occasionally described these moods to me and mentioned that they prompted the staff at her group home to call her "hyper." I had only recently begun to see this emotional state in her myself. Rhana shared that her ophthalmologist had partly attributed her eye problems to the fact that her eyes were small. We both laughed, and I found myself thinking how funny, witty, and flirtatious Rhana was and how nice it was that we were able to share humorous moments.

The remainder of the session followed one of Rhana's frequent patterns: using the session to update me on numerous issues in her life. We ended up talking about her anticipating Ray's arrival. Rhana wanted me to meet him. As the session ended, she practiced introducing us by saying, "Here is my therapist"; then she added in a more serious tone, "You're really more than a therapist to me."

During that particular session, I felt very loving toward Rhana. Yet, only shortly after this session, which was approximately 14 months into our work, the treatment began falling apart. She increasingly missed sessions, and 6 months after this session, the treatment ended. I wonder at times whether my investment in Rhana was becoming too big. Did I care about her so much that I was beginning to miss Rhana's cues? Had she sensed how much I cared about her and felt overwhelmed or uncertain about it?

The last phase of our work together started when I moved to a new office, causing a break in our consistency. We seemed to have difficulties adjusting to the new space, which was not a problem I had with other clients.

After only two sessions in the new office, Ray arrived. Although Rhana had planned on coming to see me during his visit, she missed both of the concurrent sessions. Rhana and Ray got engaged while he was visiting. She shared that their plan was to get married in 6 months. Subsequently, they were going to move to Florida, where Ray was going to be stationed next. This plan had me worried because it would mean that Rhana would give up her entire support system and rely solely on Ray. I also felt sad at the thought of our work together ending.

Mother's Day had fallen right after Ray's visit. Rhana said, "I hate Mother's Day." She mentioned that she had called Ms. Abahd and Ray's grandmother, with whom she had developed a good relationship, to wish them well. Later in the session, she became tearful when she talked about how hard it would be to leave me. Again she said, "You are more to me than a therapist," but then admitted that she believed she was not supposed to feel that way. On my way home that night, I thought of her words and was touched by how much I meant to her.

In retrospect, I wonder again about the intensity of both of our feelings. I wonder whether I developed too strong a need for recognition from her, which created blind spots; these intense feelings of caring surfaced alongside inklings that the treatment was becoming disrupted. Were we at an impasse that I was unable to recognize (Shane & Shane, 1995)? Anybody working with foster care children is at risk for a strong urge to take in a child. Of course, there are much subtler ways to act on such feelings. The consultation group was a good place for me to talk about my own emotions in relation to Rhana. On the one hand, perhaps the feelings of caring should have been addressed more in the work with Rhana. On the other hand, the fact that Rhana felt cared about may have encouraged her independence.

Certainly, the theme of loss was becoming stronger again. Not only was Rhana planning on leaving after marrying Ray, but I was going to be gone for 4 weeks in the summer. My absence would immediately follow Rhana's birthday, which again proved to be a difficult time for her. Once I came back, we did not have a session for an extended period because of Rhana's school schedule. Soon after, she started a new full-time job that made it hard for us to schedule sessions, and she frequently did not show up for our appointments.

During the late summer, Rhana made a statement that indicated ambivalence about her choice of marrying Ray. She mentioned that he had compared her with his mother. She did not like him saying that.

Rhana told me, "If he says that one more time, I am not going to marry him." Asked if she had told him this, Rhana replied, "No, it wasn't the right time, and I didn't want to do it over the phone. Also, it is not that important."

Using humor in my tone I said, "If you are thinking about breaking up because he is saying it, it seems important enough."

Rhana laughed in reply, but it was clear that talking about this topic with him would be very hard. In retrospect, I wonder if she was beginning to look for reasons to break up with Ray. Until that point, I had never heard anything bad about Ray—Rhana had idealized him. I wonder whether the planned marriage and the resulting complete dependence on Ray were starting to scare and overwhelm Rhana.

In the early autumn, Rhana commented on a previous missed session: "I'm gonna be honest with you—I didn't want to come. I was feeling happy, but then I was also sad, but I was happy, and I didn't want it to be disturbed by talking when I come here." She quickly moved away from this topic by updating me on various topics, but I said, "I don't want to move away so quickly from you not coming last week—what happened?" Again, she talked about her good mood and her bad mood. She also talked about feeling shame about admitting to others that she was in therapy. Finally, she talked about her fear of being dependent on me. She mentioned that she had cried earlier in the day about her mother not being around, but then she drifted back to talking about her brother, her father, and her father's girlfriend. Toward the end of the session, we were able to return to Rhana's fear of being dependent on me. She also addressed her discomfort with being dependent on the child welfare system.

Rhana missed the next two sessions. Waiting for her to attend the third session, I became furious. It was my last session of the day, and I was very tired. I had recently asked Rhana to let me know when she could not make an appointment. Nonetheless, she had not called, and I had no patience left. I called her 5 minutes into the session.

Rhana said, "I really don't want to come."

I said, "I really think you should come and talk about why you don't want to come."

Rhana lived 5 minutes from my office, but by the time she arrived at the office, only 20 minutes of the session remained. I felt angry and wanted to share some of that anger, but I also tried to restrain myself. Rhana commented that my anger made me seem human. She talked about simply not wanting to come and that she felt this way with everybody at the moment. She had not talked to friends or Ms. Abahd. At some point, I raised the issue of her leaving for Florida soon. She said she was not leaving. She had told Ray that she was not ready to marry him yet. I compared how I was feeling to how she was feeling: angry, frustrated, rejected, abandoned. Maybe this was the only way she knew how to share these feelings with me. She sat there swallowing hard several times. When I gently asked, "What are you swallowing right now?" Rhana started to cry. She talked about her feelings a little bit but still seemed to be holding back. Eventually she asked if she could go—we had about 3 minutes left. I let her go but felt very bad about this session. Rhana did not come to the following session, and I wondered whether she was mad at me. In discussing the situation with my consultation group, the group members and I wondered whether I had repeated something that had happened to Rhana many times before in her life. It seemed to me that I had been intrusive.

The group members and I also speculated that Rhana was in a real bind. On the one hand, she was trying to become more independent; on the other hand, seeing me made her feel very dependent. Was she therefore experiencing a normal conflict of adolescence, or did her attachment difficulties reach back to her early childhood? Levy-Warren (1999), following in the footsteps of Blos (1962, 1967), considered separation and individuation the tasks of adolescence. Early adolescence is dominated by the attempt to separate—that is, to figure out "where I stop and you begin" (Levy-Warren, 1999, p. 10). Rhana had tremendous difficulties with this concept. How could she afford to separate when she had experienced so much involuntary loss? I think that either being close or separating may have felt too threatening. The group consensus was that I should call and simply inquire how Rhana was doing, maybe commenting that our last session had been difficult, and invite her to come in again.

When Rhana answered the phone, her voice sounded constricted, and she said she could not come for our next appointment. We ended our conversation by saying that she would let me know. Later, I received a message stating that she was not sure if she wanted to continue therapy. I reached her at the group home and said, "I got your message. Thank you for leaving it. It sounded like you are not sure if you want to continue coming to see me. It is okay if you decide not to, but I suggest that we sit down and talk about it. If you decide to leave it will give us a chance to say good-bye." Rhana replied that she was not sure if she could say good-bye. I suggested that we could talk about why it would be difficult to say good-bye. She agreed to come.

Rhana arrived almost 20 minutes late for what would be our last session. She apologized and said that she had been meeting with the head of the group home.

When I asked her what the meeting was about, she said, "Everything we'll talk about today—I am leaving the group home."

"It sounds like a lot has been happening."

"Yes, there has. This feels like a confession—anyway." She took a deep breath and went on to tell me that she had a minor injury in July and was taken to the hospital when she could not sleep because of it. That is when Rhana met Tony, who worked at the hospital.

Rhana said, "He came back when I was done at 3 A.M.—it was nice that he cared. He asked me for my phone number." She went on to tell me that she ended up going to the beach with Tony and some friends. At first she kept it secret from the group home. She also kept on telling Tony that she was engaged and not to get his hopes up. At the group home, people soon started speculating that Rhana was dating someone.

Rhana continued, admitting, "I guess that is why I didn't tell you. I was worried you'd be asking the same questions the others were asking— are you sleeping with him? What about Ray?"

I said, "So you were worried that I would judge you in ways that did not feel accurate?"

Rhana replied, "Yes, and then when I got my high school diploma— that is when I decided that I was not ready to go to Florida with Ray. Getting my diploma made me feel like I could do it—that I did not need to be dependent. I feel like I need to do it on my own. Ray understands. . . . Anyway, the last thing I could handle right now is be dependent on a man—on any man—I just have to prove that I can do it on my own. I was going crazy for a while. I even AWOLed . . . When I came home the next day, [my caseworker] asked, 'Why are you lying to me?' I tried to explain that I just needed to get away for a night. She started pressuring me by asking why I did not just sign myself out. She had the paper all ready, and I would have signed it if it hadn't been for [another staff member]. That same time the mailman arrived with my papers for the apartment subsidy."

We talked a little bit about Rhana's plans to move out, her plans to go to school, and her current job. Rhana mentioned that "the head of the group home believed it was not a good time to end therapy." Earlier in the session, Rhana had reported that the group home director had also said that therapy is for people who want to live a better, healthier life. I silently thanked the woman. "And plus," Rhana continued, "I don't know how to say good-bye."

We were out of time. Hoping to keep the conversation open, I said, "Maybe we don't have to make a decision right away."

"It's like if I stop, then I can't say good-bye; maybe that's why I have had such a hard time coming lately."

"So it's like if you end then you can only drop out—or you continue?"

"Yes."

"Maybe for now we can say we'll continue, but we'll leave it open whether you may end it, and we can talk about what would be so hard about saying good-bye."

Rhana replied, "Mmh."

We settled on a time for our next appointment. When Rhana left, I was not worried that it might be the last time I would see her. Somehow I believed we would be able to continue working together. However, when I presented this material to my consultation group, the assumption was that I cried once Rhana left. This observation confirms my thoughts about having had blind spots in the treatment. Rhana's desire to end therapy immediately was so obvious to the others and yet I still hoped it would continue. After consulting with the group and experiencing two more missed sessions, I felt the need to set a limit. I wrote Rhana a letter that reviewed our work, talked about closure, and invited her to contact me should she ever want to.

Rhana had initiated the termination of treatment. Endings tend to bring up feelings of loss, and loss had been the dominant theme in our work. It seems that Rhana might have terminated our work together early so that she could be in control of the loss. Most of the losses in her life were out of her control (e.g., her grandmother's death, the loss of contact with her mother, the loss of her father's care). Her rejection of me reminds me of her running away from her father. I wonder whether Rhana knew that her romantic interests would eventually create an insurmountable conflict with her father. Maybe she was trying to avoid addressing the feelings around the possibility of his throwing her out. However, once Rhana ran away and found that her father would not take her back, she had to experience the full blow of his rejection. This in turn made the loss a traumatic event. It makes me think of Cournos's (1999) account of her childhood, in which she lost both father and mother and then was rejected by her relatives, who sent her and her siblings into foster care. Events that were already sad and difficult became more traumatic because those Cournos expected to be supportive turned against her. In fact, for Rhana this might have only been a repetition of an early feeling from when she experienced her family turning against her during the accusations of molestation.

It is curious that Rhana left me in the dark about her new romantic development for 2½ months despite the fact that we had been working together for 1½ years. This warrants speculation that she was again repeating something. One can draw a parallel to her father's discovery of her having a boyfriend. Maybe Rhana was worried that I would be as disappointed with her as he had been and that I would reject her. A parallel also can be drawn to her experience of being molested. Presumably, the molestation was a secret for some time before the truth came out and the perpetrator was pursued. It seems that her interest in Tony was in part sparked by her mixed feelings about getting married. Unable to address those feelings, she began acting them out.

RENEWED CONTACT

More than a year after we terminated treatment, Rhana contacted me. I was at home when I received Rhana's call on my cellular phone, which I used for business purposes. She was surprised to reach me in person, as I had only used voice mail in the past. I was surprised to hear her voice after such a long time. Being slightly off guard due to my surprise, I quickly shared that I had an infant, who happened to be babbling in the background. My intention was to explain that I was somewhat limited in talking to her.

Rhana updated me, mentioning that she was no longer with Ray. She lived by herself, and Tony had become her boyfriend and was helping her out with bills. She mentioned that she was going to school and that she was just about to leave her job of 1½ years. Rhana also told me that she had met with her older half sister, who had come to the United States, and that she had traveled to visit her mother. Rhana expressed surprise that I had a child. When I asked her in which way this was surprising, she said that it made me human and it made her think about me in a new way: that I had a life.

Rhana and I had discussed the issue of self-disclosure at some point of our work in the past, and it became clear that Rhana liked not knowing about my life; it made her feel safe. This discussion had been initiated by my canceling a session on short notice due to a doctor's appointment. I had not told her that I had cancelled because of a miscarriage. Rhana came in for our following session 5 minutes early and brought me a beautiful flower as a get-well gift. My own feelings about my miscarriage still felt too raw for me to help her explore her feelings about the cancelled session. Rhana missed the following session, but 2 weeks later we discussed Rhana's feelings about my canceling on short notice due to a medical procedure. She shared that it humanized me and appreciated that I thought of her as mature enough to be told, but she also shared associations about having to feel more concerned if I were sick. She described a sense of burden in potentially having to worry about me.

Given the knowledge that Rhana preferred to not know too much about me, I wondered about the impact of Rhana learning that I had had a child in her absence. I wonder if this stirred up painful feelings relating to her mother, such as intense envy toward the sister who her mother favored and fierce feelings of being excluded. The sudden burst of knowledge about my life might have triggered similar feelings of being excluded from my life.

When I asked Rhana what had prompted her call, she said that she wanted to come in for therapy again. As we arranged a time to meet, the question of the fee arose. Rhana reassured me that she was still part of the child welfare system as long as she was in school, but it was clear that we would have to address remaining questions around the meaning of my value to Rhana and her value to me. This brief interaction reminded me that I had never found the right time to talk with Rhana about the pro bono structure of CPP.

The fact that therapists in CPP work without monetary compensation raises particular and important issues, including questions about whether, when, how, and under what circumstances the structure of the organization that supports the treatment should be introduced as a topic at play in the therapeutic relationship. Clearly the discussion needs to allow for an exploration of the client's feelings on the subject. When working with an older adolescent in foster care such as Rhana, the clinician has to take into consideration the adolescent's natural urge to move toward independence. I have wondered whether Rhana might have felt in my debt because I was not paid. She might have felt safer if I had been paid, because it would have created more of a sense of neutrality, without the threat of my caring too much about her. Rhana also mentioned that she did not want her appointment to take away time from my child. I reassured her that I always worked at the office on the day of the week for which we scheduled our appointment. This concern about impinging on my time warranted some speculation. It seemed that Rhana might be burdened with the feeling that she now had to care for me or was experiencing feelings of sibling rivalry. Or perhaps she believed that a good mother should not work and therefore was disappointed in me. After all, she had been free to project any image onto me previously. The information she gained in the phone conversation seemed to offer the perfect opening to explore her feelings around taking care of others, because it was so pervasive in her relationships. Yet, of course, for this to have happened, Rhana needed to participate in therapy on a regular basis.

Rhana was late for the appointment. I knew that some public transportation in the area was delayed, and I did not know which line she was using. Nevertheless, feelings of frustration, helplessness, and anger began to arise. This made it hard for me to be as warm and welcoming as I would have liked. When Rhana finally arrived, we only had 10 minutes left. My body language was slightly frosty. I remember being slow to get out of my seat and somewhat stiff and formal. This was in spite of the fact that I was excited and happy to see her. I sensed that Rhana was taken a little aback, or maybe she was insecure as to how to greet me after such a long break. She apologized for her lateness and explained that her bus had been delayed. It is striking that we seemed to pick up the transference exactly where we had left off. I was experiencing a strong reaction toward the uncertainty of the treatment created by Rhana's ambivalence.

One of the reasons I felt frustrated was that there were a couple of issues that I had hoped to address over the course of the session. One was the question of what had brought Rhana back. I was considering two of several possibilities. Perhaps she was in some sort of a crisis and needed help. In this case, there might be a sense of time pressure in this initial period (N. Altman, personal communication, January 7, 2004). Or maybe she was in a more stable place in her life and felt more ready to be in therapy. Perhaps she now felt she had greater resources to explore emotional issues (E. Kandell, personal communication, January 16, 2004).

The second issue that I wanted to discuss was the fee. It was clear that this issue was stirred up during our phone contact and that it would be important to address. Yet during the actual appointment, I was not sure whether we would have time to discuss the issue. We had approximately 10 minutes to talk, and I wanted to let Rhana take the lead. She discussed what had happened to her since we had stopped working together, especially details concerning the visit to her mother. We then talked about what made her come back: She said it was the letter I had written to her after she dropped out of therapy more than a year prior. She had held on to it, and it seemed to have come to symbolize me in the way of Winnicott's (1971) transitional object. The letter had helped Rhana keep our work in mind. I brought up the question of whether she might have come back to therapy because she was in crisis or because she was ready to explore her feelings further. She confirmed the latter.

Finally, with just a few minutes left, Rhana raised the question of the fee. I felt that I was in a real bind. I did not really feel comfortable talking about it with no time left to explore her thoughts and feelings, but I also wanted to be straightforward. I now wish I had said, "Listen, let's talk about it first thing next time we meet." Instead, I told her that I was part of a group of clinicians that met together regularly to discuss our work and that we worked without collecting a fee in exchange for consultation. I doubt that Rhana fully recognized the value the peer group had for me. If she had a reaction to what I told her, she did not show it.

I had told Rhana that I would be away for approximately 2 weeks following our first meeting, and we scheduled another session for a few weeks later. The morning of the next session, she left me a message saying that she could not make it because she had to buy books for school. I could not reach her because she had no answering machine. She did not show for the following session, either. I decided to write another letter rather than call again. In the letter, I commented on Rhana's experiences since we had stopped working together and invited her to come back when she felt the need or wish.

Overall, I have a sense that she idealized me during our break and was disappointed with the real me upon her return. I have wondered whether she terminated treatment after more than 1½ years because she was warding off the knowledge that she was "merely" my client. Perhaps she harbored a wish to have me as real mother but was well aware that this was not possible. When she came back, she found out that I now had a child. This might have been devastating because it emphasized the fact that she was not my child. At the same time, finding out that I was not getting paid for my work with her might have felt confusing. It might have meant that she was special, but also might have stirred up the longing for more extended contact with me: Because I had volunteered my time, Rhana may have believed that I had already extended myself beyond a professional frame, which would therefore make even more time together possible. Maybe these feelings were too complex and overwhelming to bear. Perhaps she preferred to "be the abuser" (Canham, 2003, p. 15): abandoning me again and leaving me with the painful questions of what went wrong. This would allow Rhana to re-create the experience she had with her father, except that she was on the other side. Her father had not been willing to talk with her since she was placed in a group home, perhaps lacking the ability to reflect on different mental states himself (Canham, 2003; Fonagy & Target, 1998). It seems that for the father, Rhana's becoming culturally assimilated and involved with a boy evoked similarities with his wife, causing problems in his differentiating the real situation from the imagined. In turn, Rhana seemed to have acted out his worst fantasies by becoming sexually active and running away.

SUCCESSFUL TREATMENT
AND REALISTIC EXPECTATIONS

As I began writing this chapter, I pondered over what constitutes successful treatment. Is it offering consistency? Is it creating a safe place in which thinking about emotionally charged material can take place? Does it require the therapist to reflect on the client's affect and state of mind? Furthermore, does an adolescent who has been in foster care require a different set of treatment goals than another adolescent? Finally, how should the clinician's expectations be set, and, again, how would they be different for a child in foster care?

When I started seeing Rhana she was 17. She was in an abusive relationship with an adolescent who was also in foster care. She was having trouble concentrating on her schoolwork, which was reflected in her grades and attendance. She was jeopardizing her graduation from high school. Her relationship with her father was tenuous at best, and she was not able to make good use of the relationships with staff at her group home. She was showing some antisocial tendencies, such as not going to school, leaving the group home without permission, and hanging out with a crowd involved with drugs. According to Hindle (1998), this behavior may have suggested Rhana's longing for a stable external force to take care of her. Williams (1982) noted that this kind of behavior is often the only thing that mitigates intense feelings of loss.

At what seemed to be the end of treatment, Rhana had graduated from high school and was in a more supportive relationship, although she was in the process of ending it. She was responsible, working in a full-time job, and planning on going to college. She had created a substantial supportive social network with the help of and including her group home staff. She was planning on finding her own apartment and living independently.

More than a year later, Rhana was living independently and attending college. She was about to leave a full-time job that she had held for 1½ years so she could concentrate more fully on school. She was receiving financial help from the local child welfare system as well as financial support from her present boyfriend. Rhana had managed to go back to visit her mother, whom she had not seen since she was 9 years old, and had established contact with her older half sister.

The following question arises: At what point do you assess the outcome of the treatment? For example, should this be done at the end of treatment or 6 or 12 months after the end of treatment? When working with a child or adolescent, you must further consider the natural course of a disorder as well as the changes that will occur in the child or adolescent due to the natural progression of development. Research has shown that child and adolescent treatment does not always show much change or success at the end of treatment, but assessments conducted months after treatment have shown improvements at the follow-up when compared with children who had not received therapy (Target & Fonagy, 1996). With Rhana, continued improvement was occurring even more than a year after ending treatment. With foster children, perhaps it is a mistake to measure outcome when therapist and client stop meeting. Instead, it appears necessary to take a long-term view of the assessment process. In fact, treatment that appears to have ended may be ongoing, as Rhana's attempt at coming back attested.

On the surface, it appears that Rhana had improved both at the end of treatment and more than a year later. At neither point did I have a chance to ask her whether she still felt depressed and was experiencing sadness, overeating, or nightmares, yet I have the feeling that she still continued to have times during which she was probably flooded by these symptoms.

Nevertheless, Rhana had continued to make positive changes after treatment, and I believe that this was in part due to her resilience. She was able to make good use of the therapy because of internal and external resources that many children in foster care do not have. She had good thinking skills and presumably had received decent parenting during early childhood (from her grandmother). Both good intellectual skills and effective parenting have been found to contribute to competence and resilience in the face of adversity (Masten et al., 1995, 1999). Furthermore, even though Rhana's father was harsh in many ways, the fact that he had high expectations of her academically seemed to have become an internalized motivator that was driving her to continue her education beyond high school.

Rhana's resilience helped her to use me as a container for her thoughts and feelings during the course of our work. She was able to benefit from our relationship and many of the insights she gained. Therapy helped her think about certain feelings and situations differently. It helped her find delineations between her own thoughts and feelings and those of other people (Fonagy & Target, 1998).

Offering consistency in the form of a regular appointment and a place to meet—as well as in the form of an empathetic, nonmanipulative, and interested adult—seems essential to treatment (Pine, 1985). Nevertheless, failure of consistency is a normal part of therapy. Therefore we must attempt to explore the repercussions. Once failure of consistency occurs, it can become grounds for discussion of the relationship between therapist and client. We must attempt to provide a safe environment for the client to feel secure enough to explore feelings, desires, fantasies, and emotional struggles. Pine called this the "context of safety" (1985, p. 132) and pointed out that individuals who have not grown up with this experience fail to progress along normal developmental lines. Many children in foster care come from disorganized backgrounds and lack the experience of reasonable stability in their lives.

It seems particularly important to provide these children and adolescents with a different experience from what they face day to day. As we reflect on clients' mental states—saying, for example, "You're upset right now" or "You feel hurt"—we help people get to know their own feelings better. Creating a new experience may further take shape in the therapist's response to the clients' transference. For example, Rhana frequently experienced people getting angry with her. Occasionally, my counter-transference to her was indeed anger. My task was to think of new ways to react to her that allowed an exploration of the situation—perhaps by asking questions such as, "What do you think I am thinking about you today?" (Moran, as cited in Fonagy & Target, 1998, p. 108).

Every foster care story is unique, and yet themes of loss and disruption permeate all of them (e.g., see Andreou, 1991; Kaplan, 1982; Kenrick, 2000). In therapy with foster care children, themes of separation and attachment invariably emerge, as the children have few if any "thoughtful and containing parents or other available adults to help them make sense of their experience" (Kenrick, 2000, p. 394). Rhana's recollection of her story had many gaps and vague areas. These seemed to reflect the lack of continuity in her parental care and her lack of ability to attach.

The aim of treatment, according to Anna Freud, is to enable the child to return to the normal path of development (Sandler, Kennedy, & Tyson, 1980). More specifically geared toward adolescence, Levy-Warren saw the goals of psychotherapy as "defined by the adolescents' need to see themselves in . . . more realistic and differentiated terms" (1996, p. 156). The therapist helps the adolescent to become familiar with his or her drives, emotions, and thought processes.

Rhana's return after a long break might indicate that past treatment had been helpful and therefore successful. At the same time, she may have felt ready to start working on issues she had not been able to address previously. Perhaps her purpose in coming back was to be able to leave me again. The fact is that children and adolescents in foster care have a history of loss and separation. They further experience loss and separation once they are in foster care due to change of placement and turnover of staff (Kenrick, 2000). As a result, this theme seems to dominate therapy. An adolescent foster care client might decide to turn the tables on the therapist and repeatedly leave.

Terr (1994) and van der Kolk (1989, 1994) described how traumatic reactions such as flashbacks and physiological symptoms can be stimulated by feeling either too close to or too separate from significant attachment figures. This in turn can inhibit a client's ability to think clearly about his or her own or others' mental states. Such a freeze might lead to impulsivity and cause treatment dropout. These dynamics must be taken into consideration by the therapist. Working with adolescents in foster care requires extra vigilance in paying attention to one's counter-transference and larger systemic issues.

Anna Freud held that most child analysts and clients are too hopeful regarding the outcome of treatment (Sandler et al., 1980). If this idea gets applied to work with foster care children, it can mean that we may hope that the therapy will go on longer and will have more consistency than is realistic. Anna Freud also suggested that an abrupt end to treatment might not signal a premature end but demands that we readjust expectations of treatment length. In fact, in work with foster care children, it may be that treatment has not ended when we think it is over.

CONCLUSION

For foster children, meeting once a week over a long period of time may not be a realistic goal. We sometimes have to alter our expectations and anticipate that our clients may periodically withdraw. The frame of therapy might have to be adjusted and become more flexible for clients who have never experienced stability in their lives. The length of sessions might occasionally have to be extended. Missed sessions—and even termination itself—might have to be viewed as part of the treatment rather than as a failure of treatment. Indeed, Rhana's struggle over whether and how to end her treatment can be seen as an ongoing attempt to work through her own fear of endings and her attempt to create a satisfying ending.

REFERENCES

Andreou, C. (1991). A sixteen year old girl's search for a good object and the need of it for the survival of the self. *Journal of Child Psychotherapy, 17*(2), 83–102.

Blos, P. (1962). *On adolescence: A psychoanalytic interpretation.* New York: Free Press.

Blos, P. (1967). The second individuation process of adolescence. *Psychoanalytic Study of the Child, 22,* 162–186.

Canham, H. (2003). The relevance of the Oedipus myth to fostered and adopted children. *Journal of Child Psychotherapy, 29*(1), 5–19.

Coates, S.W. (1998). Having a mind of one's own and holding the other in mind: Commentary on paper by Peter Fonagy and Mary Target. *Psychoanalytic Dialogue, 8*(1), 115–148.

Cournos, F. (1999). *City of one.* New York: W.W. Norton.

Fonagy, P., & Target, M. (1998). Mentalization and the changing aims of child psychoanalysis. *Psychoanalysis Dialogues, 8*(1), 87–114.

Freud, A. (1958). Adolescence. *Psychoanalytic Study of the Child*, *13*, 255–278.

Garber, B. (2000). Adolescent mourning: A Paradigmatic case report. *Adolescent Psychiatry: Developmental and Clinical Studies*, *25*, 101–117.

Hindle, D. (1998). Loss and delinquency: Two adolescents' experience of prison as an external container of psychic pain. *Journal of Child Psychotherapy*, *24*(1), 37–60.

Kaplan, A. (1982). Growing up in foster care: One boy's struggles. *Journal of Child Psychotherapy*, *8*(1), 57–65.

Kenrick, J. (2000). "Be a kid': The traumatic impact of repeated separation on children who are fostered and adopted. *Journal of Child Psychotherapy*, *26*(3), 393–412.

Levy-Warren, M.H. (1996). *The adolescent journey: Development, identity formation, and psychotherapy*. Lanham, MD: Jason Aronson.

Levy-Warren, M.H. (1999). I am, you are, and so are we: A current perspective on adolescent separation-individuation theory. *Adolescent Psychiatry: Developmental and Clinical Studies*, *24*, 3–24.

Masten, A.S., Coatsworth, J.D., Neeman, J., Gest, S.D., Tellegen, A., & Garmezy, N. (1995). The structure and coherence of competence from childhood through adolescence. *Child Development*, *66*, 1635–1659.

Masten, A.S., Hubbard, J., Gest, S.D., Tellegen, A., Germezy, N., & Ramirez, M. (1999). Adaptation in the context of adversity: Pathways to competence resilience and maladaptation from childhood to late adolescence. *Development and Psychopathology*, *11*(1), 143–169.

Moran, G.S. (1984). Psychoanalytic treatment of diabetic children. *Psychoanalytic Study of the Child*, *38*, 265–293.

Murray, H.A. (1943). *Thematic Apperception Test*. Cambridge, MA: Harvard University Press.

Pine, F. (1985). *Developmental theory and clinical process*. New Haven, CT: Yale University Press.

Sandler, J., Kennedy, H., & Tyson, R.L. (1980). *The technique of child psychoanalysis: Discussions with Anna Freud*. Cambridge, MA: Harvard University Press.

Shane, E., & Shane, M. (1995). A self psychological view of therapeutic impasses. In B.S. Mark & J.A. Incorvaia (Eds.), *The handbook of infant , child, and adolescent psychotherapy: A guide to diagnosis and treatment*. Lanham, MD: Jason Aronson.

Target, M., & Fonagy, P. (1996). The psychological treatment of child and adolescent psychiatric disorders. In A. Roth & P. Fonagy (Eds.), *What works for whom? A critical review of psychotherapy research*. New York: The Guilford Press.

Terr, L. (1994). *Unchained memories: True stories of traumatic memories, lost and found*. New York: Basic Books.

van der Kolk, B. (1989). The compulsion to repeat trauma: Re-enactment, revictimization, and masochism. *Psychiatric Clinics of North America*, *12*, 389–411.

van der Kolk, B. (1994). The body keeps the score: Memory and the evolving psychobiology of post-traumatic stress. *Harvard Review of Psychiatry*, *1*, 253–265.

Williams, A.H. (1982). Adolescents, violence and crime. *Journal of Adolescence*, *5*, 125–134.

Winnicott, D.W. (1971). Transitional objects and transitional phenomena. In *Playing and reality*. New York: Penguin Books.

CHAPTER 9

Many Parents, One Child

Working with the Family Matrix

Diane Ehrensaft

Winnicott (1960) once said there is no infant without a mother. In like fashion, there is no foster child without a foster parent. Yet, unlike Winnicott's babies, there also is no foster child without birth parents, a social worker, the court, and a foster parent. This is the parenting matrix in which the child does his or her best to grow. This chapter shares what we Children's Psychotherapy Project (CPP) therapists have learned about working with parents, which means, by necessity, what we have learned about working with all of the people who come together so one child can go on being. I am looking through the lens of one of the founding members of CPP; I am looking through the lens of a senior consultant who has had the privilege of bearing witness to the rich, complicated, and often painful work of the clinicians who have come together over the years in my consultation group; I am looking through the lens of a therapist who has worked with a foster child through CPP.

The following vignettes present a glimpse of the various parenting scenarios found among foster care children:

Mr. Gardner is furious. He is in the midst of a reunification evaluation and wants his daughter back permanently. He only brings his daughter to therapy because he has to. He just wants everyone to leave him alone. He sputters out at his daughter's therapist, "You're just doing it for the money." The therapist anticipates that she will never see this child again once the father regains legal custody.

Ms. Anderson is one of the best foster parents in the county. She is trained to work with medically fragile children as well as with emotionally disturbed children. Yet, she is getting on in years and even she cannot tolerate the strain of 4-year-old Amanda's out-of-control behavior. With a heavy heart, she tells Amanda's therapist that she can no longer care for Amanda, after more than a year of trying.

Kimmie is 23 years old and one of the oldest children receiving treatment from CPP, as we also see youth older than age 18 if they have come out of the foster care system. In a moment of frustration, sobbing, she challenges her therapist, "Why should I keep coming? You can't help me. I need a mom, not just someone to talk to once a week."

The vignettes present three stories, three therapists in CPP confronting the challenge of one child, many parents—or alternatively, one child, no parent. As we try to stop the revolving door of our young clients' ever-changing parenting matrix, we, the therapists, can find ourselves vacillating between the Mighty Mouse theme song, "Here I am to save the day," and the old gospel hymn, "Sometimes I feel like a motherless child." Absorbing the feelings of the children, the feelings of the parents, and our own experiences as the children's therapist, these lyrics signify two of the strongest counter-transference feelings that infuse us as we work with the children and *all* of their parents, "real" and assigned.

Working with foster families involves working with a large field of players: the foster child, the foster parents, the foster child's birth parents, the foster child's biological siblings, the foster child's foster siblings, the social worker, and the court—just for a start. It is enough to make any therapist want to stick his or her head in the sand. Through the support of our consultation groups, we can resist that temptation. Instead, our work together is to help each other keep our heads above water and to remind ourselves that our job is not to save the day, but to forge the positive development of the children who may be both motherless and mother-ful, with not two hands but many—perhaps too many—overseeing their care. We have learned over and over again that the place that often makes or breaks the treatment of the children in CPP is not the work done with the children in the consultation room but the alliances that we build and the services we provide to the birth parents, the foster parents, and the assigned parenting figures in the social welfare and court system. It is this piece of the work that this chapter discusses.

FOSTER PARENTS: THE KEY PLAYERS, THE MALIGNED PLAYERS

This discussion begins by focusing on the parents with whom we have the most contact—the foster parents. To talk about working with foster parents is to talk about working with any parent, but it is also to talk about the unique situation of the foster parent. The discussion must address the paradox of the simultaneous commonality and conflict between the child's foster parent and the child's psychotherapist.

One day when I checked my office mail, I picked up the November 13, 2000, issue of *Time* magazine to read on the cover, "The Shame of Foster Care." Needless to say, as a member of CPP, I was immediately drawn to the feature article inside. Then I paused for a moment: "What would it be like for one of the foster parents in our project to read this headline?" Although the article specifically targeted the government system of foster care for its ineptness and corruption, foster parents were not exempt. According to the article, foster parents molest their foster children; they leave the children unattended to drown in swimming pools; they neglect or abuse the children at a rate that is feared to be significantly higher than that found in the general population; they murder their foster children, even if they are relatives of the child rather than strangers; they beat, break the bones of, and brutally shake foster children and then lie in the emergency room about the cause of the injuries; they beat the children with belts, throw knives at their foreheads, and force them to say that they molested another child; they have no training to watch children; they have unchecked criminal backgrounds; and they keep in their homes unsecured knives, broken glass, inoperable smoke detectors, and toxic substances within reach of children. The article asserts that counties are not aware of "the full extent of harm children may face in foster care" (Roche, 2000, p. 79). Throughout the entire article, I located only three positive references to foster parents: 1) "Many foster parents . . . continue to act selflessly as important way stations for at-risk kids while their biological parents get their lives together" (p. 75); 2) "Even the most devoted of foster parents are dropping out of programs, frustrated at times by a lack of support—as well as legal roadblocks to adopting the children if they so choose" (p. 81); and 3) a sidebar titled "When the System Works," which shows positive photographic images of three different sets of foster parents (p. 81).

Moving from my mailroom back into our clinical offices, I thought of how a foster parent comes to see us knowing about this perception of foster parents. The not-good-enough-parent or worse has been infused in the culture, and the foster parent certainly may wonder if it is infused in us as well. Is it any accident that the situation might be fraught with difficulty?

Who are foster parents, anyway? They are parents like any other parents—some are better than good, some are good-enough, and some are less than good. They are adults who get paid to take children into their home. They are adults who pick up the ball for a relative who can no longer take care of their child. They are adults who foster a child in the hope of adopting that child later.

Anyone who becomes a foster parent will inevitably hold for the child the tension between hopelessness and resilience. A child comes to the foster parents with broken attachments and the challenge of building new ones. A child who enters a foster placement has perhaps lost a parent or maybe never had one after leaving the birth mother's womb. That child may have no clear documented history, just a few facts and a plastic bag packed with scattered possessions from the past. The child may appear with a lot of bruises, both physical and psychic. The child may be lethargic, a child who has given up, a child who has lost hope. He or she may be an upstart, a child who is still full of life and holds on to hope.

The foster parent is the person who inherits this child, but maybe not for long, for somewhere out there is a parent or a relative who will come to claim the child, or another foster placement, or a group home, or maybe the streets. The foster parent has in his or her care a child who may be beaten down or perhaps a child who hopes for something better.

Our main work is to support the foster child's resiliency to meet the challenges of a disrupted life and to go on being and growing. Hand in hand comes our second piece of work: to foster the foster parents, and whoever else is active in the parenting matrix, so they can give the child the support, nurturance, and containment that are the vital elements of the foster child's facilitating environment. As we do both these pieces of work, we find ourselves holding for both parents and child the feelings of hopelessness that come from broken attachments and their aftermath while simultaneously building the resilience in both parents and child that will allow the child to go on growing.

FUSING AND LOSING: COMMONALITY
BETWEEN THERAPISTS AND FOSTER PARENTS

One way to grasp the experience of foster parents is to liken it to our experience as therapists. When a child enters CPP, both therapist and foster parent have a shared mission: to heal, to provide a corrective emotional experience, and to promote the child's forward development. We are both asked to accomplish this mission under the following condition: getting very involved with the child in our care while holding the expectation that that child will leave us.

The difference between us and foster parents, though, is that as therapists we have a frame around our involvement. We see the child once a week (sometimes more) and then carry that child in our mind at other times. Foster parents are asked to get involved 24/7. They are asked to become parents with the expectation that their parenting role may suddenly stop, sometimes with no advance notice. They are asked to become parents to a child who may come to them fully defended against having them as parents. Conversely, they are asked to become parents to a child so hungry for nurturance that the parents fear being swallowed whole.

To prepare themselves for any of these possibilities, foster parents may hold back from building an attachment with the child. Fusing and losing becomes an ongoing tension with which the parents have to contend. Those who are most successful discover that it is better to have loved and lost than to have never loved at all, both for the foster parents and for the child—but most assuredly for the child. Even for foster parents who really did not want to become parents, as is often the case in relative foster care (especially grandparent foster care), the psychological challenge of fusing with the anticipation of losing can wreak havoc on one's emotional life. For example, Ms. Yates was getting on in years and had left parenting behind decades ago. However, when her grandchild was removed from her son and his wife after a report of abuse and neglect, she grudgingly stepped in to care for her grandchild. Ms. Yates was like a tough mother hen with this child but made it very clear that her primary goal was to get this child back to her parents, where she belonged. Yet, as steps toward reunification began, Ms. Yates was the first to swoop in and block her granddaughter from any harm she worried might befall the child in her own parents' care. Ms. Yates wanted to lose this child but also was fused with her, and she worried about what the losing would mean for this child's future.

As we explore our own reactions to getting intimately involved with our young clients' lives, knowing they may leave us prematurely as they are moved from place to place, we come to understand and join with the foster parent's emotional conundrum of being asked to throw oneself into the care of the child with the understanding that it may not be for keeps. Yet, while recognizing the common experience of losing and fusing, we have learned that being in the same boat does not necessarily make for good friends. Often, as both therapists and foster parents go through their parallel experiences of fusing and losing, rather than cooperation and collaboration, a sense of competition and resentment surfaces. Sometimes a therapist, in identifying with the foster child's precariousness, can grow to believe "*I* am the mother of this motherless child." We are particularly ripe for this kind of distortion because our work with children in CPP so often goes beyond the traditional boundaries of psychotherapy, extending to "extra-therapeutic" actions. We make arrangements for transportation or bus fare to get the children and their families to their sessions, we search for classes in the community to support the children's interests and talents, we make phone calls to locate a parent or social worker missing in action, and so forth. The problem with this type of situation is that the foster parent may also have established him- or herself as the mother of this motherless child, at least for the time being. The foster parent has his or her own sense of expertise, and the common mission—to heal, to provide nurturance, and to promote forward growth—is a difficult job to share if each participant believes that he or she is the primary and only person for the job. The problem is further exacerbated when the vying parties, therapist and foster parent, are separated by age, ethnicity, race, or class.

Therapists have neither the expertise nor the same role as foster parents. Therapists have the job of getting their fingers on the pulse of the child's inner self. Foster parents have the job of getting to know the child inside and out, day and night. These are different ways of knowing. If a therapist and a foster parent can identify together the commonality of their losing–fusing experience with the foster child, they are then freer to step back and report what they each see about the same child from their unique perspectives. From there, they can join together to complete the picture of the child's experience and to think together about the interventions that will work best with this child.

As the therapist and the foster parent do this, two other participants in the matrix are also undergoing their own experience of losing and fusing. The first is the child. The second is the biological parent or parents. Each may see the situation through a very different set of lenses, generating views in total opposition to those of either the therapist or the foster parent. Instead of an integrated picture, these opposing views can become fertile ground for splitting, for projections, and for any number of primitive defenses among participants in the foster family matrix. Once again, the work of the therapist is to fit *all* of the pieces together to make a composite picture, rather than leaving them as a pile of ragged shards.

LIKE WORKING WITH ANY PARENT, LIKE WORKING WITH NO OTHER PARENT

As with any parent we work with while conducting child psychotherapy, the task with foster parents is to discover their subjective experience: What is it like to be raising this child and to be meeting with a therapist because of that child? Like any other parent today, the foster parent may be suffering from what I call the new diagnosis of the millennium: chronic parental anxiety. With no time to parent, threats of violence and terrorism, and a social mandate to raise a perfect, happy child with no accompanying supports, parents often come into my office as if they are tripping off a battlefield (Ehrensaft, 1997). Like any parents, foster parents are involved in an attachment matrix with their child, even if it does not start at birth. As with any parents, therapists may not necessarily know foster parents' motivation for parenting, and the foster parents might not know either.

However, we have learned that foster parents are *not* like other parents. Unlike other parents, child saving, service to society, and keeping a child within the extended family may be strong motivators to having a foster child in their home. Unlike other parents, foster parents cannot assume a permanent parent–child bond. Unlike other parents, as a stated policy, foster parents can return a child to the social service system if that child proves too difficult to parent. Unlike other parents, foster parents stand to have a child taken from them at a moment's notice, even when they are parenting well. Unlike other parents, they are paid to parent their foster child. Unlike other parents, foster parents have parents who supervise their parenting—the court and the social service department responsible for foster care in their county. Unlike other parents, foster parents will inevitably be in a co-parenting situation. They may find themselves in a co-parenting relationship with strangers they have never met or would never care to meet under other circumstances. They may find themselves linked to a hostile birth parent. They may have to parent in conjunction with a relative who has failed as a parent and may not have good relations with the rest of the family. In the case of grandparent fostering, they may find themselves painfully reminded of their own failures as a parent to their child who is now unable to parent.

BUILDING RATHER THAN BURNING BRIDGES IN WORK WITH FOSTER PARENTS

As noted, there is no foster parent without a foster child and many other adults as well: birth parents, social workers, and the court. This discussion addresses yet another adult to add to that list: the therapist. We have learned that our therapeutic work with foster parents is most effective when we pay attention not only to their external reality and to the parenting matrix but also to the unconscious processes of *all* of the participants. Often, there is a tendency to polarize the inadequate and the idealized parent. For example, the foster parent is a saint saving the child from the living hell of an abusive father. Or, the birth mother is a victim of a racist and class-based system that has removed the child from her care simply because she had her electricity turned off and discovers that her child has been placed in a foster home situation where she has been molested.

From the child's point of view, the foster parent can be quickly turned into the bad object while the biological parent is preserved as all good; alternatively, the foster parent becomes the saint and the birth parent the devil. There is no room for ambivalence. From the foster parents' point of view, the biological parent threatens to pull the yarn on the sweater that the foster parents are so carefully knitting; they perceive themselves to be the ideal parents who will save this child from the hands of an evil mother or father. There is no room for ambivalence. Alternatively, in grandparent fostering, the foster parents have exhausted all of their resources and can only see the parent, their own child, in the most positive of lights. Their strongest desire is to send the child back to the parent because they are so tired. In order to get some respite, they may ignore or even deny or repress evidence of the parents' drug use, criminal activity, negligence, or psychological disorganization. There is no room for ambivalence. For the biological parent, the foster parent can be construed as the devil incarnate in the business of child stealing, while the parent remains a beleaguered victim of the unjust legal system. There is no room for ambivalence. Alternatively, the biological parent can idealize the foster parent as the fairy godmother who will bring good fortune to all, including the floundering and needy birth parent. There is no room for ambivalence.

In this atmosphere of splitting, potential abounds for the eruption of bad objects in every domain. Heineman (1999) talked about the capacity of the child to transform the good parent into the bad parent, and in the case of abused children removed from their homes, the target is often the foster parent. The same transformation can happen to the therapist: Through unrelenting psychic attacks, the child has the capacity to transform the good therapist into the bad therapist. Repeatedly, therapists in CPP come back to their consultation groups to report, often with shame, a moment in which they "lost it" during a therapy session or felt themselves to be hostile attackers rather than benevolent therapists. It can happen even when the therapist has made the best of interventions. I recall a foster child I worked with many years ago. She approached her teacher in her therapeutic school after a weekend visit with her father.

Angela reported to the teacher, "My daddy says I'm a stupid fool."

Her teacher quickly responded, "Oh, Angela, that's not true. You're a very smart little girl."

Angela spit right back, "Are you callin' my daddy a liar?"

When an infant cannot be soothed, he or she has the capacity to turn a good parent into a frustrated, distraught, or even abusive parent. The infant does not do this out of conscious choice; it just happens as a consequence of his or her poor regulatory system. As the child gets older, he or she may then get involved in an unconscious dynamic or strategy in transforming the good into the bad parent. The older child is involved in a repetition compulsion of sorts, stemming from the need to recreate the bad object parent, the one he or she has always known. The child often does this to his or her foster parent with either the unconscious hope of working it out better this time or with the longing to stay in touch with a lost parent, even if that person is a bad parent. The re-creation of the bad object parent facilitates continuity—it may be the only way the child knows to be and the only kind of person the child has known. From the child's perspective, hell is knowable, and knowable, even if bad, is preferable to the unknown.

In this atmosphere of splitting, we therapists are at risk for having any possibility of ambivalence foreclosed for us as well. If this happens, we are rendered unable to think, and our alliance with the foster parents is put in serious jeopardy. We find ourselves caught thinking in black-and-white terms—seeing only the bad foster parent and the good social worker, the horrible biological parent and the saintly foster grandmother, and so forth. We are pressured both from within and from without. Anyone who has been asked to weigh in on a placement decision for a foster child knows the pressure from the legal and social service system to say in simple terms that one placement will be good, the other bad. There is no room for nuances or shading or even for a creative solution, such as a co-parenting arrangement.

We have learned in CPP that our work with the parenting matrix goes best when we can make room for ambivalence on everybody's part, including our own. It is common in therapeutic work with all parents to uncover resistance to having any murderous thoughts toward their children. Sometimes parents end up enacting the thoughts instead, in destructive or abusive acts. Sometimes they flee the thoughts so forcefully that they end up being an underaggressive parent who is afraid of asserting any authority with the child. We help such parents by allowing them to bring those murderous thoughts to the light of day, so they can be metabolized and worked through. The same applies to work with the parenting matrix surrounding a foster care child, except it is much more complicated because we are inviting everyone in the matrix to have myriad feelings—some nice, some not so nice—about everyone else in the matrix as well as about themselves. Allowing room for everyone's ambivalence fills the field with complexities, but it makes the work in the consultation room far more real and ultimately gives all of the parenting figures a better chance to think things through regarding foster care situations in which there are rarely easy or clear answers.

The signal that it is time to attend to allowing room for ambivalence is when "saints" and "devils" keep popping up. For example, 6-year-old Amber was placed with her maternal grandmother. Both of Amber's parents were drug abusers. Amber's father had successfully completed a drug treatment program; her mother had not. The father, who was the same age as the maternal grandmother, wanted his child back. Amber and her parents were going through a reunification process. The grandmother had her own health problems and then suddenly had to care for her mother following a medical emergency. The grandmother would get Amber to her therapy appointments regularly, but Amber's parents, who took over responsibility for Amber's psychotherapy, were not as reliable in getting Amber to her appointments. Amber's mother disappeared onto the streets, and Amber's father was granted temporary care of his daughter; however, the grandmother still held legal guardianship. Occasionally, Amber's father showed up for Amber's Saturday morning appointment with the smell of liquor on his breath. He was residing in a supportive living community and had to travel a fair distance to get Amber to her therapy appointments—when he showed up at all.

It was tempting for the therapist, along with all of the members of his consultation group, to vilify the father and to long for the return of the reliable maternal grandmother. Instead, everyone joined together to support the therapist in holding the father in mind as both a parent who kept falling down on the job but also a parent who genuinely cared for his child and wanted her back. The therapist also did a superb job of being able to meet the father in his vacillating feelings about the therapist—the therapist was his right-hand man, the therapist was the man he shouted at across the phone, accusing him of sabotaging his relationship with his daughter. As often happens, regrettably, the child was not seen in CPP "for as long as it takes." Instead, her father discontinued bringing Amber as soon as the therapy was no longer court ordered. Then a year after the therapy ended, as if from nowhere, the father called the therapist—just to let him know that things were going well and to thank him for helping their family. The therapist's ability to both allow for and hold everyone's ambivalence, including his own, facilitated this father's ability to recognize Amber's treatment as a healing experience rather than a prison sentence.

Just as the therapist's job is to avoid splitting and facilitate ambivalence, the therapist must also pay attention to the power of transformative fantasies if he or she is going to have a working alliance with the foster parents. In the transformative fantasy, the intent of a foster parent is to morph a "bad" foster child into a "good" child and bring the child into the fold of the family. The reality, as noted previously, is that there is equal potential for the foster child to transform the good foster parent into the bad foster parent while stubbornly maintaining his or her status as the bad child. The child may do this to test the resiliency of the system, pushing against the walls to see if they are solid. Perhaps the child cannot tolerate the toxic waste that he or she carries within and has to deposit it somewhere else. So the child dumps the psychic waste into the foster parents, who do not always have the strength to hold such poisonous material. Add to all of this the foster parents' frustration if denied their own means of discipline and limit setting and dictated to discipline the way the law and the social service system tell them, with the threat of removal of the child and the loss of their foster care license if they do not comply. Typically, this means absolutely no form of corporal discipline. Add on one more stressor: The foster child, typically well aware of this mandate, may seize the only mode of control possible by threatening to report the foster parents at the first sign of a raised voice, let alone a raised hand.

Sometimes foster parents need to create their own bad object, the child, to rid themselves of their own toxic waste. Those parents are also holding a transformative fantasy: Either the good child will be transformed into the needed bad child or the bad child will come along, not to make things right in the family but to make them different. Negative transformative fantasies are as likely to fail as positive ones when put to the test of reality. The child will either resist being bad or, in succumbing to badness, will not actually relieve the parent of the toxic waste or make the family anything but what it was before.

To establish empathy and build an alliance with foster parents, we therapists have learned to address the disappointment in the transformative fantasy—it rarely works out as anticipated. It takes resilience to bear witness to the fantasies, particularly the negative ones but also the positive ones. In each case, the child is reduced to the parent's subjective object rather than holding his or her own agency and status as an individual who comes to the family from elsewhere, with a history and with a personality in place. The foster parent may not even be consciously aware of these fantasies, so the therapeutic work is to facilitate this process, helping the foster parents make the unconscious conscious. The next step is for the therapist to help the foster parent and the foster child recognize and cope with not just the stresses but also the losses that they are experiencing and the mourning they must do—for the ideal family, for the ideal child, and for the real people who have already been lost or stand a chance of being lost or of losing.

The operative term here is *evolutionary*. The work we do with foster parents is the work we also do within ourselves regarding our therapy with the children in CPP. As much as we wish it were so, nothing we do is miraculously or quickly transformative, and that is a reality with which both therapists and foster parents have to come to terms. Instead, the work is gradual and unfolding, even when we have only a short amount of time in which to do it. CPP was founded with the idea that the children who need long-term psychotherapy with a consistent therapist the most are typically the children who receive it the least—children in the foster care system. After more than a decade of work, we have learned that the reason we need that kind of time is not just because of multiple and broken attachments but also because the work is slow and gradually unfolding. It involves developing trust, making alliances, peeling away layered psychic armor and replacing it with a firmer core of resilience, and building bridges between all of the people who are coming together to facilitate the foster child's growth. The positive changes will remain evolutionary.

FOSTER PARENTS AND FAMILY REUNIFICATION: HEAVEN OR HELL

It is not unusual for us to remain in limbo, never knowing if the child we are seeing will remain in his or her present home, return to the parents, or be sent somewhere new. Our work is to do the therapy, but often we are called on by other members of the team or experts in the field to weigh in on a child's best interests—to reunify with the parents or not, to terminate the parents' rights or not. The philosophy and policy in the United States vacillate between reuniting children with their parents wherever possible and moving to place children in adoptive homes as soon as possible. Although the merits of "social parents"—that is, those who care for children but have no biological relationships to those children—are frequently acknowledged, social service agencies still often operate under the assumption that blood is thicker than water. At the same time, clinical work and research evidence show that some bonds are better broken than mended. Tensions about good-enough parenting, parental rights, blood ties, and attachments could be no more prevalent than when we confront the issue of reunification. It is very difficult for professionals and parents alike to recognize that the issue of reunification is rarely clear-cut. More than any other facet of clinical work, this is the time to leave room for ambivalence.

From the perspective of a foster parent who has invested in and attached to a foster child, therapists are right at the cusp of fusing and losing when the issue of reunification enters the therapy room.

An example from my clinical work, not with CPP but as an expert for the court, illustrates this point. Nine-year-old David was referred to me by the juvenile court judge for a series of clinical interviews to determine how he felt about his mother. His paternal grandmother, Mrs. Sanders, was his legal guardian. She told the court that David screamed every time he had to have a visit with his mother. David had been in his grandmother's care since the age of 6 months. She had spent several anxiety-filled days tracking him down in an emergency foster care home following his removal by child protective services from a crack house where David's mother resided and abused drugs. David's mother had since completed a drug treatment program and was clean and sober. The court awarded her weekly visits with David, with an eye toward reunification. Mrs. Sanders insisted that David was distraught and disrupted by the visits, screaming, "Please don't make me go." David's mother told a completely different account. She said that she never saw David protest the visits and that he was very happy to see her.

I had David's mother bring him for appointments. He showed no fear of his mother in my office. He played games with her and invited her to sit next to him as he drew pictures for her. He seemed excited to have her with him. Although somewhat tentative in her interactions with David, she showed genuine love and concern for him, and wanted to know my impressions of how he was faring, both at school and at home. I also had Mrs. Sanders bring him for appointments. Although she was much sterner than David's mother, David seemed strongly attached to her and calmed down in her presence. David defied gender norms and carried a miniature Barbie doll in his pocket, which he proudly showed me. Mrs. Sanders, a conservative, church-going woman, left plenty of room for David to play with his dolls, unfazed by his gender-bending.

My assessment was that David's mother loved him very much, but that she was not yet ready for the task of full-time mothering. Perhaps she never would be. Mrs. Sanders was clearly the anchor in David's life, and he would probably lose ground if he lost her as his primary caregiver. With David, my job was not to work with the family but to send a report back to the court answering the question, "How does David feel about his mother?" As is often the case in court-ordered reports, I never found out what ultimately happened with David, but if I had been the therapist, here is what I would have been thinking. I would have hoped for a co-parenting arrangement, in which David would remain with his grandmother but gradually increase time spent with his mother. For this to be at all possible, I would have worked with mother and paternal grandmother to call a truce and try to recognize their respective roles as being complementary rather than combative. To do this, I would have needed to allow each of them to air their grievances toward the other and express their fears both about fusing and losing. I would hope we would get to a place that moved beyond splitting and projections to a place of forgiving and gratitude, with enough room for everyone's ambivalent feelings. While all this was going on, I would work with David to negotiate his own experiences of fusing and losing and to develop an internal world that would have room enough for two mothers—the mother who bore him and came back to him and the mother who found him and raised him. I would understand that this would probably be a slow process, most likely occurring over several years. I would be able to think about David in this way because of the lessons learned in CPP regarding the parenting matrix, fusing and losing, leaving room for ambivalence, and recognizing change as evolutionary.

CONCLUSION

This chapter concludes with the wisdom we have learned from working in CPP. The challenge of holding all of the many participants in the parenting matrix in our head—with all of the issues of fusing and losing, splitting and ambivalence, transformation and evolution, and overall impermanence—while juggling treatment of a child at the same time makes it very hard to do the work as a solo practitioner. We have discovered that our weekly consultation groups, in which we can share our successes, failures, and foibles, are invaluable in moving the work forward for the therapist, the child, the foster parents, and the birth parents. Nowhere is it clearer than in our work with foster children that when it comes to helping children grow, it takes a village.

REFERENCES

Ehrensaft, D. (1997). *Spoiling childhood: How well-meaning parents are giving children too much, but not what they need.* New York: The Guilford Press.

Heineman, T. (1999). In search of the romantic family: Unconscious contributions to problems in foster and adoptive placement. *Journal for the Psychoanalysis of Culture and Society, 4,* 250–264.

Roche, T. (2000, November 13). The crisis of foster care. *Time,* 79–82.

Winnicott, D.W. (1960). The theory of the parent–infant relationship. In *The maturational processes and the facilitating environment* (pp. 37–55). Madison, CT: International Universities Press.

CHAPTER 10

Beyond the Comfortable Edge

The Experience of Being a
Therapist for Foster Children

Richard Ruth

Ilike watching cop shows. I think it is because in the therapy work that I do every day, I see a part of the world most people never see (or, maybe more accurately, never know or admit to themselves that they see). I like the acknowledgment, coming to me through the airwaves, that what I see in my work is real. In their own odd way, cop shows help me settle and help me think.

Other authors in this book have written about what happens in therapy with foster children, their families, and the communities and systems involved with them. Their ideas are accurate and very important, and their experiences are very moving. Yet, as a therapist and a psychoanalyst, what keeps me sharp and useful begins with listening for what goes unsaid, what lies beyond the known and comfortable edge. When I read over this book's outline and wondered what contribution I might make, I realized that the most difficult and interesting edge of my experience (spanning almost 30 years of work with foster children) has involved listening for what it has been like inside me. In writing about this issue, my aspiration is to be like a good cop show—to tell some of my stories in a way that might help readers think differently about some of aspects of their own experiences.

THE INTERNAL EXPERIENCE OF BEING A
THERAPIST WORKING WITH FOSTER CHILDREN

Some people think that psychoanalysts work with rich individuals whose problems are of their own making and not all that serious. As with many stereotypes, this perception is not as inaccurate as analysts might wish. It is true that Freud discovered the psychoanalytic approach to therapy in his attempt to help affluent women who had lost important parts of their emotional selves in privileged but stifling, and abusive, settings. Yet soon into his work, Freud began thinking actively about how his insights might well be useful to dispossessed people. While on a vacation, Freud spoke with a boy who worked on a farm and had some problems, and Freud found he was able to be of significant help to the boy (Freud, 1955/1919). Some of his early disciples became intimately involved in work with delinquent youth from poor backgrounds (see Altman, 1995, for a thorough discussion). What seems obvious and foundational to therapists' work with children today—that children have meaningful conflicts and feelings and thoughts of their own—was Freud's radical discovery.

Fast forward to the early 1970s. Immersion in the activism of the 1960s led me to graduate school in clinical psychology. Like everyone in my graduate school class, I was idealistic and wanted to help people; however, as the only bilingual/bicultural person in the class, I defined *people* differently than most of my classmates. Early in my professional development, I became interested in working with people with whom others did not want to work, especially those whom people in authority had declared beyond the reach of psychotherapy. The initial unconscious motivation was not difficult to draw out in my personal analysis—if those people were beyond reach, then so was I.

Initially, this led to a highly uneasy relationship with the psychoanalytic theories and approaches that I was being taught. They seemed a bit off target, if not irrelevant or harmful, to the community that I was living in and wanted to serve.

However, over several years, I began to appreciate that the open-ended, in-depth search for meaning in subjective experience offered by psychoanalytic approaches made a lot of sense to me and to my clients. Something about being listened to in that way was healing, and it led me to a less ambivalent embrace of psychoanalytic psychotherapy. Along the way, I learned that other socially minded and socially committed people had traveled similar journeys (Altman, 1995; Jacoby, 1983; Langer, 1989)—not that my teachers had even hinted of that in graduate school, except for one professor, who got fired for his openness and courage.

However, there was a tension in my developing professional identity. On the one hand, I was a developing psychotherapist/psychoanalyst like any other, with a range of clients. On the other hand, I was seeing some clients, including several foster children, who were very different from the kinds of clients my peers were seeing, and I did not know how (or even whether) to think about that.

I first worked with a foster child when I was an extern. I could say that I *accepted* the child as a client, using the traditional language of therapists, but that would be only partly honest—externs do not get to select their clients, and I did not select him. However, I knew he had a highly disrupted life; I did not reject him, and I met him with an open mind and an open heart. Perhaps because of that, I liked working with him, and he liked working with me. That was as far as my conscious thinking went, at that early point in my development, and it seemed to be enough—to everyone except my supervisor at the time, who was somehow suspicious of me because a client who was not supposed to be able to get better was getting better. My client became less angry, did better in school, and did not annoy his foster mother so much. Feeling good about the experience—and seething and feeling covertly defiant because my supervisor kept implying I was somehow at fault for feeling good about it—I was open to seeing other foster children. The clinics where I worked, as an intern and then as a junior psychologist, were eager to give me more than my share. This was done not to teach me anything about the foster care system or the inner lives of foster children—except for one beloved supervisor, to whom I am enduringly grateful, there was no such teaching—but to give me plenty of cases. The clinics had far too many children who needed to be seen.

Conscious understandings, however, are deceptive. It took me longer to understand what attracted me to this work. Part of me identified with, and in turn felt the most intimately connected with and the most useful to, my clients in foster care because I had also been cut adrift from my natural home and therefore was still, in some ways, a foster child. As a young child, I moved from a housing project, where I felt more or less comfortable, to a middle-class suburb, where I did not. At the point in my professional development about which I have been writing, I was doing therapy almost completely in Spanish—a comfortable fit for me—in clinics where I had almost no Spanish-speaking colleagues—a very uncomfortable fit. I was going home every day after work to an urban neighborhood where I felt at home but where the professionals with whom I worked did not. My identifications would whipsaw back and forth, between a personal identity that I held onto inside me and an evolving professional identity that I wore like poorly fitting clothes. I have subsequently come to know that many foster children have similar, but much more intense, kinds of fragmentation and conflict around issues of identity.

This sharpened for me, one day out of the blue, in a supervision experience. I was supervising a Caucasian therapist from a privileged background, who was doing a psychological evaluation of a foster child. She was smart and had substantial depth, but her work in the case we were discussing seemed hollow, out of tune, and dismissive of the child. She began speaking in a way that put down the child, and I called her on it—in hindsight, in a tone that was too harsh to be helpful. She became quite upset, and I felt angry at her for being upset. Only in reflection did I realize I was angry with her because I felt she was dismissing me, because I was too much like her client for her to be comfortable in the presence of either of us.

This personal discovery was both disquieting and freeing, but it is not simply a personal discovery. Many therapists (and many people who are not therapists but are involved with foster children) have similar elements in their inner experience—or need to find them. Perhaps these parts are necessary to the vocation of a truly empathic and effective therapist, as Coltart (1992, 1996) has argued, and never more than in work with foster children.

The edge of my experience has involved trying to integrate my work as a therapist with foster children into my identity—something more involved in who I am than in what I do, something that I want to do more than something I long ago fell into. It has been interesting, for example, to feel that I am part of the child welfare system, at home with colleagues who are judges and lawyers and social workers, and not some kind of professional "tourist." This aspect of my experience is still evolving, but I value it and the communities in which it offers me membership.

BEING SEEN AS A THERAPIST
WORKING WITH FOSTER CHILDREN

One line of my career's story is that the systems I thought I would work in forever have collapsed around me, one after another. When an agency where I had spent several fulfilling years began to feel unbearable, I began a private practice—mostly as a way to have space and autonomy to do the kind of work I wanted to do, although I was not averse to fantasies that my income might rise as well.

When I started my private practice, I was at a point in my professional development where I was beginning to be seen as someone senior. I had some involvement in teaching and supervision. I had substantial experience in community mental health work, especially with traumatized children—something a recognizable minority of psychoanalysts have long embraced (Altman, 1995; Heineman, 1998). I hoped that my private practice might extend my experience in new and interesting directions, without losing my roots; thus, I hoped to attract a variety of clients, including a majority who would pay me the fees that other private practitioners in my area were charging and that I believed I merited.

A pattern developed that at first I found gratifying and then found problematic. Colleagues began referring difficult cases, often involving clients who could not afford a full fee. I needed to fill hours and was interested in and not afraid of complexity. I welcomed the referrals; callers often stroked my ego, telling me these were cases few other were willing or able to treat. I did not hear the edge—that these were cases most of my colleagues *did not want* to treat.

As my practice began to fill up, it started dawning on me that colleagues were holding back from referring patients who could pay my fees. I had become negatively identified with my clients' privations. My willingness to work with traumatized foster children seemed to be generating a perception among colleagues that I was somehow "less than," someone to be held at a distance, treated differently, set off—like a foster child. So my struggles with identity, as with the similar but more life-and-death struggles of foster children, seemed not to remain purely internal after all.

It is possible to talk about this with the benefit of reflection and perspective, but it was enraging and very difficult, as well as quite powerful, to realize that I was being treated like a foster child. In talking about it, my purpose is not to vent feelings or recriminate but to try to draw out similar experiences of other therapists who work with foster children. Sharply etched lines divide the psychotherapy community: public-sector and private practitioners, well-paid and poorly paid therapists, people with thriving practices and people who struggle to make a living, people who are effective in their work and people who fall into routines that cause them not to be productive with their clients. Too much of the field's professional literature is written for those on the privileged side of these divides and not enough for those on the underprivileged side—or for those who, like me and other therapists working in the Children's Psychotherapy Project (CPP), straddle the various psychotherapy worlds.

I do not believe that these dynamics of advantage and disadvantage in psychotherapy are the product of external, market forces alone, but rather that they have something to do with things that go on, things that are difficult to think about, in the inner lives of therapists. To write about these things entails a risk, not necessarily intentional or desired, of public disclosure, challenging conventions, and taking professional risks. Yet, such a realization is an entry-way into my point.

I do not subscribe to "identity politics"; I think the concept is simplistic. Yet, I do think that who we are, how we think about who we are, and how we act out our values and identities, based on this kind of hard-won self-knowledge, affect what happens to us to a large extent. My experience of being treated like a professional "foster child" has resonated with my experiences being bilingual, being bicultural, and having been economically disadvantaged as a child, as well as with other ways that my life has taken a different course from the mainstream.

For example, a well-respected tutor, someone I would value getting to know, called to ask if I would evaluate a foster child attending a well-endowed, independent school. The tutor began by praising my reputation, in particular my reputation as someone who "knew Latino issues." He was looking for a thorough evaluation of a foster child, whom he had been tutoring but who did not seem to be improving in his schoolwork. The school was paying his hourly fee for the tutoring, which I knew from the grapevine to be not too distant from my hourly fee for therapy. The tutor wanted me to see the student because I spoke Spanish.

I asked the tutor if he spoke Spanish, assuming that if the child needed a Spanish-speaking psychologist, he probably also needed a Spanish-speaking tutor. In hindsight, I also was probably a bit excited that I may have found a professional "buddy." With an uncomfortable tone in his voice—notes of hurt and confusion—he responded that he did not and that the child did not seem anything less than fluent in English. Sensing I was already in trouble, I did not ask what I wanted to ask—and what perhaps my caller was in the moment beginning to think about—which was how he knew, or whether he knew, if his client was indeed fluent in English and, if the child was, why he needed a Spanish-speaking evaluator.

The conversation then changed, and the tutor went on to explain in a more soothing tone that he needed me to see this child for free, as the school had used up all its available resources for this student by providing the tutoring. The soothing tone vanished when I attempted to explain I did not have an opening for a pro bono patient in the near future. I wondered but did not inquire about why I was being asked to work for free when he was being paid.

Based on working through experiences such as this one, I began to again reframe my area of expertise with foster children *as* an area of expertise and to set different kinds of demands about what I would do, under what circumstances, and for what kinds of fees. This has led some colleagues to see me as hostile or dangerous instead of vulnerable—in a way that identifies with another aspect of how foster children are seen.

Beyond the lesson of learning to manage myself in emotionally charged circumstances that touch on issues of identity, I have also learned from this line of experience the path to its undoing. I come back to my enjoyment of cop shows—in this instance, as someone who has had something of an underdog life and identity, I nevertheless identify with police officers, at least their good sides. The deeper I get into work with foster children, the more new and different referral sources seek my expertise, which they value and find ways to compensate. The clearer I am about how I see myself, the more I find that others look at me in more satisfying ways. The parallel to what therapists at CPP hope to achieve for the foster children we treat is compelling.

THEORETICAL IMPLICATIONS FOR THERAPY

It is often said that many foster children have part–object modes of experience (Boston & Szur, 1990)—that is, that they see people and experience events as only part of who and what they are, as black and white and oversimplified, not as ambiguous, gradated, and complex. This happens, these theorists state, because these foster children internalize potent experiences of deprivation, abandonment, traumatization, repeated rejection, lack of attention and misunderstanding. Like all individuals, they are in process, but they are different in outcome; they think the world is more or less as they have experienced it to behave. It also seems to be true, as Terr (1990) wrote, that external, traumatic events shape the experience of foster children as much as the workings of their psyches. As both these positions seem to be true, many therapists assume they are complementary. Yet, they are in tension, and the tension seems to matter.

Therapy with foster children based on the internalization-of-experience perspective focuses logically on certain elements:

- A safe and reliable therapeutic "frame," meaning regular times, boundaries, and rules for what is allowed to happen in meetings with the therapist (Langs, 1976, 1979)

- The therapist holding safely and bearing without judgmental reaction what the child puts out in the sessions and, metaphorically, puts into the therapist by means of misperceptions and misattributions (containment) (Bion, 1962)

- The therapist digesting inside him- or herself what the child cannot yet digest, as a way to helping the child begin to digest what he or she has lived through (metabolization) (Klein, 1986/1935, 1986/1940)

- Collaborating with the child to make meaning of the child's experience of the therapist and what happens in the therapy

- The therapist's interpretations of the unconscious content of what the child says and does

Therapists are encouraged to resist pressures to achieve quick behavioral change, or to focus directly on behavioral change very much if at all, and to keep to fairly classical models of psychoanalytic psychotherapy. Much of my experience working in therapy with foster children has been shaped and guided by this perspective. It is has been undeniably helpful to many children and has served me as a useful starting and reference point.

Yet, to be a foster child is much more often like being caught up in a cop show: The plot never stops twisting, and the good guys lose in the end. Many, if not most, foster children experience chronic retraumatization, which is caused both by what is done to them and by their internal psychological processes. Many foster children trigger powerful reactions in others, more because of who they are and what they embody than because of what they do. Placements change abruptly, for reasons foster children cannot fathom; valued possessions, relationships, and even memories are treated shoddily by professionals with excellent intentions but too many responsibilities and not enough resources or time, and are often lost or destroyed (Heineman, 1998; Solnit, Nordhaus, & Lord, 1992).

Such experiences show that perhaps what therapists do needs to shift as well. Perhaps there is a therapeutic way of intervening with not just individual children but also whole systems and in roles of evaluators and advocates as well as, or as part of, being therapists.

I am *not* talking here case management and multisystemic approaches, which generally do not include psychotherapy that is long term, child focused, empathy and relationship oriented (rather than behavior oriented), and conducted for as long as it takes. Instead, many case management and multisystemic approaches end up substituting whole-system interventions, evaluation, and advocacy for psychotherapy (Boston & Szur, 1990; Coffey, 2004). Nor am I talking about the kinds of limited adjunctive work that go along with traditional child psychotherapy (Arnold, 1976). Rather, I am talking about the value of committed therapists opening themselves to difficult but potentially exciting and useful decisions about how they will work and specifically to possibilities of combining powerful, intensive, child-focused work with more systemic interventions woven together into the fabric of workable therapies of a new kind. Many of the other writers in this book have described such work.

I will add my voice to this chorus by mentioning a recent experience. I work with a boy in kinship foster placement. His caregiver seems to have good intentions and more challenges in life than she can handle; there are too many loose ends, and things go undone. The county agency that has placed the child is no longer able to provide the supports to foster families (e.g., parent aides, regular transportation assistance) that used to help in such circumstances. Its budget has been cut too deep and too hard. As a result, despite assurances that this child would come every week without fail, there have been many missed sessions. Everyone (including the child and I) was trying his or her best and failing.

My client experienced this with no distortion. It was the reenactment of his initial parental abandonment, in scarcely attenuated form, each and every time, over and over again. He was hurt and angry, at me and at the world and everyone else who lives in it—except for the parents who abused and neglected him. They are not around for him to be angry with, so he idealizes them in fantasy.

Early in the therapy, I was tempted to call a halt. Undeniably, the therapy was hurting the client more than helping him. I was feeling incompetent, ashamed, and belittled, just like my client. Minimum traditional conditions for therapeutic success were not being met.

I was fortunate to be able to discuss the case with my colleagues in CPP, and I want to focus on how that changed something inside me. My colleagues helped me see how powerfully my client was reacting to the initial sessions and to see the hope in that. They encouraged me to see what I could do to meet some of the foster mother's needs, by "feeding" her metaphorically—that is, giving her some attention and some perspectives that could sustain her when I spoke with her. I felt differently and began to think about what I might do with a few more degrees of creative freedom. I began to fight to continue the therapy rather than to end it or, by my passivity, to allow it to find its own end.

Two things changed in short order. First, the foster mother mobilized her whole family system to work together to bring the child to sessions. One week, her elderly mother brought the child, beaming with her accomplishment as she sat in my waiting room without taking off her hat or coat, seemingly indicating that she felt the occasion was special. Another week, a young adult uncle brought him. The uncle initially seemed uncomfortable speaking with a professional of a different ethnicity and was pleasantly shocked when I offered him my hand in gratitude.

The second change was that, out of the corner of my eye, I saw the child watching these scenes and, in turn, beginning to feel comfortable and welcome in my office. My place was becoming his place and was starting to feel like a good place, one with more possibilities than problems. This, it seemed, was the fulcrum in my client; it extended from him to his foster family, around which events began to take a more hopeful turn, and it paralleled a fulcrum process in my own internal experience.

CONCLUSION

Having CPP as a professional home—quite different from the alone space or vague professional networks that more often guide professional thinking and development for therapists—has changed my experience of, and thus my thinking about, how to work with foster children and the systems that are the context for their lives. For me, the experience of having a CPP chapter as a professional place of connection has felt as close as I can imagine to what it might be like for a foster child—or at least the foster child part of me—to finally come home.

REFERENCES

Altman, N. (1995). *The analyst in the inner city: Race, class, and culture through a psychoanalytic lens.* Hillsdale, NJ: The Analytic Press.

Arnold, L.E. (Ed.). (1976). *Helping parents help their children.* New York: Brunner/ Mazel.

Bion, W. (1962). A theory of thinking. *International Journal of Psycho-Analysis, 42,* 306–310.

Boston, M., & Szur, R. (Eds.). (1990). *Psychotherapy with severely deprived children.* London: Maresfield Library.

Coffey, E.P. (2004). The heart of the matter 2: Integration of ecosystemic family theory practices with systems of care mental health services for children and families. *Family Process, 43,* 161–173.

Coltart, N. (1992). *Slouching toward Bethlehem.* New York: The Guilford Press.

Coltart, N. (1996). *The baby and the bathwater.* Madison, CT: International Universities Press.

Freud, S. (1955/1919). Lines of advance in psychoanalytic therapy. *Standard Edition, 17,* 157–168.

Heineman, T.V. (1998). *The abused child: Psychoanalytic understanding and treatment.* New York: The Guilford Press.

Jacoby, R. (1983). *The repression of psychoanalysis.* New York: Basic Books.

Klein, M. (1986/1935). A contribution to the psychogenesis of manic-depressive states. In J. Mitchell (Ed.), *The selected Melanie Klein* (pp. 115–143). London: Penguin.

Klein, M. (1986/1940). Mourning and its relations to manic-depressive states. In J. Mitchell (Ed.), *The selected Melanie Klein* (pp. 146–174). London: Penguin.

Langer, M. (1989). *From Vienna to Managua.* London: Free Association Press.

Langs, R. (1976). *The bipersonal field.* Lanham, MD: Jason Aronson.

Langs, R. (1979). *The therapeutic environment.* Lanham, MD: Jason Aronson.

Solnit, A., Nordhaus, B., & Lord, R. (1992). *When home is no haven: Child placement issues.* New Haven, CT: Yale University Press.

Terr, L. (1990). *Too scared to cry: Psychic trauma in childhood.* New York: Harper & Row.

Clinical Moments

Case Studies for Exploration and Discussion

The clinicians in the Children's Psychotherapy Project (CPP) have all benefited enormously from hearing each other's work and thinking through clinical moments with one another. We would now like to afford you the same opportunity: to read vignettes from our therapy with the children and think about what you might have done in a similar situation or what insights come to you about the child, the family, the therapist, the clinical work, the social context, and the intersection among all these forces in each of the following case studies.

We have chosen case material to represent the full developmental spectrum of children and youth in foster care—from infancy to early adulthood. We have also highlighted core issues that appear again and again in our work with our young clients: attachment and bonding, developmental disruptions, neglect and abuse, resiliency, reunification, the healing force of foster care, and the negative impact of foster care.

After each case study we have provided study questions to promote further exploration and discussion of clinical work with children in foster care, informed by the common themes that run through the chapters in this volume. When mental health professionals begin their training, their work deepens and grows as they continually practice answering the key question about interventions with their clients: "Why am I doing what I am doing when I do it?" This is a question we never stop asking, and we invite you to apply it to each of the five case studies, addressing both the therapist and yourself if you were to imagine yourself in the same situation: "What would I do? Why would I do it? Why would I do it at that moment?"

Infant–Parent Psychotherapy

Barbara Reed McCarroll

This clinical vignette illustrates the challenges encountered by one infant, Lilly, and her family as they navigated the disruptions of separation, foster care, and reunification. Interruptions of attachment are particularly significant during infancy and early childhood, when healthy brain development relies on consistent, contingent caregiving. This narrative describes an infant's extraordinary attempts to survive the multiple breaking of primary bonds and the efforts of a family to reconnect.

LILLY'S FAMILY HISTORY

Lilly's parents, Jill and Mark, had extensive histories of homelessness, drug and alcohol dependence, and drug-related incarcerations. Each of their children from previous relationships experienced removal from the home by child protective services and placement in foster care due to severe neglect. Two of the older children had drug-related problems and had spent time in juvenile hall.

Mark was incarcerated at the time of Lilly's birth and when released from jail was sent to a residential recovery program for men. At birth, Lilly tested positive for methamphetamines and was removed from Jill's care at age 2 days. She was returned to her mother 2 weeks later, and Jill was ordered by the court to participate in a substance recovery program. Following relapses in her mother's recovery, Lilly was removed from her mother's care. Each time she was returned to Jill from foster care homes. By her first birthday Lilly had experienced five disruptions of primary caregiving and safe havens were few.

TRANSITION TO CHILD CARE

When Lilly was 9 months old and in her third foster home, Jill rejoined her drug treatment program as a condition of reunification. Two months later, Lilly was enrolled in a therapeutic child care center staffed by teachers, a psychologist, a psychiatrist, and a special education teacher. The center was designed to provide child care for young children whose parents' substance abuse and other psychological disorders made them vulnerable to attachment and mental health disorders. The therapeutic program had a preventive focus that included assessment of all developmental domains and treatment when concerns emerged.

Prior to attending the therapeutic center, 11-month-old Lilly was visited in her fost-adopt home by me, the psychologist. She seemed to have an emotional connection with her foster mother, Sarah, who had cared for Lilly for 2 months. Lilly seemed curious about me as the visitor, crawled to a nearby table, and cautiously initiated a game of tapping on the table. Sad, weak smiles were Lilly's responses to reciprocal tapping. It was evident that the infant was capable of attending to her world and interacting purposefully. However, her affect was constricted, and there seemed to be minimal energy and pleasure during exchanges. Throughout the visit, Lilly was silent and she frequently made eye contact with Sarah. Her foster mother gently supported Lilly's mild curiosity about me and was warm in her responses to the infant's soundless bids for reassurance.

During daily activities at the child care center, Lilly was found to have difficulty remaining calm and attentive during exchanges with caregivers and peers. When calm, she was able to engage in Peekaboo and other games, to which she responded slowly and with her characteristic sad smile that did not reach her eyes. Exchanges were brief and often lacked vitality. In addition, her appetite was poor and her sleeping patterns included frantic flailing when falling asleep and frequent sleep disruptions.

Prior to walking, Lilly's activity range was narrow. She was regularly seen sitting and observing her peers and caregivers, and she frequently aborted attempts to initiate interaction. When she became ambulatory, Lilly often toddled aimlessly, making quiet whimpering sounds. She tended to wander from toy to toy without showing interest for more than 15 seconds. When Lilly made bids for attention, she waited for a response and then quickly ran away.

Lilly's emotional capacities were found to be at age level, but her affect was generally constricted and her ability to be intentional and reciprocal was vulnerable to stress. Her overall development was screened at 2-month intervals using the Ages and Stages Questionnaires® (ASQ; Bricker & Squires, 1999). Lilly was repeatedly found to be at age level in the cognitive, communication, gross motor, fine motor, and personal-social skills domains. Sarah completed the Preventive Ounce Temperament Questionnaires (Cameron & Rice, 1999), and the results suggested that she thought of Lilly as being easily frustrated and slow in adapting to changes and novelty.

FAMILY REUNIFICATION

After 2 weeks at the therapeutic center, Jill began having unsupervised biweekly visits with Lilly. Initially Lilly seemed confused and somewhat fearful as she clung to caregivers and avoided looking at Jill. Throughout the 2 months of gradual reunification, routines and connections were regularly interrupted and Lilly seemed chronically stressed by the changes thrust on her. She needed considerable support to regulate herself to a calm state.

Eventually, during visits with Jill, Lilly began toddling in circles and exhibiting clowning behaviors that engaged and enlivened her mother. Jill was frequently distracted and often jokingly criticized her child's attempts to gain attention. The toddler worked diligently to be the focus of her mother's attention. Lilly's behavior with Jill was contradictory, as the infant sometimes avoided her mother and at other times frantically demanded to be held. Jill's efforts were often intrusive and lacked empathy. She seemed to be uncertain about how to interact with her daughter and perhaps did not understand how to begin to repair the relationship.

Jill tended to speak in a sad, pressured voice and focused on her own challenges with housing and economics and her wish to reunite with Mark. She was more appropriate in her interactions with Lilly's peers and was more of a spectator than a participant with her daughter. Jill frequently spoke about having failed Lilly and her fears of making mistakes again.

As Jill's visits with Lilly commenced, weekly visitation with Mark was initiated. Lilly and her mother were transported to Mark's residential treatment facility, and Jill reported that the encounters were successful. Within a month, Mark returned to live with Jill and began to participate in a local day treatment program.

During visits with his daughter at the therapeutic center, Mark's calm demeanor and his capacity to follow Lilly's lead seemed to engage and soothe the toddler. Mark was able to pause and allow Lilly to respond to his overtures. His visits included time with Lilly outside in the yard, where the toddler was often observed leading Mark around the path and looking over her shoulder at her father with smiles and quiet giggles. Father and daughter seemed to enjoy their outdoor ritual of shuffling back and forth along the pathways. Lilly began to brighten during the visits with Mark, and there was noticeable joy growing between them as they shared attention and experience.

Jill seemed overwhelmed by her own emotions and unable to soothe her daughter. Lilly appeared to be burdened by the dramas of her mother and her fost-adopt family, and the adults seemed paralyzed by their own disorganized states. Jill expressed fear that Mark would relapse, and she talked about her difficulty managing her feelings of guilt regarding Lilly and the older children. An older son had recently been incarcerated in juvenile hall, and Jill blamed a variety of agencies that she believed were impeding the family's progress. The blaming was often preceded by expressions of guilt. In addition to coping with her relationships with her children, Jill frequently spoke of the challenges of managing withdrawal, relapses, and attempts to incorporate new behaviors.

Sarah's family coped with the grief of losing Lilly. The family of five had hoped that Lilly would join them permanently. Although Sarah was appropriate in her support of Lilly's reunification, her affect revealed the sadness that was present. Following reunification, Sarah and her children continued to visit Lilly until Jill reported that Lilly was confused by the visits. One month following reunification, Jill suggested that it was in Lilly's best interest to terminate the visits with Sarah's family.

DIAGNOSTIC IMPRESSIONS

The Diagnostic Classification of Mental Health and Developmental Disorders of Infancy and Early Childhood (DC: 0-3; ZERO TO THREE Diagnostic Classification Task Force, 1994) guided the consideration of a

diagnosis for Lilly. I found that she met the criteria for a prolonged be-
reavement reaction. She exhibited emotional withdrawal that included
lethargy, a predominantly sad facial expression, and low interest in age-
appropriate activities. In addition, Lilly's sleeping was frequently disturbed.

DC: 0-3 Axis II addresses the characteristics of the parent–infant relationship. Behavioral interaction, affective tone, and psychological involvement are considered when making a diagnosis. In addition, the assignment
of a DC: 0-3 Parent–Infant Relationship Global Assessment Scale (PIR-
GAS) score of less than 40 is compatible with an Axis II diagnosis. Jill was
found to be insensitive to Lilly's cues and often misinterpreted Lilly's intentions. Affective tone within the dyad was sad and constricted. These elements are features of an uninvolved relationship. The findings for Lilly were
as follows:

- *Axis I: Primary Diagnosis*
  Mood Disorder: Prolonged Bereavement/Grief Reaction

- *Axis II: Relationship Disorder Classification*
  Underinvolved Relationship Disorder (mother)

- *Axis III: Medical and Developmental Disorders and Conditions*
  Methamphetamine and Hepatitis C exposure in utero

- *Axis IV: Psychosocial Stressors*
  Moderately severe effects of enduring stress

- *Axis V: Functional Emotional Developmental Level*
  Interactive intentionality and reciprocity (needs some structure or
  sensorimotor support to evidence capacity—otherwise manifests capacity intermittently or inconsistently; earlier levels of mutual attention
  and mutual engagement are not at age-expected forms of capacity)

- *PIR-GAS 30: Disturbed*
  Maladaptive interactions and distress in both members of dyad

THERAPEUTIC INTERVENTIONS

Lilly's mood symptoms and her chronically changing living situation required the attention of staff and family. The therapeutic team identified
interventions designed to treat Lilly's grief, foster her capacity for attach-

ment, and prevent the development of rigid maladaptive patterns. In addition, the parent–child relationship needed therapeutic intervention. Jill and Mark, who had chronic mental health issues that interfered with recovery and the capacity to parent, were referred for individual psychotherapy.

Lilly's depressed mood and associated symptoms were a primary focus of therapeutic intervention during my daily time with Lilly. In the infant classroom, I used an interactive therapeutic model that focused on Lilly's symptoms and addressed the vulnerabilities of her emotional development. A major component of treatment involved the teachers who were supported to be consistent and patient as they helped Lilly calmly attend to her world and gradually participate in back-and-forth exchanges. Predictable routines and reliable caregiving were provided by the trained staff. In addition, the staff anticipated Lilly's distress and offered soothing care. They helped her to soothe herself with her blanket when she was distressed and challenged by daily events. The familiar object had been with Lilly since birth, and Jill brought her daughter to child care wrapped in her blanket. Lilly frequently carried it around with her when tired or upset.

The therapeutic team considered areas of Lilly's emotional development that had been impeded by the multiple disruptions in her primary care. Goals for Lilly included strengthening both her ability to attend to her world and her capacity to participate in a broad repertoire of emotional exchanges with predictable caregivers. In addition, the team wanted to support her emerging efforts to initiate interactions.

The parent–child relationship was another focus of treatment and was approached utilizing an infant–parent psychotherapy model. I met with Lilly and Jill twice weekly. Initially Jill had difficulty focusing on her infant and seemed overwhelmed and unavailable for interaction. Gradually and with modeling and encouragement, she gained confidence and began to follow her daughter's lead and be reciprocal. Jill also learned to wait for Lilly to initiate and respond.

Mark was incarcerated again on drug-related charges, so he did not participate in the regular child–parent interventions. When released from jail, he visited Lilly daily and the two resumed their play rituals. He met weekly with the psychologist and began to participate in child–parent therapy.

Lilly's parents had repeatedly failed Lilly but were willing to join in therapeutic work with their daughter and to participate in their own psychotherapy. Although Jill and Mark are vulnerable to relapse, they have continued to participate in therapeutic interventions. Mother and child are beginning to experience some joyful exchanges, and both parents struggle to maintain sobriety.

Lilly's range of affect is less constricted, but the characteristic sad smile remains a common feature that conveys the enduring effects of the relationship disturbances that have marked her short life. Although Lilly suffered multiple losses during her infancy and lacked sensitive, consistent care, she gradually absorbed what was offered by caregivers who understood her vulnerability and uniqueness and were willing to wait for her gradual responses. Her energy level and interest in her world have increased, and her capacity for mutual attention and engagement has matured. Lilly also has developed strong representational capacities.

Lilly is now with a group of toddlers at the therapeutic center and spends much of her time in domestic play. She plays with peers in the play kitchen pretending to eat from toy plates, and she has been observed using a block as a phone. However, most of her attention is focused on tending to her baby dolls. She is sensitive to perceived baby doll cues, spends much of her time arranging a blanket around the dolls, and regularly puts her finger to her lips and says, "Ssh. Baby night night." She seems to enjoy being with peers, and when they are in distress she responds. Once when a peer cried, she left her lunch table to go and give him a kiss. Lilly thrives on routines and rituals at the center. She is a resilient little girl who is making gains in her challenging world.

⋙⋘

QUESTIONS

1. Lilly was removed from and returned to her mother's care five times during her first year of life. What criteria would you use if you had to decide whether Lilly should return to her mother's care or remain in foster care?

2. The therapist noted that Lilly had difficulty focusing, whether in solitary play or with a caregiver, for more than a few seconds. How might you relate this observation to Lilly's pattern of relationships?

3. Jill and Lilly are described as beginning to share some joyful moments. What, if anything, does that say about the prognosis for this mother–child relationship? What factors might influence a good or poor outcome?

REFERENCES

Bricker, D., & Squires, J. (with Mounts, L., Potter, L., Nickel, R., Twombly, E., & Farrell, J.). (1999). *Ages & Stages Questionnaires ® (ASQ): A parent-completed, child-monitoring system*, (2nd ed.). Baltimore: Paul H. Brookes Publishing Co.

Cameron, J., & Rice, D. (1999). *Cameron-Rice Temperament Questionnaires.* Retrieved April 4, 2005, from http://www.preventiveoz.org

ZERO TO THREE Diagnostic Classification Task Force. (1994). *Diagnostic Classification of Mental Health and Developmental Disorders of Infancy and Early Childhood (DC:0-3).* Washington, DC: ZERO TO THREE.

A Boy Referred for
Alleged Sexual Perpetration

Thetis Rachel Cromie

Empirical clinical research suggests there are multiple factors that contribute to the development of children who engage in problematic sexual behavior (e.g., see Araji, 1997; Friedrich, 1993, 2002; Friedrich & Luecke, 1988; Gray, Pithers, Busconi, & Houchens, 1999; Johnson, 1999). These children's families frequently manifest many markers of chronic distress, including high rates of poverty, physical and sexual abuse within the family, arrest for criminal behavior, and impaired attachment between parent and child. Many of these factors appeared to have been present in the following case, which involves a boy whom the state labeled as a sexual perpetrator at age 5. The case study describes several different challenges that I confronted as a psychodynamic psychotherapist who considered the important contexts of trauma and child development during the course of this boy's treatment.

Jerome, a 5½-year-old boy, had a 15-year-old half brother, Mark, and a 2-year-old brother, Michael. His parents were separated. Their marriage was conflicted from the start. Mr. Johnson had a history of poly-substance abuse, and the family was economically stressed due to ongoing underemployment. Both parents worked in seasonal jobs.

When Jerome was 3½ years old, he was sexually abused by Mark. When Mrs. Johnson learned about this from Jerome, she spoke to a school social worker. The social worker, a mandated reporter, called the child welfare agency hotline. The agency removed Mark from the home and placed him in a residential treatment facility for adolescent sex offenders. Jerome did not receive any psychotherapy at the time.

When Jerome was 5 years old, a relative discovered Jerome and Zina, his same-age female cousin, playing together with their clothes off. She stated that it appeared to her that Jerome had his face against Zina's bare crotch. The relative called the child welfare agency hotline, fearing that sexual perpetration had become contagious in her family. The agency removed Jerome from his parental home. The case worker wrote a protective plan for Jerome, requiring supervision at home, at school, at church, and in other situations. His name was placed on the state child and adolescent sex offender database. The agency referred Jerome to psychotherapy for child sex offender treatment.

HISTORY OF TREATMENT

Jerome entered twice weekly psychotherapy 5 months after his foster placement with relatives and 6 months after the alleged incident of sexual perpetration against Zina. Parent guidance sessions were scheduled for twice monthly. In the beginning phase of treatment, I worked to establish rapport with Jerome, his parents, and his relative foster parents. The story of Jerome's sexual perpetration was contested by his parents, who expressed considerable animus against the relative who called the hotline. Their own marital disagreements not withstanding, they were united in the opinion that they and their son were involuntary patients, coerced by an impersonal child welfare system.

Jerome appeared anxious and overstimulated at the assessment interview. Scarcely a session went by that I did not have to contain his impulses to run out of the office, to cover his face and hide under the desk, or to throw objects. He disavowed any knowledge of his sexual behavior that brought him to treatment. He covered his ears and shouted, "I'm not listening! I'm not listening!" He disavowed feeling angry, often stating that he was tricking the therapist when he threw things around the room.

In parent guidance sessions, Mr. Johnson complained that the child welfare agency intruded into the family's life. He was directed by the agency to undergo drug testing and enter a substance abuse rehabilitation program. He refused. Soon after, he withdrew from the parent guidance sessions and any involvement with his son's treatment. Mrs. Johnson remained, feeling pressured by the agency and the juvenile court to complete parenting classes and to comply with making therapy appointments for her son and herself. The court warned that no cooperation would delay Jerome's return home.

During the early sessions, I saw transferential elements in some of Jerome's kicking and throwing. On one occasion, he smashed a doll against a chair and grinned. He said this is what he did with his younger brother's toys. He noted that his brother was sitting in the waiting room alone with their mother. Jerome commented that things were bad for him because he had to live with his relatives, but not as bad as they were for Mark, who had to live with strangers in the residential program. Jerome felt exiled like his older half brother; he felt his younger brother had their mother all to himself. He also felt angry with his mother who, in his mind, had messed a good thing up by having baby Michael. The therapist learned that Mark had abused Jerome at the time Mrs. Johnson was pregnant with Michael. Perhaps Jerome felt like a little prince, dethroned by his younger brother, much as Mark may have years before.

During the first 5 months of treatment, Jerome brought a well-worn plastic suitcase to his sessions. He pointed out to me that it had many pockets and places to hide things. I thought about the suitcase as a representation of Jerome's self, with many parts concealed from both himself and his therapist. Twice a week, he used the suitcase to bring something to his session. He regretted that many of the things he liked were lost in the messy garage at home. I thought about Jerome with his suitcase as a kind of displaced refugee, expelled from home because of the allegation of sexual perpetration. My office became a psychological home for him. Jerome asked for stickers, pencils, rubber bands, paper, and paper clips to take with him when he left the sessions. These objects became a way for him to remember his relationship with me and to assure his anxious self that our relationship was ongoing.

As I got to know Mrs. Johnson better in scheduled parent guidance sessions, I observed that although Mrs. Johnson deeply loved her son, she seemed to lack a genuine interest in his needs and uniqueness. It was hard for Mrs. Johnson to think about Jerome's psychological world on a consistent basis. At times she appeared to understand the impact of the family disruptions and losses on her son. At other times, she was no longer in touch with that reality, stating that she had to get over things in her life, and so did Jerome. Her lack of genuine interest in him was evident on one occasion when she took him with her to her friend's house. While talking with her friend, she let Jerome go upstairs with her friend's son. Soon enough, both boys were running around with their shorts off. Her friend, aware that Jerome was labeled a sexual perpetrator, wondered if he had abused her son. She called the child welfare agency. As a result, Jerome lost his twice weekly overnight visits with his mother and brother for several months. Mrs. Johnson was angry. Determined to supervise her son better in the future, she removed all of the bedroom and bathroom doors in her house. She told me she had long ago begun to have both Jerome and Michael sleep with her during overnights so she could ensure that nothing happened between them. When I raised the issue of personal boundaries, Mrs. Johnson was angry. She viewed her behavior as evidence of maternal care. I could scarcely raise an issue without Mrs. Johnson becoming upset and unable to think through the problem. The parent guidance sessions were often most comfortable for Mrs. Johnson when I gave her written material to read on subjects such as parenting, discipline, and children's behavior problems.

After 6 months, Jerome was calmer and could end his therapy sessions without becoming disruptive. The middle phase of treatment began when he stopped bringing his suitcase and started bringing more of his own self to the sessions. It took a while for Jerome to feel that I was genuinely interested in him, in how he felt, and in what concerned him.

During the 2½-year period when Jerome received treatment, he lived in one relative foster placement. His mother had liberal visiting hours in addition to Jerome's overnight visits at her home. Living with his relatives, Jerome experienced more predictability and regulation than in his own home. However, his relatives were often worried about his distractibility at school, his problems organizing his school material, and his difficulty with completing class assignments. They worked with Jerome's teacher and me to structure his school experience. The relative foster parents were also confused about what was usual and unusual sexual behavior for the child. When one of the foster parents discovered Jerome in the bathroom masturbating, he scolded Jerome and called me and the agency. I tried to reassure the foster parent, saying that Jerome's behavior did not appear compulsive and took place in the privacy of the bathroom. The foster parent, a devoutly religious and conservative man, was not convinced. Jerome used his next session to play out the scene on the toilet. He used a Bart Simpson doll to say, "Can I have a little privacy please?" I supported Bart's request as a reasonable one. Jerome described Bart as Frankenstein. He began to throw pieces of crayon around the room and said, "Bart doesn't want to be Frankenstein anymore." I told Jerome that I had spoken with foster parents and told them that Jerome was not a bad boy because he had masturbated in the bathroom. Jerome appeared calmed by my words.

In my view, Jerome's sexualized behavior was related to the over-stimulating environment that surrounded him. This included his older brother's sexual behavior toward him as well as his mother's failure to es-tablish appropriate physical and emotional boundaries that could have helped Jerome manage his own intense feelings.

In his sessions, Jerome slowly felt more confident in me and the rela-tionship developing between us. Jerome wanted me to sit next to him and to draw pictures with him but not to draw the same thing. He wanted me to color with him but was concerned that we used different colors. I be-lieved that this behavior indicated Jerome's growing sense of autonomy. The increase in autonomy was also expressed when Jerome asked me how long a second and a minute were. He tolerated time passing in the sessions with greater equanimity. When he came to his sessions, he decided to sign in by himself at the office manager's front desk. His wish to have something from me between sessions changed. At first, this behavior appeared to have a largely anxious and reassuring quality; later, it seemed to be more a feel-ing of connection that he had in mind.

In the middle phase of treatment, Jerome began to consolidate some of his experiences of himself. He saw himself warring between good and evil. He represented this struggle in drawings of CD covers. Sometimes he was an angel and sometimes he was a devil. He represented himself as the Mini-Me character in the Austin Powers movies, but he added the detail of biting penises. At other times he saw himself as a Frankenstein monster giving the finger and laughing. At other times he represented himself as a good boy.

An important part of the middle phase of treatment was a 45-minute apology session that was set up by the child welfare agency and involved Jerome and Mark. The meeting signaled the end of Mark's residential treat-ment as well as a possible conclusion to Jerome's. Mrs. Johnson was very much in favor of the meeting, viewing it as a reunion party after so many years of separation between her sons. She was upset that she could not be there to take pictures; however, it was important that the mother did not intrude on the meeting with her own emotional agenda. I emphasized to Mrs. Johnson the purpose of the meeting in terms of Jerome's treatment and the context of the early sexual abuse. Jerome was anxious about the meeting but wanted to go. During the meeting, Jerome and Mark had a significant emotional exchange solely in the presence of their respective therapists.

The termination phase was highly influenced by the pressures of the juvenile court. The juvenile justice system wanted a clear ending to the case, requiring a conclusion to treatment. During the six sessions, Jerome reviewed with me the reason for his coming to therapy and shared with me his experience of treatment. He also thought about the new things in his life, such as a new friendship at school. Jerome allowed me to talk in some detail about why he had come for treatment. He was able to say that he knew he came to see me because of " S-E-X." He listened as I unpacked what I believed he meant by "S-E-X." During the conclusion, Jerome did not feel the need to flee from the room with anxiety.

During the 2½ years of treatment, Jerome engaged in the one reported incident of sexualized behavior, which occurred at the beginning of treatment. No sexualized behavior toward other children occurred during the remaining course of treatment. He appeared to improve in school, develop a capacity to play by the rules, pursue his interests, and make a friend. He was able to handle himself better, feel more in charge of himself, and feel more secure about boundaries. It is important to note that Jerome was able to move through the emotionally loaded incident surrounding his masturbation in the bathroom. The feelings of shame that pressed him to hide under desks and chairs, cover his face and ears, and run out of the office in the beginning of treatment diminished.

◈◈

QUESTIONS

1. Jerome was sexually abused at the age of 3 but not referred for treatment. If he had been referred at that time, would you expect to see any

particular themes in his play? What themes would you expect and how would you locate them in the context of his individual development and family situation?

2. Jerome was identified by the state child welfare agency as a sexual perpetrator at the age of 5 ½. In what ways, if any, would your clinical knowledge of trauma and child development inform your diagnosis and treatment of this child?

3. The therapist understood the suitcase that Jerome brought to his early therapy sessions as a representation of himself. How would you think about the suitcase, and how would you approach your understanding with Jerome?

REFERENCES

Araji, S. (1997). *Sexually aggressive children: Coming to understand them.* Thousand Oaks, CA: Sage Publications.

Friedrich, W.N. (1993). Sexual victimization and sexual behavior in children: A review of the recent literature. *Child Abuse and Neglect, 17,* 59–66.

Friedrich, W.N. (2002). *Psychological assessment of sexually abused children and their families.* Thousand Oaks, CA: Sage Publications.

Friedrich, W.N., & Luecke, W.J. (1988). Young school-age sexually aggressive children. *Professional Psychology Research and Practice, 19*(2), 155–163.

Gray, A.S., Pithers, W.D., Busconi, A., & Houchens, P. (1999). Developmental and etiological characteristics of children with sexual behavior problems: Treatment implications. *Child Abuse and Neglect, 23*(6), 601–621.

Johnson, T.C. (1999). The development of sexual behavior problems in childhood. In J.A. Shaw (Ed.) *Sexual aggression* (pp. 41–74). Washington, DC: American Psychiatric Association.

Therapy in the Process of Reunification

Susan R. Bernstein

My work with Darlene, an 11-year-old African American girl, began as her previous therapist was preparing to depart for maternity leave. This disappearance would be yet another in a long series of losses for this "diamond in the rough," as Darlene's foster mother affectionately called her. Exposed to drugs in utero and born prematurely, Darlene was initially removed from her biological mother and placed with her biological father. Years later, Darlene was removed from her biological father due to his extensive drug use, neglect of his children, and failure to protect Darlene from sexual abuse. He and other members of her biological family were marginally available. At the time our work together began, Darlene was graduating from elementary school and leaving her much-beloved school counselor of 5 years. In addition, Darlene was struggling to settle in with her relatively new foster mother.

Darlene's frightening and unpredictable early childhood constantly affected her, as manifested in her daily interactions. For example, a typical day at school for Darlene contained at least one visit to the school counselor. Darlene's history of failed attachments prevented her from internalizing a dependable attachment figure and from developing a secure base. Consequently, a primary goal of Darlene's long-term treatment was to develop a sense of a secure base to support Darlene in her interpersonal relationships. Embedded in this therapy was the ambiguous possibility of Darlene's reunification with her father.

Given Darlene's history, our work on forming a new attachment began with some nervousness and skepticism on both our parts. At times, Darlene would act hostile and demanding; at other times, she would abruptly withdraw. For Darlene, risking vulnerability often seemed overwhelming and unthinkable, leaving her with an all-or-nothing approach to her emotions. This presentation was likely a reflection of her mistrust of relationships as well as a simultaneous longing for connection. It was this desire for connection that allowed Darlene to push past feelings of shame and humiliation in search of emotional intimacy and understanding.

Several months into the therapy and past the initial testing period, Darlene had become better able to modulate the intimacy of the therapeutic relationship as she negotiated emotional closeness and distance. A brief vignette transpired over several weeks and continued to emerge periodically, illustrating how Darlene was confronted with the ongoing intricacies of reunification. The significance of this process encompassed more than Darlene's relationship with her father. She wrestled with a complex matrix of questions: Who do I want to live with? What happens if I leave my foster mother? Can my father really take care of me? Why didn't my grandmother take me in? What about my own mother? Where do I belong and who am I? If I move in with my father, do I lose my foster mother? Will I still see my therapist? Is my foster mother going to kick me out? Where will I be living for Christmas?

Leaving the many adults in her life to confront the legal, social, and psychological implications of the reunification process, Darlene developed her own useful metaphor in therapy. I felt honored to witness this unfolding of her unconscious that offered an uncanny depiction of her life in the foster care system. Engrossed in play therapy, Darlene created a modified game of kickball to work through the emotional complexities associated with her various attachment figures (e.g., biological father, foster mother, grandmother, therapist)—that is, her "home bases." Darlene's personalized game of kickball consisted of four bases plus home plate. After kicking the ball, Darlene connected visually with me as she strategized her run. With vigilance, she took in all the subtleties of my responses to her newly launched ball. Darlene's intensity was palpable. Every so often, the tension was lessened by a shared laugh about one of my errors. Darlene scrambled around the room, grabbing pieces of furniture that represented the bases. Making certain that she was safe on each base, as if symbolically testing different attachment figures, Darlene strove to ensure that she did not get thrown out, both literally and figuratively. In a literal sense, that meant being tagged as out and having to start over. More important, in a figurative sense it meant guaranteeing that Darlene was not suddenly pulled from anyone's care, including that of her father, foster mother, grandmother, therapist, teachers, social workers, and after-school program staff.

As the game progressed, Darlene evaded and tricked me while constantly revising the rules to assure attainment of her ultimate goal: home base. She sustained her omnipotence by transferring her sense of hopelessness and futility to me. She rushed around the bases with tension-filled excitement, and then hesitated before connecting with home plate. Wavering between the fourth base and home plate, Darlene waited for me to position myself between her and home. In that moment I appeared to embody all of her loyalty conflicts, ambivalence, and trepidation about the reunification process. Confidently, Darlene stretched her body, one hand on the couch, the other reaching for the door, also known as "home." She appeared pleased with her resilient self and the focused connection between us. She ran home and boldly shouted, "Come on, try an' get me out!"

Variations of the game evolved as Darlene and I mutually agreed on safety requirements; meanwhile, Darlene continued to randomly dictate new rules. As in Darlene's life, the rules changed frequently and unpredictably. She conveyed her experience of the world to me, leaving me confused and unable to win. No matter what obstacles I created, Darlene always devised a situation in which she got home safely. Eventually, she was able to symbolically work through some of her feelings about the reunification process via acknowledgment of me as a challenging yet surmountable obstacle. It is noteworthy to mention that this play sequence reappeared on the anniversary of Darlene's original removal from her father's care.

It was never clear who home base represented; the work mirrored Darlene's constant sorting through of the intricacies of the reunification process. The play therapy provided Darlene with a medium to express her complex and conflicting feelings about the possibility of leaving her strong, committed foster mother to live with her previously neglectful biological father. Often it was tempting to offer Darlene interpretations of the play, by linking her in-the-moment experiences with prevalent themes of reunification. However, my interpretations were usually met with hostility and a shutting down or turning inward. Direct interpretations appeared to be too confrontational for Darlene and frequently triggered a disconnection between us. Developmentally, Darlene's emotional needs and interaction style were similar to those of a toddler; she required close attention and understanding from inside her world, not the sidelines. Consequently, my ultimate role with Darlene was to play ball rather than to interpret from a distance and inflict yet another loss.

QUESTIONS

1. The therapist understood Darlene's version of kickball as an expression of her concerns about having many homes and not knowing for sure which would eventually be her "home base." Do you agree with this analysis? Why or why not?

2. The therapist says that Darlene would shut down or turn inward when she tried to connect the play with possible feelings about reunification. How would you understand this? Would you continue to try to put words to Darlene's play? Why or why not?

3. The process of reunification often causes great emotional upheaval for foster children, particularly as they approach adolescence. How would you understand the conflicts that reunification raises in an adolescent?

Resiliency in the Context of Foster Care

Michael LoGuidice

Maria entered foster care in crisis and received therapy through the Children's Psychotherapy Project (CPP) for 2½ years in her mid- and late adolescence. Looking through the lens of resiliency allows consideration of how the therapeutic process enabled Maria to mobilize and build on her strengths in order to grow.

Maria was born in a small village in Mexico. At the age of 3 years, Maria's mother and father immigrated to the United States. Maria, her sister (age 7), and her cousin (age 2) were left in the care of Maria's paternal grandmother and aunt. Maria has no conscious recollection of her parents' departure. Her earliest memories of her mother and father came from phone conversations and photographs. When Maria was about 4 or 5, her grandmother and aunt moved to the country's capital, leaving Maria, her cousin, and her sister to fend for themselves. Maria described her caregivers as "fake," visiting weekly or monthly to drop off food, dress up the children, and take photos for Maria's parents and stealing the money that Maria's parents sent for Maria, her sister, and her cousin.

Maria attended school when she wanted and did not master the fundamentals of reading or writing. Much of her language was acquired through conversation with her sister and among a largely illiterate population. Traumatized by the sudden and inadequately explained departure of her parents and the neglect of her grandmother and aunt, Maria had minimal opportunity to develop a consistent object relationship with primary caregivers.

When Maria was about 4 or 5, her aunt's husband sexually abused her. The extent and frequency of this abuse is unclear. When Maria was approximately 12 years old, her mother, Ms. Lopez, discovered that the grandmother and aunt were stealing the money she sent for the children. It was at this time that all three children immigrated to the United States. There the two sisters lived with their mother and Maria's younger brother (age 7), who Maria then met for the first time. Although Ms. Lopez was very nice to Maria for the first 2 weeks, her treatment of Maria abruptly shifted to being abusive. Maria soon assumed the responsibility of the household chores and described her mother as hating her, threatening and hitting her when she did not clean or cook correctly. One time, Ms. Lopez even threatened to kill herself in front of Maria as she brandished a hot iron. Maria was struck with an electric cord once, leaving a scar on her elbow. She was not permitted to have any friends and was repeatedly told that she was "retarded." Her mother repeatedly told Maria, "I hate you; you are the worst thing that ever happened to me."

After Maria opened up to a teacher about the abuse she was enduring at home, gears were set in motion to remedy the situation. Maria and her brother were removed from the home and placed in foster care. Maria was referred to CPP, with me as her therapist.

Maria's visits to court were traumatic. Ms. Lopez fought diligently, hiring her own lawyer to help exonerate her from the charges of abuse and maintaining false claims that Maria was a gang member, used drugs, and stayed out late. After her court appearances, Maria grew to understand that she was not going to return home nor get the mother that she desired. Nonetheless, Maria yearned for the connection with her mother that she never had. She was protective of her mother even though significant amounts of session time were dedicated to her defending herself from her mother's charges against her. As time passed, Maria became more depressed and missed her younger brother immensely. The focus of treatment was help-ing her adjust to the changes and loss.

As the therapy progressed, my role evolved from therapist to advo-cate—visiting the foster care agency and the school, making phone calls, and writing letters on Maria's behalf. My efforts yielded minimal results yet served to strengthen Maria's trust in me. As I entered deeper in her world of chaos and incompetence, Maria was able to say, "Now you under-stand how I am living."

Maria was motivated to succeed because of her mother's prediction that she would become nothing. She also wanted to be out of foster care. Maria worked on Saturdays and Sundays as a caterer and took classes to become an emergency medical technician (EMT) as part of a bridge program offered to select students. Despite the fact that the program was academically difficult for her and required that she travel 1½ hours each way to another school, her mood in the sessions following her enrollment in this program was elation; she noted, "I finally found something I like."

However, Maria was growing tired—from her physical work and from her emotional work in therapy. High school graduation was near, and her self-imposed deadline of signing out of foster care was rapidly approaching. In one session, she told me that I had no understanding of what it is like to be in foster care, that her talking in therapy once a week did nothing to affect the challenges she faced in her life. I commented in return, "Having me in your life only once a week is not enough. You wish that I could be in your life more," to which Maria replied, "Now you got it . . . finally."

Maria exhibited many resilient qualities over the course of her therapy. Despite her many ongoing traumas, almost every adult who came in contact with her found her to be charming and likable. She made a proactive decision to participate in CPP to help herself and possessed a reflective temperament that enabled her to connect feelings to behavior.

Maria had the good fortune of being placed with an exceptionally loving and committed foster mother. Slowly, Maria began to compare and contrast what she was experiencing in her relationship with her foster mother with what she had not experienced in her relationship with her mother. Most important, Maria was able to take in these experiences and feel worthy of special treatment (e.g., Maria's foster mother let her pick out the color of paint for her room). In her foster mother's care, Maria was continually being exposed to a new way of life in a family where the members respected and looked after each other. As much as Maria hated being in foster care, she was keenly aware of how her experiences with her foster family were opening up her world view. In one session, shortly after her foster mother's son entrusted Maria to babysit his children, Maria said, "I just see things differently now. . . . I really feel part of the family." The stability that Maria experienced in her foster home and in her therapeutic treatment provided her with two dependable parental objects who anchored her emotionally as she made a very difficult, complicated, and often painful developmental push toward an emotional separation from her mother.

Maria's strength was most evident during her high school graduation, as she announced, "I must be the happiest person here." The positive force behind this statement showed promise for her future and a window into the resiliency that helped her survive her past. She did not minimize the uphill battle ahead of her, but she also did not fear the future so much so that she could not celebrate the present moment.

Maria's ability to use our relationship and connect to me helped her feel anchored enough to leave therapy knowing that I would be there as she explored and figured out her new world. Not just with me but also with others, Maria sought strong adult relationships that she could use in place of a relationship with her mother and thereby receive parental support and guidance.

Maria was able to construe her experiences in a positive and constructive way, recognizing that although her experiences were negative, she nonetheless grew and gained valuable life knowledge. For example, she explained that the autonomy that she had as a young child, as a result of the neglect in her upbringing, allowed her to think for herself.

Coherence refers to a basic belief that life makes sense and that one has control over what happens. Coherence speaks to the place of psychotherapy with children in foster care, and it is the characteristic that most embodied my work with Maria. A new foster home, the welfare system, the school system, and all of the system's players tugged at the boundaries of Maria's freedom. I cannot overemphasize the depth of feeling and impact that foster care had on Maria, as well as how much this experience challenged her to develop and exercise an internal sense of control while her external world was suffocating her (a key factor in resiliency). Maria's own assessment of why she had decided to move to another city and essentially discontinue treatment reflects that essential quality of resiliency; she said she could no longer stand living in foster care because she wanted to be in control of her life. Her dream was to become a psychiatrist so she could help other children who had been through experiences like hers. She often spoke of her brother, for whom she felt responsible. Maria had a reunification fantasy in which she would graduate from school, get an apartment and a job, and rescue him from their mother's home.

I spoke to Maria two months after she had left treatment and relocated. I reminded her about CPP and how we began working together. I spoke with her about resilience—that is, how certain people go through very difficult situations but somehow have the strength and courage to continue to grow in spite of their obstacles. She remained silent. I finished by saying, "That's you, Maria." I listened into the silence and heard her faintly crying. It was a strangely familiar and comfortable silence as we had been through many such moments before. She knew I was being sincere in reminding her how much I respected her courage, knowledge, and strength. I wondered with her if being out of foster care had accomplished what she had hoped—freedom from confinement and other people's control. Maria replied, "It's been real hard. I'm not gonna lie . . . but, yeah, it does feel good to be out of foster care. I feel like it's my own life I'm living now."

QUESTIONS

1. Maria reported that her mother frequently said that she "hated" her, yet Maria continued to long for a connection to her mother. How do you understand the wish of children to maintain a close relationship with abusive parents?

2. Maria tells her therapist, "You have no idea what it's like being in foster care." If a child or adolescent said this to you, how would you respond and why?

3. The therapist describes Maria as being particularly resilient. Based on the information you have, do you agree with this assessment? Why or why not?

Parents Bonding with Nonbiological Children

Barbara Waterman

In working with parents bonding with nonbiological children (Waterman, 2003a), I have found that no matter the child's age, the attachment process proceeds with the same developmental steps as with a biological child. What makes this challenging for foster parents—tempting them to give up on the newly placed child—is that few therapies with foster children build in meetings with the parents designed to contain and empower them, so the foster parents are not pulled to act out with "their" children the highly primitive affects that may create a rupture in the fledgling bond. A recent case is an illustration of the dilemmas for fost-adopt parents; these ripple throughout the system of professional workers attempting to facilitate and finalize an adoption and need to be addressed by clinicians treating the foster children.

Siblings Tanya (age 8) and Shawna (age 12) were placed with a biracial lesbian couple. The two girls had been through a number of foster homes between periods of reunification with their birth mother, who had a recurring substance abuse problem. Public sector attorneys and social workers in the birth mother's hometown—several hours away from the foster home—as well as a social worker in a private adoption agency working with the aspiring parents were involved in the process of terminating the birth mother's rights. Shawna began individual therapy with my colleague, Dr. Smith, and Tanya began therapy with me. Dr. Smith and I built periodic conjoint meetings between the two therapists and the fost-adopt parents into the treatment plan.

Initially, Shawna carried all of the loyalty to her birth mother and Tanya carried all of the longing for a new and more stable life. Paradoxically, Shawna immediately called her foster mothers "Mom" and was physically affectionate, in contrast to Tanya, who was more cautious about engaging in these new relationships, calling her new parents by their names and reserving physical expressions of fondness for much later. Because of these stylistic differences in attachment, the siblings diverged in their approach to their foster parents: Shawna formed a closer bond with the stay-at-home foster mother, Sherry, while Tanya formed a closer bond with the out-at-work foster mother, Denise.

From the outset, Dr. Smith and I realized that we would have to find a way to help contain this dichotomy, lest the split ripple through the system and destroy the chance for long-term placement or adoption. The adoptive social worker, Bernice, was caught up in Shawna's resistance to the adoption. She called me to take Tanya's adoption "temperature" fairly regularly, and I had to keep reminding her that Tanya's hesitancy was a normal part of pushing the fost-adopt envelope on the way to permanent placement. Dr. Smith spoke with Bernice and gave her the same message. Because Bernice had several decades of experience in the adoption field, her joining in the questioning of parent–child fit made me wonder if she was responding to unconscious feelings as well as openly expressed doubts.

Conversely, when the social service workers claimed that the birth mother might manage reunification, Bernice responded to my concerns with a near-blind faith in the adoption finalization process, suggesting a split between agencies, with those pushing for reunification on one side and those looking to adopt on the other. In fact, the girls' mother was quite active in trying to undermine her daughters' sense of stability in their new home. In phone calls, she made promises about giving them money from a lawsuit as soon as they returned home to live with her. She also pursued legal appeals, attempting to forestall the termination of her parental rights. Thus, the attorneys assigned to protect the girls' rights, as well as social workers from the foster care system, were working at cross-purposes to Bernice's private agency and its commitment to pursuing adoption.

What unfolded in the collateral meetings was that Sherry, who was in charge of the mothering (Waterman, 2003b), identified with the children's futility/despair about having missed out on a home base. They projected all of their sadness into her in a preverbal mode of communication crucial to building attachments, called *projective identification* (Bion, 1962). Sherry passed these feelings from the girls' past to me in a parallel manner, causing me to feel like I was an awful, unempathic therapist who dismissed her suffering as a beleaguered foster mother. No matter how much I normalized Sherry's unbearable feelings, I could not soften Sherry's hateful feelings toward me. Sherry's rancor was in part legitimate because she had to bear the children's projections full time, whereas I only experienced Tanya's ruthlessness and aggression—resulting from her previous deprivation—for an hour each week, once she felt safe enough with me. I also suspect that Sherry unconsciously chose to blame me, rather than Dr. Smith, for her mothering struggles because Sherry's relationship with Tanya was harder for her than her relationship with Shawna. I relied heavily on my colleague for consultation in order to metabolize Sherry's negative projections, just as Sherry relied heavily on Denise for containment of excruciating feelings she absorbed from the children.

Over time, these primitive emotions, which were communicated non-verbally, shifted valence with astonishing rapidity for any particular dyad in the system. By 9 months into the therapy, Tanya had me convinced of the futility of the adoption quest in her verbal determination to find the ideal (i.e., heterosexual) family while I experienced her indifference about ending our therapy—a test no doubt to see whether I would claim her instead of joining her in her easy-come, easy-go detachment. At that point I could identify with the experiences of Sherry as parent, and Bernice as adoption worker more directly, because I, too, fell into Tanya's projections with her, joining the other caregivers in feeling like chopped liver. By year 2 into the therapy, the attachment Tanya and I had woven was not so easily torn; when she protested her need for further therapy after a particularly upsetting phone call with her birth mother, I did not miss a beat in telling Tanya that she was stuck with me for at least the next 8 years, when she would legally come of age. Tanya's relief at my response was palpable.

Meanwhile, Shawna gradually stopped longing for her birth mother and took over Tanya's spirited testing of limits at home and in therapy, suggesting more engagement in her new life, mixed in with early adolescent developmental behavior. Parent collateral meetings became more focused on Shawna's tendency to form indiscriminate (especially heterosexual) attachments and risky self-destructive behavior, with Denise taking Sherry's place as the parent overwhelmed with her antagonistic feelings toward this foster daughter. With Sherry back at work, Denise became the more primary mother, falling into a long journey of "prebuyer's remorse" as she struggled with the girls' constant, ruthless use of her, taking over Sherry's role of absorbing the children's rejections while needing co-parent containment. Simultaneously, maternal aggression shifted to Dr. Smith, who then had to live the darker feelings with Shawna and Denise. It was Denise's turn to feel dismissed by Dr. Smith about her feelings of inadequacy to ensure Shawna's safety; therapist input at the level of problem solving around Shawna's dangerous behavior did nothing to alleviate Denise's sense that Shawna was so damaged that no amount of caring could make a difference. Denise's temptation to detach from the girls emotionally in order to cope with her overwhelmed state paralleled the girls' knee-jerk response, "Fine, I'm outta here," whenever foster parent–child conflict deepened. As Denise's hateful feelings were exacerbated by her more central role as lightening rod for the girls' negative projections, Tanya shared her enjoyment at relaxing into being a child with me, and both girls communicated their acceptance of adoption to Bernice.

Prior to the adoption's becoming final the projection of loving feelings on the part of Tanya and Shawna into foster parent, birth mother, or therapist tended to be split off from the projection of hateful feelings. For example, while there were brief moments when Tanya could express both aggression and caring towards me in a single session, more typically one parent was preferred over the other, the birth mother idealized over foster parent, therapist bond revered in lieu of that with the foster caregiver on the front lines. This kind of splitting is endemic to clinical work with fost-adopt children as well as their adoptive parents, because it is very dangerous to invest all of one's hopes and dreams in a single relationship while the legal fate of that relationship hangs in the balance. Helping such children and their future parents manage ambivalent feelings toward one another is part and parcel of the development of a secure bond. While the weaving of such attachments takes time, having legal backing for "the buck stops here" security is a vital step in reducing the temptation for black-and-white, all-or-nothing coping mechanisms that children project into parents and therapists on the way to permanency.

The clinical question inferred from this case is how therapists working with foster children in long-term therapy can enable foster parents to resist falling into hopelessness about their efforts to provide their children with a corrective emotional experience, especially when the children re-create their early childhood exchanges with a birth mother who did not provide a secure attachment in order to test the resilience of the new foster parent–child bond. Clinician containment throughout the system becomes a crucial intervention for preventing ruptures in foster placements so that children may have a better chance of finding a secure base to call home.

⤜⤝

QUESTIONS

1. According to the therapist, the attachment to a foster child follows the same developmental progression as a parent's attachment to a biological child, regardless of the child's age at placement. If so, how would you explain this? Do you have reason to question this statement? If so, why?

2. The therapist describes a pattern of "splitting" that occurred on many levels—from individual to systemic. How do you understand splitting as a common response to those living and working in the foster care system? What factors intensify or diminish this reaction?

3. The therapist says that foster parents are vulnerable to hopelessness as they try to help children overcome the residues of maltreatment in their earliest relationships. How do you understand foster children's pattern of re-creating old relationships with new caregivers? What kind of intervention(s) might be most helpful in addressing this issue and why?

⤜⤝

REFERENCES

Bion, W.R. (1962). *Learning from experience*. London: Maresfield Library.

Waterman, B. (2003a). *The birth of an adoptive, foster or step-mother: Beyond biological mothering attachments*. London: Jessica Kingsley Publishers, Ltd.

Waterman, B. (2003b). Winnicott meets *Daddy & Papa*: How gay men father and mother. *Fort Da, IX*(1), 59–76.

Epilogue

Toni Vaughn Heineman and Diane Ehrensaft

Shortly after we began the Children's Psychotherapy Project (CPP), Anne Alvarez visited San Francisco and graciously accepted our invitation to meet with us. She generously shared her clinical wisdom with the therapists who gathered over coffee and pastries to hear the presentation of one of our very first cases. Not having yet established a firm foundation, we were surprised and delighted to hear Anne warmly embrace and endorse our new work with "You should write a book!"

Several years later, in the spring of 2003 and as the chapters of CPP were expanding, we gathered the clinical directors from the seven chapters then in existence for our first annual weekend retreat. Near the end of the weekend, as we sat around the breakfast table, thinking together about the direction of the newly formed A Home Within, Richard Ruth, the Washington, D.C., clinical director, mused, "If we want to move beyond treating individual children to changing policy, we will have to write a book." With Anne's proclamation still ringing in our ears, the confidence that had grown over our years of experience, and the contributions from CPP clinicians across the continents, we did finally write a book.

We write this epilogue while sitting at a table at the third annual retreat. The book will soon go to press. We are two of the founding members of CPP. As proud mothers we have watched a very simple idea flourish and grow in all of its accompanying simplicity and complexity. We have learned how simple our guiding principle "One child, for as long as it takes" can be. One therapist agrees to be available for as long as that child needs a therapist—and maybe even beyond. We have learned how complicated "One child, for as long as it takes" can be. Glitches in the system, placement changes, unforeseen circumstances, and resistance of children and families sometimes compromise our ability to follow through on our plan for long-term psychotherapy.

The year 2003 marked the tenth anniversary of the original group's gathering around a dinner table to think together about providing long-term psychotherapy to foster children through CPP in San Francisco. In 10 years, CPP had grown to reach from coast to coast. Over the years since we began, we have gathered around many tables, in small and large groups, in cities and towns across the country, to think and talk together about the internal lives of foster children and the systems that try but often fail to support them.

We have wondered about where we fit in the communities surrounding these children, who, for a variety of tragic reasons, must grow up without the consistent, nurturing care of their parents. Many themes—the reality that there are some children we have to turn away, the tension between the system's demand for action and our demand for time for reflection, the importance and difficulty of establishing collaborative relationships, or the challenges of adapting the private practice model—find their way into every discussion. Other themes seem more pertinent to a particular child, time, or place. However, our recognition of the crucial importance of relationships among individuals, groups, and systems remains the cornerstone of our discussions and work and transcends all variations in needs, locations, or resources. Indeed, after 10 years of these discussions, it did seem like a good time to write a book.

In reviewing the contributions of the CPP clinicians to this book, we realize how much we have all learned from each other and from the children and families we treat. We have learned that we are "doctors forever." We have learned that forever is inside. We have learned that we are part of a stack of nesting dolls—from the smallest, the child, to the therapist, to the consultation group, to the parenting matrix, to the system of care. We have learned in our work with foster children that not coming to sessions can be as important as coming. The space created by missed sessions is a place where children learn that relationships do not necessarily collapse in the midst of absence; we are still there when they come back. We have learned that our work in CPP demands that we extend ourselves in unexpected ways. Some children tell us, "You are more than a therapist to me," creating fertile ground for adoption fantasies—theirs and ours. Above all, in rereading the book we came to realize, in ways that we had never fully appreciated, the absolute importance of the consultation groups. As we launched CPP more than a decade ago, we had an inkling that the consultation groups would be central to our success. We now know that they sustain the life of our project.

We have learned that the lives of foster children are more complex, more fraught with uncertainty and unexpected disruptions, and more confusing than anyone who does not have contact with the foster care system can even begin to imagine. Someday, in a better world, there may be no need for foster care; children would be able to live with their own families in their own communities. That will be a long time in coming. Because we have no illusions that we will see dramatic changes in the foreseeable future, we remain firm in our resolve. "One child, for as long as it takes" is our ideal— one we will hold to as we challenge the social forces that prevent children who need this therapy the most from getting the most of it and until it is no longer an ideal but standard practice for children and youth in foster care. To that end, we invite others to join us and help us build on what we have learned. As we continue to learn, we will keep on doing what we have learned to do best—offering "One child. One therapist. For as long as it takes."

Index

Page numbers followed by *n* indicate footnotes.